HARVARD HISTORICAL STUDIES

Published under the direction
of the Department of History
from the income of the
Henry Warren Torrey Fund

Volume XCIII

**Map 1.** Peru

# Conquest and Agrarian Change: The Emergence of the Hacienda System on the Peruvian Coast

*Robert G. Keith*

Harvard University Press
Cambridge, Massachusetts
and London, England
1976

Library of Congress Cataloging in Publication Data

Keith, Robert G
  Conquest and agrarian change.
  (Harvard historical studies; 93)
  Bibliography: p.
  Includes index.
  1. Haciendas—Peru—History. 2. Peru—Social con-
ditions. 3. Encomiendas (Latin America) 4. Agricul-
ture—Economic aspects—Peru—History. I. Title.
II. Series.
HD1471.P45K45     333.3'23'0985     76-7354
ISBN 0-674-16293-5

For Anne

# Acknowledgments

Of the many debts I have incurred while working on this book only a few can be recognized here. Professor J. H. Parry of Harvard directed the original dissertation and has since been an unfailing source of advice and help. Professor Alvaro Jara encouraged my initial interest in Latin-American economic history and gave freely of his knowledge about colonial Peru. My thanks go also to Noble David Cook, for providing me with demographic material gathered in the course of his own research, and to John V. Murra, Karen Spalding, Thomas Patterson, and Glynne Evans for reading and criticizing earlier drafts of the manuscript. Among those who helped me in Peru, I particularly wish to express my gratitude to Guillermo Lohmann Villena, José Matos Mar, and the staffs of the Archivo Nacional and the Biblioteca Nacional. Finally, my greatest debt of all is to my wife, without whose support and encouragement the book could not have been completed.

Jamaica Plain, Massachusetts

# Contents

# Tables

# Maps

# Conquest and Agrarian Change

# Introduction

The history of any society can theoretically be studied from two different perspectives, one of which might be described as sociological and the other anthropological. From the former, the society would appear as a hierarchical structure of social classes and occupational or other society-wide groups which can be taken apart and analyzed. From the latter perspective, it would have the aspect of a network of small social systems (or "part societies" as Redfield termed them), whose principles of operation have to be known if one is to understand the society as a whole.[1] These two points do not, of course, exclude each other. In a metaphorical sense, the one offers us a wide-angle lens, permitting the observation of large areas and groups of people, of nations, of societies, of "civilizations." The other provides a telescopic lens which makes it possible to observe the intricate local life of the small communities which constitute a society.

Social history has traditionally been written from a sociological rather than an anthropological perspective. It has concerned itself with the larger social groupings and treated individuals chiefly in terms of class, status, and economic role. Since about 1930, however, historians have come to realize the importance of understanding smaller social systems, not for their own sake, but because of what they reveal about the whole society. The pioneer of the new approach was Marc Bloch. His book, *Les caractères originaux de l'histoire rurale française* (1931), brilliantly demonstrated the value of getting beyond the uniformity of the written law to the diversity which characterized the operation of real manors and peasant villages. Bloch's work had a profound influence on the writing of European history, encouraging scholars to study the life and organization of manors, peasant villages, and towns, and more recently to examine local demographic patterns as well as the structure of family life.[2] In Latin-American history, this trend has been far less pronounced and, with several notable exceptions, the investigation of local patterns has been left largely to anthropologists.[3] Historical studies of haciendas, towns, and villages have therefore been rare, and though historical demography has become a major interest in recent years, it has depended primarily on tribute records rather than on local parish registers as in Europe.

This book is concerned with haciendas as local social systems which existed within a larger colonial society. The main question it attempts to answer is how and why this particular type of social system arose when it did. Was it primarily a product of Spanish history and culture? Was it an inevitable result of the conquest? What did it owe to Indian customs and traditions? To local geography? To economic and social conditions?

What exactly was an hacienda? We usually think of it as a large, inefficiently managed estate which mixed agriculture with stock raising and possessed a labor system resembling that of a medieval manor. Though this was not inaccurate for the highland districts of Middle America and the Andes, it did not apply very well in many other areas. In northern Mexico, for instance, haciendas were usually large cattle ranches; on the south coast of Peru they were vineyards tended by Negro slaves; in Cuba they were small tobacco farms (*vegas*) or large sugar plantations. The hacienda was basically a hybrid institution which established itself chiefly in areas where the Spaniards had lived for some time; its characteristics in each case were largely determined by the circumstances in which it developed. Serving the needs of Indians or Blacks as well as Spaniards, it could not ignore their diverse customs and traditions. This hybrid character distinguished it from the traditional Indian community, whose basic patterns of organization dated from long before the conquest, and likewise from the Spanish town, whose form and style reflected the fact that it had originally served simply as a means of transforming a band of Spanish soldiers into a civil administration.

In a general sense, of course, the hacienda can be defined as an income-producing agricultural estate with a paternalistic form of social organization, the Spanish-American offspring of a family which included the European manor and the plantation of Brazil and the West Indies. Its most characteristic feature was the sharp social distinction between masters and servants or, following Freyre, between the big house and the slave huts.[4] It did not have to be a large estate; nor was it necessarily "feudal" in the Marxist sense. The wine haciendas of the southern coast of Peru were, in fact, highly commercialized and profitable enterprises, often no larger than New England farms. It is true that the manor-like haciendas of the Mexican and

Andean highlands were large and had some "feudal" traits, but the reasons for this must be sought in the circumstances which gave rise to this type of hacienda, not in the general characteristics of the institution.

We have tended to think of the hacienda as an institution brought to the New World by the Spaniards, who were of course familiar with large estates in their own country. The diversity among haciendas, however, suggests that they were far from being based on any single model. Furthermore, there is no reason to think that we can adequately understand the hacienda system in terms of the cultural heritage of the Spanish settlers alone. Attributing the emergence of the hacienda to a land-grabbing mentality fostered by medieval wars against the Moors is no more satisfactory than attributing the rise of the New England town meeting to the English tradition of the rights of individuals. The distinctive institutions of the New World clearly did owe something to the traditions and customs of the European settlers; but they owed at least as much to the new and unprecedented local situations with which these settlers had to deal. The landed estate has, after all, been an almost universal phenomenon. In a general sense its appearance after the Spanish conquest hardly needs an involved explanation. What is intriguing is why such estates appeared in some parts of Spanish America but not in others, why they used Indian peons in some areas and Negro slaves in others, or why they were profitable in some areas and economically backward in others.

These and similar questions can only be answered if we look at the local circumstances out of which haciendas arose in each region. Chevalier has set the example with his remarkable study of the hacienda system in central and northern Mexico. The present book examines the rise of the hacienda system on the Peruvian coast, a smaller region but one which was very important within the Spanish empire. Like central Mexico, it was attractive to Spanish immigrants for its temperate climate and because it was suited to the cultivation of traditional Spanish food crops. In the latter respect, indeed, it was better off, since on its soil Spaniards could produce both wine and olives while in Mexico they were never very successful with either. The coastal area also resembled central Mexico in its position of economic dominance within a larger region, the result of its control over the trade routes leading to mining regions farther inland.

At the same time the coast differed from central Mexico in two fundamental respects. It was a lowland region where transportation, whether by water or by land, was relatively cheap and easy. This advantage was all the greater because the region's dependence on irrigation encouraged the concentration of its population in a small part of its total area. On the other hand, the coast suffered under one great handicap. Its Indian population, like that of most lowland regions in Spanish America, died off very rapidly, creating a labor shortage which could be alleviated only by the massive importation of Negro slaves. As a result of these factors, the haciendas which developed on the Peruvian coast were generally smaller than those of central Mexico and depended on African rather than local Indian labor.

Fundamentally, however, this book is less concerned with the broad trends of social and economic change on the coast than with local patterns of change and how they varied from valley to valley. It is therefore based on an investigation of the conditions and circum- stances found within individual valleys, as they appear mainly in the wills, bills of sale, contracts, and other legal documents drawn up by local notaries. Since the entire coast proved too large an area to study in this detailed fashion, the area of local research was narrowed down to the seven major valleys of the central coast, extending from Huaura south to Ica. What follows, then, is both a general account of the rise of the hacienda system on the Peruvian coast and an analysis of the processes of change found in a number of valleys within the larger region. It is a story which begins even before the conquest, since we need to have some idea of how the traditional societies of the coast were organized before the arrival of the Spaniards, and of what changes were already occurring within them; and it reaches a natural conclusion in the early years of the seventeenth century, by which time the hacienda system had been consolidated in most of the coastal valleys. In a broad sense, it may be seen as the story of how the Spanish settlers of the coast established the economic foundations for their aristocratic colonial society of the seventeenth and eighteenth centu- ries.

# 1 / Coastal Society before the Spanish Conquest

The ancient civilization of Peru is synonymous, in popular usage, with the civilization of the Incas. Yet the Incas were relative latecomers to the stage of Andean history, having appeared only in the fourteenth century. They have been described as the Romans of ancient Peru, excelling in law and engineering—like the Romans, their best-known achievements were their roads and bridges—and borrowing many other aspects of their civilization from their predecessors, as the Romans did from the Greeks. But who were the Greeks of the Andean region? The evidence suggests that this role was played by the peoples who inhabited the Peruvian coastal valleys. It was on the coast that large cities and bureaucratic states first appeared. It was there that the finest pottery was made and the finest cloth woven. It was there that the technology and management of irrigation was developed to a level of efficiency that has never since been matched in Peru. There were, indeed, early centers of civilization and urbanization in the highlands, of which Tiahuanaco is perhaps the most famous example, but those who created these civilizations, down to the Incas themselves, seem to have borrowed heavily from the civilizations of the coast.

There is another parallel between the Greeks and the coastal Peruvians. Both found it impossible to maintain their political independence. The golden age of the independent Greek polis was followed by subjugation to rulers from outside: Macedonians, Romans, Byzantines, and Turks. Similarly the coastal states, which had passed through their golden age during the first centuries of the Christian era, found themselves successively conquered by the highland states of Huari and Tiahuanaco, by the Incas, and finally by the Spaniards. As in the case of the Greek cities, conquest encouraged the diffusion of coastal influences throughout the Andean region, but also undermined the vitality of coastal society itself.

If we are to understand how this society was transformed during the century following the Spanish conquest, then we must have some idea of what it had been like previously. This chapter will examine the physical environment within which it existed, analyze its patterns of political, economic, and social organization, and attempt to assess how it had already been changed by incorporation into the Inca empire.

## The Environment

To the traveller approaching Lima from the sea, the Peruvian coast seems one of the least suitable regions for human habitation. The climate is temperate for its latitude, and the humidity very high — Lima normally stays cool and damp under a thick cloud bank for more than half the year — but neither the city nor the coast as a whole receives significant amounts of rainfall. The landscape is thus one of desert mountains interrupted at intervals by oases which receive their water from rivers originating in the higher reaches of the Andes to the east. When rain does occasionally fall here, it is not something to be welcomed, but rather a disaster which destroys crops, buildings, and irrigation works.

The primary reason for the lack of rainfall on the coast is the presence to the west of the cold Peru or Humboldt current.[1] This chills the air as it moves toward land, creating a stable high pressure system over the coast which is held in position by the barrier of the Andes. As the chilled air runs up against the mountains, it is forced to rise, which cools it still further. This does not produce rain but, instead, a heavy mist called *garúa*, the one regular form of precipitation known on most of the coast. In Lima, the garúa coats streets, sidewalks, and windshields with water, and at higher elevations (between 2,000 and 5,000 feet) it provides seasonally enough moisture to support quick-flowering plants and grasses, making the desert suddenly appear to bloom. Areas where this occurs regularly are known as *lomas* and have been used as winter pastures since before the Spanish conquest. The seventeenth-century Jesuit historian Bernabé Cobo tells us that in some cases loma grass grew high enough to hide the animals grazing on it.[2]

There are also subterranean sources of water on the coast. *Puquios* or wells are common in all the valleys and have provided water both for household use and for irrigation from early times. In a few areas, where the water table was close to the surface, the ancient Peruvians discovered they could provide moisture for their crops by excavating their gardens and allowing the subsoil water to seep up to them. Such sunken gardens were known as *mahamaes* to the Indians and as *hoyas* to the Spaniards; in the seventeenth century they were thought to produce better fruit and wine grapes than did soil irrigated from the rivers. The amount of subsoil water available was usually less than was brought down by the rivers, however, and it was normally found only in the river valleys, not in the desert areas between them.[3]

The distinctive features of coastal geography stand out more clearly when we compare the region to the Nile Valley, which is similar in many ways. The Nile, which annually carries some eighty-four milliards or cubic kilometers of water to Egypt from Lake Victoria and the mountains of Ethiopia, is much larger than any of the rivers of the Peruvian coast. Only three of the latter—the Chira, the Tumbes, and the Santa—carry more than five milliards each year (an average flow of 159 cubic meters per second), and none of these has enough irrigable land to use all of its water (see table 1).[4] Both the Nile and the coastal rivers are subject to seasonal fluctuations in the volume of water they carry, but in the smaller Peruvian rivers these fluctuations are much more extreme. The level of the Nile rises and falls regularly, but many of the coastal rivers simply disappear during the dry season. Even a relatively large and important river like the Chicama on the north coast fluctuates between a peak flow of more than 300 cubic meters a second and a minimum flow of less than 10 in the dry season. It is not surprising, then, that Egypt has traditionally irrigated more land than could possibly be irrigated on the Peruvian coast. In 1880, Egyptians had about six million acres of land under cultivation and had probably cultivated a similar amount in the age of the pharaohs. On the Peruvian coast, it has been estimated that some 1.8 million acres were cultivated before the Spanish conquest.[5]

Both the Nile Valley and the Peruvian coast may be described as narrow elongated rectangles. The former, which is seldom more than ten miles wide above the delta, extends roughly 600 miles between Alexandria and the first cataract. The latter, stretching approximately 1,200 miles from Tumbes to Tacna, is no more than forty miles wide on the most liberal estimate, except at its northern end, where the mountains are farther removed from the sea. But in spite of this general similarity in shape there is a fundamental difference: the Nile flows lengthwise through its rectangle while the Peruvian rivers flow crosswise.[6] The Nile Valley therefore became a continuous ribbon of cultivated land while the Peruvian coast remained a series of oases separated from one another by long stretches of desert. The difference is accentuated by the fact that the Nile has always provided an excellent

**Table 1.**   Land and Water in the Major Coastal Valleys, c. 1960

| Valley | Irrigated area (thousands of hectares) | Average flow of water (cubic meters per second) |
|---|---|---|
| Tumbes | 6 | 216 |
| Chira | 27 | 344 |
| Piura | 60 | 69 |
| Lambayeque & La Leche | 87 | 44 |
| Saña | 19 | 13 |
| Jequetepeque | 30 | 72 |
| Chicama | 40 | 42 |
| Moche | 20 | 14 |
| Santa | 9 | 192 |
| Pativilca | 21 | 55 |
| Huaura | 32 | 32 |
| Chancay | 22 | 12 |
| Lima (Rímac and Chillón) | 39 | 48 |
| Cañete | 24 | 60 |
| Chincha | 24 | 36 |
| Pisco | 25 | 34 |
| Ica | 21 | 15 |
| Acarí | 7 | 24 |
| Camaná | 8 | 72 |
| Vítor | 13 | |
| Moquegua | 3 | 2 |

*Source:* Romero, *Geografía económica*, pp. 62, 174-176.

highway for communication and the transport of goods. The coastal rivers could not be used in such a way, and the ancient Peruvians never learned to use the ocean as their highway, as the Spaniards were to do later on. They did use the Pacific as a source of food, however, and this may have made up for the lack of navigable rivers, since the waters off Peru were one of the richest fishing grounds in the world.

Because cultivation and settlement on the Peruvian coast were concentrated in areas physically separate from one another, political and economic unification was more difficult to achieve than in the Nile Valley. While Egypt was politically unified virtually from the beginning of its known history, the coastal peoples were seldom able to build up states embracing more than three or four neighboring valleys. Only the Chimús, who consolidated the northern half of the coast in the fifteenth century, proved an exception. And the Chimú empire, with its elaborate canals which transferred water from valley to valley and carried it to desert lands between the valleys, was perhaps the only one of the coastal states which developed something like that large continuous band of cultivation which existed in Egypt.[7]

Man's adaptation to the coastal environment was a gradual process with several distinct stages: a nomadic stage, a stage of dependence on the sea, and an agricultural stage.[8] The earliest inhabitants were hunters and gatherers who built temporary camps in the lomas during the season of the garúa and moved to the shore when the lomas dried up. In time they learned to exploit the resources of the sea more effectively and to grow edible plants like squash, beans, and maize on small strips of land along the rivers or next to springs. At first, it was fishing rather than agriculture which provided these early Peruvians with a stable basis of subsistence and allowed them, after about 2000 B.C., to abandon their migratory life and settle down in large permanent towns close to the sea. Later, though the coastal inhabitants continued to depend heavily on seafood, the construction of large irrigation systems greatly increased the amount of land they could cultivate. This in turn resulted in rapid population growth and shifted the primary base of subsistence from fishing to agriculture. Little is known of when and how the irrigation systems were built. The period of growth and development probably lasted from around 900 B.C. to about 600 A.D. There were additions and improvements after that time, but by the latter date the relationship between the coastal peoples and their natural environment had stabilized in patterns which would not change greatly until after the Spanish conquest.

## The Indian Society of the Coast

Our knowledge of how coastal society was organized is limited. The inferences which can be drawn from the archaeological evidence do not take us very far in the absence of concrete verbal evidence, either written or oral. Since the Indians of Peru never developed a means of written communication, evidence derived from oral tradition, as later recorded by Spaniards, is particularly important. But on the coast the speed of the demographic collapse after the Spanish conquest largely erased the memory of the old traditions and way of life before they could be documented. In the highlands, on the other hand, the collapse was less drastic, and more of the oral tradition survived to be written down; thus we know more about how the society was organized.

Our account of pre-conquest coastal society, then, must rely heavily on the memory and traditions of highlanders—particularly the Incas—and on the observations of Spaniards in the years immediately following the conquest. Neither Spaniards nor Incas were unbiased observers, however. The former saw themselves as bearers of Christianity and civilization to the rude and barbarous tribes of the New World; and the latter, according to Garcilaso, believed themselves sent on a divine mission to give their subjects "precepts and laws by which they would live as reasonable and civilized men."[9] These views, so similar to each other, clearly encouraged the growth of myths and prejudices concerning the conquered peoples in both empires. The Incas, for example, considered the people of the coast to be "soft, lazy, corrupt, and arrogant."[10]

Lack of evidence, however, has not precluded the recognition that the civilizations of the Peruvian coast were highly developed and that they bore a definite resemblance not only to those of Middle America, but also to the older civilizations of the Near East, particularly those of Egypt and Mesopotamia. Karl Wittfogel, the most systematic student of this subject, argues that all these civilizations were "hydraulic" ones; that is, they were based on an agriculture which involved "large-scale and government managed works of irrigation and flood control." To Wittfogel this implied that they possessed certain definite traits which clearly differentiated them from other kinds of societies—"feudal" or "industrial" for example.[11] In the first place, they were dependent on large and complex irrigation systems to provide themselves with adequate supplies of food. Secondly, they developed around core areas of irrigated agriculture, within which population, wealth, and power all tended to be concentrated.* Thirdly, they possessed highly centralized

---

*The concept of the core area allows Wittfogel to distinguish between two different types of hydraulic societies. A "compact" hydraulic society is one in which the core areas are economically dominant over the areas of non-hydraulic agriculture. A "loose" hydraulic society, in contrast, is

administrative systems which permitted the organization of the population as a labor force for large building projects, such as irrigation
canals or pyramids. Wittfogel also suggests that in the course of building up a centralized system, "hydraulic" societies tended to assimilate
government and religion to one another, creating "established" religions which were dependent on the state, and frequently turning
priests into officials and kings into gods. He also argues that they
tended to limit private ownership of land, and sometimes private property in general, thus preventing the rise of a true landed aristocracy.[12]

Wittfogel's theory has not been received uncritically. It has been
condemned on the one hand as overly deterministic, since it appears to
argue that despotic systems of government result from the building of
large irrigation systems. On the other hand, it has been criticized for
claiming more universal validity than it has, for ignoring cases in
which dependence on large-scale irrigation works failed to produce
centralization. In southeastern Spain, for instance, there were traditionally two patterns of regulation in irrigated areas, one centralized
and under the control of municipal governments, the other highly
decentralized. In the irrigated plain of Valencia, control over the irrigation system rested in the hands of eight separate irrigation communities — one for each of the major canals — and "the basis of authority
was the consensus of all the irrigators" who used a canal. This decentralized pattern was not something introduced by the Christians in the
thirteenth century, but had clearly been present under Moslem rule.[13]

The theory also runs into difficulty with respect to the regions of
wet-rice cultivation scattered through southern India, Ceylon, South-
east Asia, southern China, and Japan, where societies traditionally
depended on irrigation systems of considerable size and complexity
and concentrated their population in intensively cultivated "core"
areas. But these societies did not have highly centralized political systems. Indeed Leach has argued that the kingdoms of medieval Ceylon
had an essentially "feudal" structure, more like that of contemporary
European monarchies than that of Wittfogel's oriental despotisms.

---

one in which the non-hydraulic areas are economically more important, but where the core area
is still strong enough to establish its political and organizational superiority. Wittfogel classifies
Egyptian, Sumerian, and coastal Peruvian societies as "compact," but Babylonian, Assyrian,
Aztec, and Inca societies as "loose."

Similarly, medieval Javanese government has been described as "a case of a maharaja controlling countless little lordships," receiving homage and tribute, but leaving local chieftains to manage their own affairs. And Japan has long been known as a classic center of non-European feudalism.[14]

Nevertheless, the criticisms do not invalidate the theory as a whole. Though societies have existed in which the development of irrigation systems and the concentration of population in "core" areas did not lead to political centralization, the three traits noted by Wittfogel frequently did occur together and may therefore be said to define a "hydraulic" type of society. We do not have to assume that this is the only type of society found in conjunction with large-scale irrigation systems. Nor is there any need to argue that any one trait is the cause of the others; more probably each one reinforced and was reinforced by the others as it evolved.[15]

Although he possessed little information about them, Wittfogel classified the Peruvian coastal societies, along with pharaonic Egypt, as among the most hydraulic known.[16] What we now know about them does not suggest that he was fundamentally wrong. The coast was a desert which depended on water imported from outside. In the absence of countervailing factors — warfare for instance — this tended to encourage the highest possible concentration of population, both because dispersion implied transporting water to more areas than was necessary and because increasing the efficiency of existing irrigation works probably raised agricultural productivity more than expanding the system into new regions.[17] Thus individual landholdings tended to be smaller in size and more efficiently farmed than they would have been in the absence of irrigation, and the density of the rural population in the valleys was capable of reaching very high levels.

Because of the scarcity of water at certain times of year, it was economically advantageous for the coastal societies to regulate their use of water over fairly wide areas. Political consolidation was thus a logical, though not invariable, consequence of the development of coastal irrigation systems. Such consolidation was especially likely in large valleys supplied by a single river and in groups of valleys which were or could be linked into a single system. It occurred on the northern coast, where Kosok has shown that valleys were linked together into great irrigated complexes. The Pativilca-Fortaleza complex, with its so-called "fortress" of Paramonga, may have been the center of a large state before its conquest by the Chimús in the fifteenth century. The chronicler

Molina tells us that under the Incas the valleys of Huaura, Pativilca, and Huarmey formed a single province. Since the Incas usually preserved existing administrative arrangements on the coast, this would suggest previous centralization. The chroniclers mention the existence of three other states to the south at the time of the Inca conquest: in the Lima and Pachacamac valleys, in the valley of Huarco (Cañete), and in the Chincha valley. They do not mention an independent state in the Ica valley, though one had existed there earlier and there is no archaeological evidence to suggest that it had been conquered; its rulers were perhaps dependent on Chincha in some way.[18]

With respect to the Lima valley, recent scholars have tended to reject Garcilaso's account of a centralized "Cuismancu" empire, citing Cobo's statement that the valley was inhabited by two different "nations" and certain archaeological evidence which suggests the existence of two separate cultures there.[19] But "nations" in sixteenth-century usage were ethnic groups, not independent states, and while it was often true that political boundaries followed ethnic and cultural lines in Peru, they did not always do so. In fact, the historical evidence indicates that the Lima and Pachacamac valleys formed a single administrative unit under the Incas — Molina says they were "all one thing" — a situation which probably antedated the Inca conquest. Considering the opportunities for mispronunciation, it seems likely that the Don Gonzalo Taurichusco who occasionally appears in Lima notarial books as the "cacique principal" of the valley prior to his death in the early 1560's was the "Taurichumbi" whom Estete described as the "principal señor" of Pachacamac in 1533, or perhaps a relative. If so, it would suggest that Pachacamac, one of the largest and most important cities on the coast, was also the capital of the Lima state.[20]

What kind of states were these? The information we have suggests that they were monarchical and that the ruler's authority was derived largely from his sacred character. According to the archaeologist Larco Hoyle, the ruler of the Moche state was often portrayed with great feline teeth, indicating his "divine origin and religious functions." Rowe's retelling of the myth of the foundation of the Chimú kingdom implies similar attributes.

A man named Taycanamo or Tacaynamo came to Chimor on a log balsa of the type used along the Gulf of Guayaquil. He was dressed in a cotton breechclout and brought with him certain yellow powders which he used in ceremonies. He said that he had been sent by a great lord from across the sea to govern the land of Chimor, but did not say exactly whence he came. He spent a year after his arrival in a building (probably a shrine) where he performed certain ceremonies with his yellow powders. During this time he learned the local language and was accepted as a ruler by the inhabitants, whereupon he took the name of "King of Chimor."[21]

Below this level, however, the character of the states is less clear. Were they "bureaucratic" ones, in which authority depended primarily on a belief in the law, and administrative officials were part of a hierarchically structured organization, had clearly defined powers and spheres of competence, and received fixed salaries? Were they "patrimonial" states, in which authority depended primarily on "an established belief in the sanctity of immemorial tradition," and the duties and powers of administrative officials were not regularized or clearly defined but rather "commissioned and granted by a chief through his arbitrary decision of the moment," and where the remuneration of such officials tended to take the form of benefices? Or were they "feudal" states, in which individuals or groups had effectively appropriated most of the powers and economic benefits of office as their personal property?[22] The answer depends largely on our perception of the local authorities on the coast, the men known as *curacas* or *caciques*. Were they bureaucrats employed by a centralized government, or were they feudal lords, or something in between?

Rowe has argued that on the northern coast at least the curacas were feudal lords. The evidence for this judgment appears in a series of colonial lawsuits which contain testimony indicating that the curacas were traditionally chosen on a hereditary basis (though succession may have been matrilineal rather than patrilineal). These documents seem to imply that the main subdivisions of the Chimú empire were controlled by certain families or "feudal dynasties," some of which continued in possession of these offices for many years after the Spanish conquest.[23]

But hereditary succession to political office is not necessarily a sign of feudalism in the sense used here. It may merely mean that, on a local level, the rulers of a large empire have found it expedient to permit the survival of certain traditional political arrangements of their subjects, adopting the kind of policy the British would later call "indirect rule." This certainly was done by the Incas, who set up the sons of the defeated Chimú ruler as hereditary lords of towns and valleys on the northern coast and generally accepted traditional rules of succession for the curacas.[24] According to the testimony of witnesses in a lawsuit from the 1590's, the death of a curaca was followed by a meeting of his subjects to nominate a successor who then had to be approved in Cuzco, the Inca capital, before he could take office. Thus it appears that on both levels certain hereditary rights were respected, but that these were the hereditary rights of families, not individuals. As one of the witnesses put the matter, "the Inca appointed the person from that family [de aquella casta] who appeared most able, sometimes naming the brother and other times the son . . . ."[25]

Such respect for traditional rights and practices was characteristic of Inca rule. The Chupachu of the Huánuco region of central Peru, for instance, were allowed to continue choosing their curacas under a stricter hereditary system—the oldest son always succeeded, provided he was of age—but as on the coast, confirmation from Cuzco was required before the succession took effect. The existence of dynasties of curacas, however, did not imply that the curacas exercised much independent authority. The Spanish official who interviewed the Chupachu leaders in 1562 was informed that their curacas had been subject to the orders of an Inca governor, to whom many powers were reserved, and that they could be deposed for any one of five major violations: disobeying orders, conspiring to revolt, failing to collect the required tribute, failing to perform the sacrifices, and demanding excessive labor from their subjects. The situation appears to have been much the same on the coast. Curacas, then, were not particularly powerful and independent under the Incas. As one of the Chupachu witnesses put it, perhaps with some exaggeration, "the Inca had such authority over them that nothing he ordered failed of accomplishment, and that if he had ordered them to hang themselves they would have done it."[26]

This evidence does not, of course, tell us explicitly about the position of curacas in the pre-Inca coastal states. Nevertheless, since the Incas seem to have borrowed the idea of a bureaucratic system of control from the Chimús, it is likely that the position of the curacas was much the same under the two empires. Chimú curacas probably went to Chanchan for confirmation just as their successors would later go to Cuzco, and their power was probably restricted in much the same way.[27]

The coastal curacas, then, were not a landed nobility in the European sense, though one sixteenth-century observer did claim that they owned the land in their valleys and rented it out to their subjects.[28] The misunderstanding is not surprising. Few European settlers in the New World, regardless of their nationality, showed much ability or inclination to understand the indigenous systems of land tenure. Coming from countries where land was bought and sold, and hoping to acquire estates of their own, they found it easier and more practical to assume that the land they wanted was "owned" by certain individuals, who could then sell it to them, than to accept the fact that there was no real tradition of private landownership among the Indians of the western hemisphere.

In the Inca empire, our ethnographic sources suggest that three main types of land were recognized: community land, land assigned to religious cults and shrines (including the Inca cult), and "government" land assigned to rulers and subordinate authorities by virtue of their office.[29] Throughout the empire most agricultural land seems to have been community land. On the coast such land was probably regulated by the centralized states which controlled the irrigation systems, though the curacas, who were the local representatives of these states, might have appeared to be landowners. If there was any private land-holding in Peru it had little importance. Rulers and curacas traditionally received land and labor with which to support themselves and their households, and the Incas do seem to have made some grants of land to individuals. But such lands did not represent a large share of the total, and it is not certain that we can consider them as private landholdings in the usual sense.[30]

The states of the Peruvian coast, then, had both bureaucratic and patrimonial characteristics. They were structured hierarchically—the famous decimal system of organization used by the Incas was probably borrowed from the Chimús—and the rights and duties of subordinate political authorities seem to have been more clearly defined than in most traditional political systems. On the other hand, these deputies seem not to have been paid salaries but rather to have received benefits and gifts of various kinds, notably labor services, cloth, servants, women, and land; and their authority was primarily based on heredity rather than on law.

This mixture of the traditional and the modern was characteristic of coastal society in general. The pattern of daily life and work for most of the population, their religious life, their methods of making war and raising children, for instance, were not fundamentally different from those of peasants the world over. At the same time, coastal society came to possess certain highly distinctive traits, due mainly to its dependence on irrigation. It was able to concentrate more people and greater wealth in smaller areas than could most traditional societies. It could regulate its economic life more systematically and over wider areas. And it could centralize power more efficiently through the creation of semi-bureaucratic political systems. All these traits merit some emphasis, because the colonial period in Peru was to be characterized by a diametrically opposed set of tendencies: the relative dispersion of population, the deregulation of economic life, and the decentralization of power.

## The Coast under Inca Rule

Between 1460 and 1480 the coast was conquered by the Incas, a highland people who had appeared as a major Andean power only in the 1430's. They seem to have met with relatively little resistance. The Chimús, having failed to keep them out of the Moche valley where Chanchan was located, survived a single season's campaign, "terrified and shut up behind their high walls," as the chronicler Cabello Balboa puts it. This was apparently enough for them, however. When the Incas returned a year or so later, they marched virtually unopposed over much of the north coast before looting Chanchan and carrying the Chimú ruler Minchancaman off to exile in Cuzco. The Chincha and Pachacamac states appear to have put up even less resistance.[31]

Only at Huarco did the Incas meet with strong and persistent opposition. Here, according to Cieza de León, the natives resisted the Incas for four successive years, forcing them to establish a permanent base of operations in the valley. The consequences of this resistance were apparently disastrous; Cieza says that "mountains of bones" could still be seen in the valley when he was there in the 1540's. And the valley would be chosen as the site for the town of Cañete in 1556 precisely because its Indian population was so much smaller than that of other valleys of comparable size. At the time it contained only about seventy Indian households, some of which had come from Coayllo and Calango outside the valley.[32] Later Spanish census figures (table 3) suggest that this depopulation may have been limited to the lower Cañete valley and did not affect other areas within the Huarco state. In the

sixteenth century, Lunahuaná, Coayllo and Calango, and Chilca and
Mala all had much larger populations than the central *encomienda* of
Huarco, which should, however, have been the largest of the four.*

There were several reasons for this lack of resistance. The Incas used
diplomatic as well as military means to extend their rule, making it a
practice to guarantee the wealth, status, and privileges of those leaders
who submitted to them willingly. The priests of the oracle of Pachacamac, for instance, were allowed to keep and even to extend their
influence over the rest of the coast, collecting tribute from as far away
as southern Ecuador. It seems likely that this helped to procure the
peaceful submission of the Pachacamac state. Chincha's submission
may also have been bought in part through the granting of privileges.[33]

More important than Inca diplomacy, however, was the vulnerabil-
ity of the coastal states to economic warfare. The reasons are made
clear in Garcilaso's description of the last phase of the Inca campaign
against Chincha.

When all this had been done, the general began to intensify the war against the
Chinchas, investing them more closely and laying waste their crops and the fruits of
the field, so that they might be straitened by hunger. He had the irrigation channels
destroyed, so that any land not laid waste by the Incas could not be watered. This had
the greatest effect on the Yuncas, for as the country is so hot and the sun burns, the
land has to be watered every three or four days or it will not bear fruit.[34]

Given their dependence on complex irrigation systems, it was risky for
the coastal states to mount a prolonged defense against an invader who
had penetrated as far as their central core. Highland peoples might
withstand such an invader by retiring to fortified hilltops or *pucaras*
and waiting him out, but on the coast such a strategy could well turn
out to be self-defeating, as it apparently was in the case of Huarco.

In the short run at least, there is little doubt that a policy of limited
resistance to the Incas was a prudent one for the rulers of the coastal

*By the late sixteenth century, the encomienda of Huarco had become so small that it was
sometimes omitted altogether from official census lists, though it was the only encomienda in the
lower valley. A compilation from the early seventeenth century shows it with only 5 tributaries,
compared with 320 for Lunahuaná, 250 for Coayllo and Calango, and 142 for Chilca and Mala.
(See Antonio Vásquez de Espinosa, *Compendium and Description of the West Indies*, ed. and
trans. Charles Upson Clark, Smithsonian Miscellaneous Collections, 102 [Washington, 1942], p.
696.) An encomienda was a group of Indians assigned to support a Spaniard, known as the encomendero (see below, ch. 2).

valleys. For the Incas were not revolutionaries. In spite of their self-proclaimed "civilizing mission," they had little desire to change things very much. Their main concern was to obtain a share of the wealth of the coast; and since the production of this wealth depended on complex social, political, and technological arrangements which were unfamiliar to them, they were inclined to avoid measures which would disrupt these arrangements. For this reason, and perhaps also because of their own traditions, they left the existing political and social structure largely as they found it. Thus most of the pre-Inca coastal dynasties were still in existence at the time of the Spanish conquest. Estete mentions rulers (señores) of Pachacamac, Huarco, and Chincha among those who met with Hernando Pizarro at Pachacamac in 1533. And though the Chimú ruler Minchancaman was exiled, his son was allowed to take his place, and the dynasty survived into the seventeenth century.[35]

To control these whole states which were incorporated into their empire, the Incas made use of a bureaucratic system probably based on Chimú models. The rulers and curacas of the coastal valleys were subordinated to Inca governors operating out of administrative centers scattered along the coast, often at the same location as pre-Inca centers of government. The principal administrative center on the central coast, for instance, seems to have been at Pachacamac. The rulers and curacas had to go to Cuzco to be confirmed, and perhaps to be educated in the duties of their offices, and like the Chupachu curacas, they could presumably be removed if they failed to obey their superiors. None of this, however, implied a fundamental change in the life of the coastal population, except perhaps at the top levels of society. These were the men who knew best how to manage the system of production, and they were probably left to run it as they had before, provided the Incas received their share. In some cases this continuity left clear traces in the archaeological record. Rowe has observed that there is little evidence of Inca influence on the pottery styles of the north coast, which continued to follow traditional Chimú patterns well after the fall of the Chimú empire. And though the cultural influence of the Incas was more apparent in the Ica valley, the violent reaction against it at the time of the Spanish conquest is testimony to its superficiality.[36]

In spite of the conservative character of their administration, however, the Incas did bring about some changes. Their conquest of the coast effected a shift in the relative power of the traditional rulers and curacas, strengthening the latter at the expense of the former. This was accomplished, as we have seen, not by removing the rulers but rather by encouraging the curacas to look directly to the Incas as well as to the old rulers for instructions and approval. The process may be observed most clearly in the old Chimú empire, where the authority of the ruling dynasty was gradually undermined by setting up Minchan-caman's younger sons as curacas in their own right. A similar tendency seems to have prevailed in the Pachacamac state, where the existence of major secondary centers at Carabayllo, Maranga, and Surco (Ar-matambo) in the Lima valley provided an opportunity for weakening the old central authority. And the division of the population of the Chincha and Ica valleys into two groups, called by the names of Lurin and Hanan as was the usage in Cuzco, may reflect an Inca attempt to decentralize the political structure of these valleys.[37]

The Inca conquest also led to a gradual decrease in the amount of agricultural land used for feeding the coastal population. Throughout their empire, the Incas appropriated land for the support of the state and the official religious cult, and they seem to have continued to do this down to the time of the Spanish conquest. Thus the Chincha Indians told their Dominican missionaries that at his accession the emperor Huayna Capac demanded new lands (*chacras*), women, and servants from all of his subjects, considering it dishonorable to use those which had belonged to his predecessors.[38] Though it occurred throughout Peru, such appropriation of land was particularly exten-sive on the coast, where the best land was found for growing maize.

A more prestigious food than potatoes, the traditional staple of the highlands, maize was increasingly in demand among the Inca nobility. Because land for growing it in the sierra was scarce, it was imported from the coast, where it had traditionally been the staple crop. But maize was not strictly speaking an article of long-distance trade or of tribute, though it probably had been grown for years by *mitmaq* colonists sent to the coast to supply the needs of their native com-munities in the sierra. Under the Incas it was grown on the coast by the state, by the official cult, and probably by some of the Inca elite, using appropriated land and labor. Archaeologists have found evidence in the Lima valley of the existence of landed estates or *villas* which probably belonged to members of the Inca elite and were used to pro-vide them with maize. Some of these estates possessed "manor houses" which were built right on the valley floor, in disregard of the coastal tradition of efficient land use.[39]

The appropriation of coastal land to grow maize for the highlands appears to have followed and partly depended on a decline in the size of the coastal population. The demographic evidence on which this inference is based is not totally conclusive, however, since it applies only to the period immediately preceding the Spanish conquest and to three areas on the central coast.

According to the chronicler Cristóbal de Molina, the four Huaura valleys (Huaura to Huarmey) and the Chincha valley each contained 40,000 households—strictly speaking, 40,000 heads of households or tributaries, as the Spaniards called them—at the time of the conquest. Cieza de León estimated more than 25,000 households at the same date in the Chincha valley, for which a later writer, the Dominican Reginaldo de Lizárraga, gave a pre-conquest figure of 30,000. Cieza's and Lizárraga's estimates probably derive from the early Dominican missionaries who worked in the valley, of whom the most famous was Fray Domingo de Santo Tomás. The 30,000 figure therefore seems reasonable for Chincha, and probably for the Huaura valleys as well, since Molina's statement would suggest that this area contained roughly as many households as Chincha. In the Lima and Pachacamac valleys, Molina estimated a pre-conquest population of 25,000 households. Since this figure agrees approximately with Cobo's statement that this area contained three *hunos* or groups of 10,000 households, it seems reasonable to accept it.[40]

But how many people were there in a household? There is no direct evidence on the subject, so we must fall back on inference. The census data collected in the 1570's during the *visita general* of the viceroy Toledo indicates that the total population of the central coast was then about 4.6 times larger than the number of tributaries.[41] We cannot, however, assume that the same ratio held true before the conquest, since the Spaniards made a number of innovations in the collection of census data.

Within Indian society, the basic unit had been the household, established with marriage and dissolved whenever the marriage ended. Each household had certain economic obligations to the state, and these were ultimately the responsibility of the head of the household, the *hatunruna*, who was generally called a *casado* in the Spanish records.[42] An examination of the census data from the late sixteenth century, however, makes it clear that the Spanish category of "tributaries" included significantly more people than did that of "casados." A census of Huaura in 1583, for instance, lists 284 tributaries and only 199 casados, the difference being a result of the fact that both bachelors (*solteros*) and widowers were counted as tributaries. If a similar proportion prevailed over the whole central coast, it would imply that in the 1570's the average household was almost half again as large as the Toledo figures suggest.[43]

Furthermore, the Incas and Spaniards may have been counting different age groups. C. T. Smith suggests that the Spaniards counted men between the ages of eighteen and sixty as tributaries, while the Inca age limits were thirty and fifty or sixty.[44] The difficulty with this argument is that most of the evidence indicates that marital status rather than age was the determining factor, but it is possible that the Inca limits reflect statistical averages rather than bureaucratic standards: that the average man did not in fact marry and set up a household until he was thirty and that he was either widowed or too old to work by the time he reached sixty. If such was the case, then the average household would have been still larger in Inca than in colonial times. In the Huaura census of 1583, for instance, more than one-third of the casados listed were under thirty. If all of them had been living with their parents, the number of households would have been reduced from 199 to 121 and their average size increased by about half.[45] While we do not know that grown sons remained at home this long, it seems likely that they married enough later than in colonial times to affect the size of households.

A third source of error in the Toledo figures was the practice of counting members of the Indian nobility, who were traditionally exempt from tribute and labor obligations and were therefore not counted in Inca censuses. The colonial regime did not completely do away with such exemptions, but they were largely restricted to the "upper" nobility of Inca descendants and curacas. The colonial censuses thus included one group of casados — the "lower nobility" — which was not counted in colonial censuses, an innovation which again served to decrease the ratio of total population to casados on which our estimates of household size are based.[46]

On the basis of this evidence, we may tentatively conclude that the average pre-conquest household on the coast was made up of somewhere between six and ten persons. From these values we can calculate maximum and minimum populations for the three areas on the central coast for which we have estimates of the number of households. And since the area under irrigation along the central coast in pre-conquest times was probably not very different from what it is now, we can give a range of values for the population density of these three areas (see table 2).[47]

These density figures, ranging from less than one to five persons per acre, all seem within the realm of possibility. Considerably higher densities have been reported in some parts of Asia.[48] More startling perhaps is the contrast between the population density of Chincha and that of the other two areas. But there is a great deal of additional evidence to suggest the extraordinary importance of Chincha in Inca times. We know that the Incas named the whole northern quarter of their empire, Chinchasuyo, after it. When the Spaniards arrived on the north coast, they soon heard from the Indians about the valley. Cieza de León tells us that Pizarro learned of Chincha, "which was the greatest and best of all," on his first visit to Tumbez in 1528; and Jérez says that Chincha and Cuzco were described to the Spaniards in 1532 as the wealthiest and most important towns to the south. Archaeological investigation has shown that the graves of Chincha were in fact par-

Table 2. Population Density on the Central Coast before the Conquest

| Valleys | Households | Total population | Irrigated area (in acres)[a] | Density (per acre) |
|---------|-----------|------------------|------------------------------|--------------------|
| Chincha | 30,000 | 180,000-300,000[b] | 60,000 | 3.0-5.0 |
| Lima-Pachacamac | 25,000 | 150,000-250,000 | 180,000[c] | 0.8-1.4 |
| Huarmey-Huaura | 30,000 | 180,000-300,000 | 150,000 | 1.2-2.0 |

Sources: Molina, "Relación de muchas cosas," p. 67; Vedia, Historiadores primitivos, II, 424; Lizárraga, Descripción breve, p. 44.

[a]These modern figures are given in hectares by Romero, Geografía económica, p. 175 (1 hectare = 2.47 acres); the area cultivated in these valleys before the conquest was probably not very different.

[b]Assuming multipliers of 6 and 10 persons per household.

[c]Romero's figure for the Rímac valley has been doubled to correct for the growth of Lima.

ticularly rich in gold and silver. Finally, we know that it was Pizarro's brother Hernando who originally took the valley as his encomienda, clearly indicating its importance in Spanish eyes.[49]

Why was Chincha so wealthy and prosperous at the time of the conquest? The evidence suggests that it may have had a more complex and developed economy than most of the coastal valleys, an economy which was relatively more dependent on industry and commerce and relatively less on agriculture and fishing. According to Lizárraga, Chincha's 30,000 households were divided into equal groups of farmers, fishermen, and merchants (merchant-artisans) who carried on their trade as far away as Chucuito on Lake Titicaca. The main exports seem to have been silverware (Chincha still had native silversmiths at the end of the sixteenth century) and painted gourds for drinking. When the Incas conquered Chincha, they apparently allowed the valley to continue providing these goods throughout the southern part of Peru. This is perhaps the meaning in economic terms of the privileged position which Chincha seems to have had within the Inca empire.[50]

Of the other major valleys on the coast, only Ica seems to have had a population density comparable to Chincha's. Projections based on later Spanish census figures suggest that it might have contained as many as 36,000 households in the 1520's, even though it was slightly smaller in size. Ica had been the most important valley on this part of the coast before Chincha overshadowed it, and like its more powerful neighbor it chose not to resist the Incas for long. Elsewhere the story was different. Pisco appears to have been conquered and partly occupied by Chincha; projections from the Spanish figures suggest that its population in the 1520's was only a third as large as that of Chincha, though the valley was roughly the same size. The lower Cañete valley, as we have seen, had been the scene of a brave but futile attempt to resist the Incas, and its population in the 1520's was a small fraction of what it had been. Farther north, the valleys of Pativilca, Huaura, Chancay, and Lima had borne the main weight of Chimú imperialism in the fifteenth century as Minchancaman's armies had advanced to Chancay before being defeated in a great battle in the valley of Lima; in the 1520's, all seem to have had populations considerably less dense than Chincha's.[51] The large valleys of the northern coast may also have

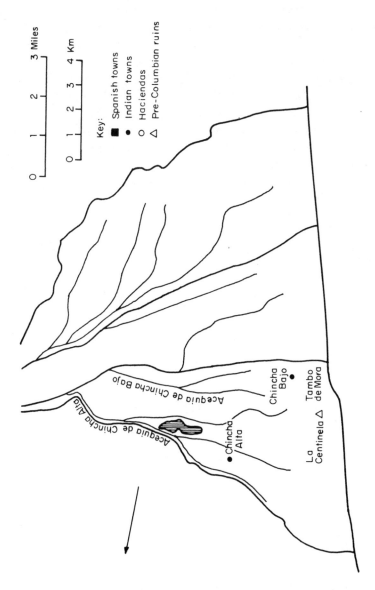

Map 2. The Chincha Valley

suffered some depopulation as a result of the Inca campaigns in the region.*

Chincha and Ica, then, were exceptional. During the years preceding the Spanish conquest, most of the coastal valleys show signs of a demographic decline — in some instances as an outcome of the Inca conquest, in others as a result of wars with more powerful neighbors on the coast. Inca interference with the traditional patterns of bureaucratic rule and the appropriation of maize land must also have contributed to the decline. Yet there is no indication that this decline was accompanied by any radical changes in the traditional way of life of the coastal population. Wars and conquests had long been a part of Andean history, and while those of the fifteenth century weakened coastal society, they did not transform it completely, as the Spanish conquest was to do.

---

*At the time of the founding of the Spanish town of Saña in 1563, the settlers found fewer than 400 Indian households in the valley. This suggests a population of considerably lower density than that of the Chincha and Ica valleys, and of about the same density as that of the Lima and Chancay valleys. (Domingo Angulo, ed., "La fundación y población de la villa de Zaña," RANP, 1 [1920], 280; see below, table 3.)

# 2 / The Encomienda System

Half a century after the Incas' conquest of the coast, their strong and well-organized empire fell to a small group of Spanish adventurers who had been fortunate enough to arrive at a moment of crisis. Several years earlier, a major epidemic (probably smallpox) had run through the country, including among its victims both the reigning emperor, Huayna Capac, and his chosen successor. This set the stage for a succession war between Huascar and Atahualpa, two of the surviving sons of the old emperor. In this struggle, Huascar received the support of most of the traditional Inca ruling class, whose power was centered in the Cuzco region, while Atahualpa was backed by Huayna Capac's army, which had been fighting to the north of Quito. Pizarro appeared on the scene in 1532, at the moment when this war was decided in favor of Atahualpa, following a great battle outside Cuzco.[1]

Atahualpa's enjoyment of his victory was cut short when he was kidnapped by the Spaniards at Cajamarca. His execution several months later might in other circumstances have united the Incas against the invaders, but in the civil-war atmosphere which prevailed, it merely confirmed the Cuzco faction in their belief that the Spaniards were their saviors rather than their enemies. Huascar's brother Manco was installed as emperor with Pizarro's approval and cooperated with him in defeating the surviving divisions of Atahualpa's army. The Spaniards were thus given four years in which to consolidate their position before Manco's disenchantment with his saviors led him to organized resistance. But by then it was too late. His forces were too weak even to overcome the two hundred Spaniards in Cuzco, and he was forced to retire to the rugged *montaña* region north of the city where he and his successors managed to maintain their independence until the 1570's.

With the overthrow of the Incas, the Spaniards became the rulers of millions of Indians living within the boundaries of present-day Peru, Ecuador, and Bolivia. But how were they to hold their conquests and to govern their new subjects? And how were they even to keep an adequate military force in the country, when the overwhelming temptation was to return home to enjoy their newly acquired wealth? The initial answer to these questions was found in the granting of

27

encomiendas, through which local Indian groups were assigned to supply individual conquerors with tribute and labor. On the one hand, the encomienda served to assure Spanish control over the conquered population. On the other, it offered a means of supporting the Spanish population from the surplus produced by the Indian economy. The effect of the distribution of encomiendas, however, was to break down the centralized Inca empire into a collection of small, loosely connected, feudal principalities, since at the beginning the crown was unable to enforce its view that the encomenderos should not possess independent jurisdiction.

The defeat of Manco was followed by a decade of civil war among the victorious Spaniards. Between 1537 and 1542 the followers of Pizarro's partner Diego de Almagro fought to gain what they considered a fair share of the benefits of the conquest. In the course of this struggle Almagro was executed and Pizarro himself assassinated. Peace was temporarily re-established when the governor Vaca de Castro, who had been sent out from Spain, defeated and executed Almagro's mestizo son. But war broke out again with the arrival in 1544 of Blasco Núñez Vela, the first viceroy of Peru. Núñez had been sent with instructions to enforce the New Laws of 1542, which would have deprived most Peruvian Spaniards of their encomiendas. Rejecting the path of compromise followed by his counterpart in Mexico at the same time, Núñez was killed in a rebellion led by Gonzalo Pizarro, a younger brother of Francisco. Royal authority in Peru seemed to have collapsed completely. In 1547, however, a new governor, Pedro de la Gasca, was able to restore control by announcing the suspension of the New Laws and winning over many of the rebels. Gonzalo's execution in 1548, followed by a new distribution of encomiendas to those who had supported Gasca, announced the definitive establishment of royal authority in Peru, but at the same time it confirmed the social and economic dominance of the new class of encomenderos.

## The Rise of the Encomienda

During the early stages of colonization, the encomienda dominated Peruvian life completely. It was the main reward given to Spaniards who had participated in the conquest. It was the basic institution for the control of the Indian population and the very foundation of the system of defense. It offered virtually the only route to the attainment of wealth and political power. In short, during these early years, Peruvian society was organized around the encomienda in much the same way that it would later be organized around the hacienda, and much as medieval European society had once been organized around the fief.

The reasons for this phenomenon are fairly clear. Ambitious sixteenth-century Spaniards not born into the higher aristocracy had three principal ways of raising their social status: procurement of liquid wealth, particularly in the form of booty or rents; acquisition of landed estates with dependents who owed them dues and services; investment with political or military authority.

While the conquest of Peru made it possible for those who had participated to satisfy these ambitions to a much greater degree than would have been possible for them in Spain, it also presented them with a dilemma. Should they remain in their rude frontier garrison towns or take their booty back to Spain, where they could use it to purchase an estate and a seat on a municipal council? Many returned, and it is likely that more stayed on with the idea of making themselves all the wealthier before they did likewise. Even Cortés says of the Mexican conquistadores that their aim was to strip the country and then to leave it; the attitude of the Peruvian conquistadores seems to have been much the same.

The conquest of Peru may best be viewed as a kind of gold rush, characterized by violence and anarchy, by the immense wealth and power of the lucky few, and by the poverty of the flood of immigrants attracted by the fabulous news of Cajamarca. The expeditions of conquest were essentially speculative enterprises whose primary purpose was the seizure of booty, particularly gold and silver. Horses and weapons were the capital, and profits were distributed according to the amount of capital each individual provided as well as according to rank. There were even cases of partnerships in which capital and profits were shared.[2]

Because of this "gold rush" mentality, Spaniards were seldom inclined to settle down in the territories they had conquered. Thus if the new conquests were to be held — and almost no one seriously contemplated giving them up — the leaders of the expeditions had to provide some inducement for their followers to become settlers. Throughout the Indies this was accomplished by distributing the conquered population among the Spaniards, making them "grand seigneurs" on a scale they could not have dreamed of achieving at home. Even this did not always work. Those who held poorer encomiendas might move on if grander possibilities beckoned. Such lures account in part for the mass emigration from the Caribbean islands after the conquest of Mexico and from Central America after the conquest of Peru.

The Spaniards established an encomienda system in most of the conquered territories, although the encomiendas were not identical wherever they were found. The richest Peruvian encomenderos, for instance, were rather like feudal lords, while Paraguayan encomenderos might be better described as tribal chieftains.[3] The legal literature on encomiendas which grew up later on tended to conceal such variations and to create the impression that the system had been imported in its essentials from Spain. But the Spanish encomienda was quite different from the institution which evolved in the New World.

This is not simply because the Spanish encomienda involved rights over land while the American did not, as has sometimes been suggested. H. B. Johnson has pointed out that late medieval grants of *señorío* in the Iberian peninsula (of which the encomienda represented one type) often conferred rights of jurisdiction, but not necessarily ownership of land. In Spain and Portugal, however, the señorío had a territorial basis, and the rights it conferred were exercised within definite boundaries. This was not true in Peru, where the encomienda bestowed rights to the tribute and labor of the subjects of certain chiefs (*caciques*), not to the Indians who lived in a certain territory. In 1534, for example, Pizarro granted Alonso Riquelme "the cacique Taparas, principal cacique of Tarama [Tarma] and Pombo, with the caciques and *principales* [subordinate chiefs] of the said province, and of the pueblos of Chacamarca and Tambo, with all their Indians and pueblos," following a form which was common in early Peruvian encomienda grants. And this language was not confined to the grants. We read in the minutes of the Lima *cabildo* (municipal council) in 1539 that Alonso Martín de Don Benito, who was "in the cacique of Sangallán" (his encomienda in the Pisco valley), had warned of a brewing Indian revolt, and that Nicolás de Ribera was therefore dispatched to bring back all Spaniards who were still "in their caciques." The language accurately reflects the realities of Indian social organization in sixteenth-century Peru. After the conquest there would grow up a class of Indian *forasteros* (Indians who lived in communities to which they did not belong), who would not be held liable for tribute and labor obligations except in their own communities, even though these might be so far away as to make enforcement impossible.[4]

The American encomienda was composed in practice of two distinct elements, one imposed by the conquerors and the other by the officials of the crown. In the beginning the institution had been known as the "*repartimiento*," a term which referred to the act of distributing Indians among the Spanish settlers, but which came to be used as well for the Indians so distributed. In both senses, the repartimiento represented the provision made locally by the leaders of the expeditions of conquest to satisfy the demands of their followers and to establish a rudimentary administration over the Indian population. The word "encomienda" appeared later, being favored mainly by officials who wished to establish greater uniformity in the chaos of local repartimientos, to bring them within the framework of the Spanish legal system, and to delimit as sharply as possible the powers, rights, and obligations of those who had received them. For these officials, the term was a useful one. The legal position of the Spanish encomienda was already well established, so that Spanish precedents could be applied to American encomiendas. Most importantly, perhaps, encomiendas were usually granted only for the lifetime of the encomendero, a precedent which could be invoked to prevent American encomiendas from becoming hereditary.[5]

In one respect, however, Spanish officials were not willing to copy the Spanish model. They did not want the American encomienda to confer governmental powers, as the Spanish encomienda frequently did, lest the encomenderos turn into the kind of feudal nobility which had plagued the Castilian monarchy in the fifteenth century. Thus American encomenderos never legally exercised civil and criminal jurisdiction over their Indians except in a few unusual cases, and the de facto existence of the encomienda as an administrative institution was never officially recognized by the crown.

The relative importance of the local and official elements in the encomienda varied with time and place. During the first years of Spanish settlement, the crown wielded little real power and was seldom able in practice to prevent encomenderos from exercising the jurisdiction which was officially denied them. Thus in Peru the encomenderos replaced the old Inca governors as the main link between the central authority and the curacas. But while the governors had been closely supervised from Cuzco, the encomenderos were virtually independent.

As time went on, growing tax revenues made possible the creation of a strong royal bureaucracy, which was able to force its conception of the encomienda on the encomenderos throughout most of Peru. In poorer regions like Venezuela or Paraguay, by contrast, the crown was able to pay few officials, and the encomenderos retained more of their power.[6]

The granting of encomiendas was generally associated with the foundation of towns, which was the basic legal mechanism for settling a group of Spaniards in any area, and encomenderos were identified in the first place as *vecinos* (citizens) of a town. The sites were selected with an eye both for strategic considerations and for the number of Indians in the surrounding region who could be distributed to the prospective vecinos. The towns were usually laid out on a gridiron plan, and land was distributed in the form of building lots (*solares*) of a quarter of a block, with larger plots of agricultural land outside the town. Vecinos were expected to maintain their personal residences in town, instead of living on their encomiendas; after 1563 they were expressly forbidden to live among their Indians for more than a few days at a time.[7] The degree to which this rule could be enforced depended on whether the Indian population was large and well enough organized to permit it. On the Peruvian coast, most encomenderos did live mainly in town, but elsewhere they might have to spend most of their time supervising their Indians if they were to receive enough to live on.

The first Spanish town located within the boundaries of modern Peru was San Miguél de Piura, established in one of the northernmost of the coastal valleys by Pizarro, while he was on his way to Cajamarca in 1532. The first vecinos were mainly older men and the sick, and the encomiendas they received were poor compensation for what they lost by not continuing with Pizarro. In 1535 a visitor in the area reported to the Council of the Indies that most of the Indians had fled into the mountains to get away from the Spaniards, and that the vecinos lived from trading with and "almost robbing" those who passed through the town. Thirty years later the governor in Lima noted continuing difficulty in keeping Spaniards of substance living in the town.[8]

As the Spanish forces progressed southward, they founded two more Spanish towns: Jauja (1533), in the central sierra to the east of Pachacamac, and Cuzco (1534), at the Inca capital. The vecinos of Jauja disliked the site of their town, which like Cuzco was located at an altitude of 11,000 feet, and in 1535 they abandoned it to found the new town of

Lima on the coast. The town of Trujillo was founded this same year next to the ruined Chimú capital of Chanchan. After Manco's rebellion and the defeat of Almagro three more towns were established: Arequipa and Huamanga (Ayacucho) in 1539, and Huánuco in 1542.[9]

There were also two ephemeral towns on the coast. In 1534 an Indian rebellion had led to the foundation of a small garrison town at the old Inca administrative center of Sangallán in the Pisco valley. But the vecinos, a group of men from Jauja under the leadership of Nicolás de Ribera, moved to Lima when it was founded the next year. The other town, located in the Chincha valley, was founded by Almagro in the course of the first civil war. It was evacuated when he left the coast with his army to return to Cuzco and was never refounded.[10]

After 1542, then, Peruvian encomenderos were distributed among seven Spanish towns: Piura and Trujillo in the north; Lima, Huánuco, and Huamanga in the center; and Cuzco and Arequipa in the south. Normally encomienda location dictated the town where one lived. On the coast, encomenderos from Huarmey to the north lived in Trujillo or Piura; those from Pativilca to Nazca lived in Lima; and those from Acarí to the south lived in Arequipa. There were exceptions, however, like Juan de Barbarán, who was allowed to live in Lima and even to become a magistrate (*alcalde*) of the city, though his encomienda of Lambayeque was on the north coast.[11] Many of the vecinos of the coastal towns had their encomiendas in the sierra: of Lima's major encomiendas only about half were on the coast, and in the case of Arequipa the proportion was much lower.

How large were these encomiendas? An approximate answer to this question is possible for the coastal encomiendas granted to the founders of Lima. We have early estimates of the number of households contained in the pre-conquest provinces of Chincha, Pachacamac, and Huaura. By comparing these with the tributary figures collected for the viceroy Toledo about 1575, it is possible to calculate ratios of decline applicable to the encomiendas which were cut out of these three provinces. We can also calculate an average ratio of decline for the whole central coast. These ratios can then be used to estimate the pre-conquest tributary population of individual encomiendas.[12]

The results of these calculations (table 3) suggest that the coastal encomiendas in the Lima district ranged in size from Chincha's 30,000 tributaries down to less than 1,000 in the case of some of the Lima valley encomiendas. Classified according to size, these encomiendas seem

**Table 3.** Tributary Population of Central Coast Encomiendas, c. 1525

| Encomiendas[a] | Tributary population c. 1575 | Ratio of decline[b] (1525-1575) | Projected tributary population c. 1525 |
|---|---|---|---|
| Huarmey | 204 | 28 | 6,000 |
| Barranca (Pativilca) | 268 | 28 | 8,000 |
| Supe | 102 | 28 | 3,000 |
| Huaura | 391 | 28 | 11,000 |
| Vegueta | 124 | 28 | 3,000 |
| Aucallama (Chancay) | 420 | 25 | 11,000 |
| Chancayllo | 94 | 25 | 2,000 |
| Zupillán | 28 | 25 | 700 |
| Surco (Lima) | 370 | 18 | 7,000 |
| Magdalena | 246 | 18 | 4,000 |
| Carabayllo | 184 | 18 | 3,000 |
| Maranga | 133 | 18 | 3,000 |
| Late | 86 | 18 | 2,000 |
| Lurigancho | 83 | 18 | 1,000 |
| Huanchoguaylas | 43 | 18 | 800 |
| Cacahuasi | 17 | 18 | 300 |
| Puruchuco | 12 | 18 | 200 |
| Pachacamac | 162 | 18 | 3,000 |
| Manchay | 37 | 18 | 700 |
| Caringas | 26 | 18 | 500 |
| Chilca and Mala | 225 | 25 | 6,000 |
| Coayllo and Calango | 397 | 25 | 10,000 |
| Huarco (Cañete) | 21 | 25 | 500 |
| Lunahuaná | 740 | 25 | 19,000 |
| Chincha | 979 | 31 | 30,000 |
| Pisco | 285 | 25 | 7,000 |
| Humay | 167 | 25 | 4,000 |
| Lurin Ica | 731 | 25 | 18,000 |
| Hanan Ica | 709 | 25 | 18,000 |
| Nazca | 630 | 25 | 16,000 |

*Source:* Cook, "Indian Population," pp. 351-353.

[a]The encomiendas are grouped together by valleys.

[b]See table 5, below. The average value of 25 is used for encomiendas outside of the Chincha, Lima-Pachacamac, and Huarmey-Huaura areas. A denominator of one is assumed in all cases.

to fall into three main groups: large encomiendas with more than 10,000 tributaries, substantial encomiendas with 5,000 to 10,000 tributaries, and small encomiendas with fewer than 5,000 tributaries.

The large encomiendas were given mainly to those who had been leaders in the expeditions of conquest. Chincha first belonged to Hernando Pizarro, the governor's older brother and second-in-command, and it was subsequently taken over by the crown. The original Huaura encomienda, which was almost as large, was taken by Almagro; after his death it may have belonged briefly to Pizarro himself before being broken up into the five smaller encomiendas of Huaura, Végueta, Supe, Barranca, and Huarmey. The first holder of the smaller Huaura encomienda was Ventura Beltrán, a latecomer whose main claim to it seems to have been that he was the oldest son of an important member of the Council of the Indies. Lunahuaná went to Captain Diego de Agüero, a member of the Lima cabildo from 1535 until his death; Lurin Ica to the older Nicolás de Ribera, one of Pizarro's thirteen companions on the island of Gallo in 1527 and the first alcalde elected in Lima; Nazca to the royal *veedor* (comptroller) García de Salcedo. Aucallama was first given to the Dominican order in Lima and, like Chincha, it subsequently passed to the crown. Hanan Ica, on the other hand, was not granted initially as a single encomienda, but rather divided between two men of lower status, Juan de Barrios (who later held the whole encomienda) and Felipe Boscán.[13]

The "substantial" encomiendas went generally to rank and file conquistadores: men like the trumpeter Pedro de Alconchel (Chilca and Mala); Pedro Navarro, who was a retainer and friend of Francisco Pizarro (Coayllo and Calango); the illiterate peasant Pedro Martín de Sicilia (Pisco). On the other hand, Felipe Boscán, who got half of Hanan Ica, was a merchant who had arrived in Peru only in 1536, and the encomienda of Huarmey was given after Almagro's death to Pizarro's Indian interpreter Martinillo.[14]

Small encomiendas, apparently considered inadequate to sustain a Spaniard of any consequence by themselves, were seldom granted separately. Thus Alonso Martín de Don Benito was given both Humay and Ate, and later on Huarco as well. More often, these small coastal encomiendas were granted along with larger ones in the sierra, perhaps to provide a more accessible supply of labor. Both Jerónimo de Aliaga and Sebastián de Torres received encomiendas in the Callejón de Huaylas along with smaller ones in the Chancay valley. The royal treasurer Alonso Riquelme, Pizarro's half-brother Francisco Martín de Alcántara, and his private secretary Antonio Picado all had small encomiendas in the Lima or Pachacamac valleys in addition to larger ones in the sierra to the east.[15]

How did these encomiendas compare with their counterparts in the highlands? In his account of the conquest, Juan Ruiz de Arce said that in 1534 the founders of Cuzco received encomiendas of from 5,000 to 40,000 tributaries.[16] The latter figure is probably too high, since it is unlikely that there were any single encomiendas in Peru larger than those given to Almagro and Hernando Pizarro (Francisco Pizarro may have received more tributaries in all, but if so they were divided among several encomiendas). It is true that by the 1570's the largest sierra encomiendas invariably contained many more tributaries than the largest coastal ones, but the sierra was depopulated less rapidly than the coast. The evidence we possess on this subject suggests that in the central sierra the number of tributaries may have declined in a ratio of five or six to one during the period 1525-1562, while in the south the ratio of decline may have been lower than two to one during the similar period 1525-1567.[17] Since there were only three or four sierra encomiendas with more than 3,000 tributaries in the 1570's, the upper limit in that region was probably close to 20,000. This was of course true of our coastal sample as well if we exclude the exceptionally large Pizarro and Almagro encomiendas. Ruiz de Arce's lower figure of 5,000 also fits well with the coastal evidence, provided we take it as applying to the total number of tributaries granted an encomendero instead of to the size of individual encomiendas. Presumably there were encomiendas with fewer than 5,000 tributaries in the highlands, as on the coast, but at least within the principal areas of Spanish settlement an encomendero usually received more than one of them.

It is not surprising, then, that many of Lima's more prominent vecinos took their encomiendas on the coast. Of the nine or ten large encomiendas within the district of the city, six were on the coast. And García de Salcedo was said to have exchanged his original encomienda of Huarochirí for that of Nazca, which was presumably larger. It was only in the 1540's that coastal encomiendas began to seem insufficient. Perhaps the earliest sign of the change was Felipe Boscán's decision to give up his half of Hanan Ica in return for a new encomienda in the sierra, because, in the words of the new grant, the old encomienda was

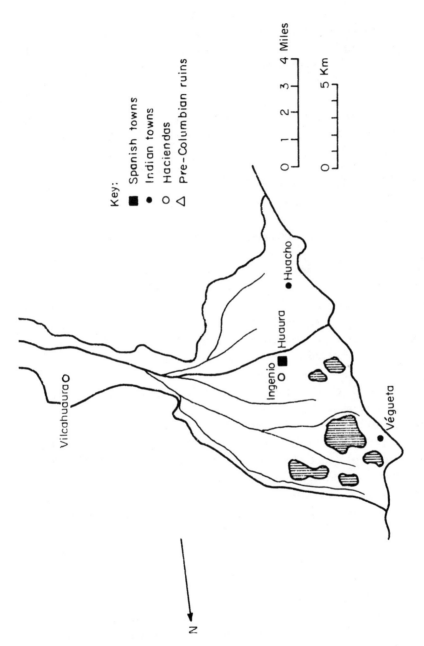

Key:
■ Spanish towns
● Indian towns
○ Haciendas
△ Pre-Columbian ruins

Vilcahuaura ○

Huacho ●

Huaura ■

Ingenio ○

Végueta ●

N

0  1  2  3  4 Miles

0        5 Km

Map 3. The Huaura Valley

too small to support a conquistador "according to the quality of his person."[18]

The social background of the vecinos of Lima who originally held these encomiendas varied. Like the conquistadores in general, few were aristocrats, though some could claim connection with noble or hidalgo families, or at least had enough education to differentiate themselves from peasants and laborers. Captain Diego de Agüero, for instance, was probably related to the Spanish Agüeros, but the exact nature of the connection is unclear. The fact that he was illiterate suggests that it cannot have been too close, and that his position in Peru depended as much on his military reputation as on his name. Similarly Jerónimo de Aliaga, a young man with some education who came to join Pizarro in 1531, may have been related to an hidalgo family in Spain, but he was never able to produce evidence to support a personal claim to hidalgo status. His reputation and position in Peru seem to have derived from his notarial training and his skill in acquiring high governmental offices for himself. Though he himself finally returned to Spain, he founded one of the longest-lived of Peru's Spanish families: there are Aliagas still living on the site of the original family house in Lima.[19] Other men with some rank and education who became vecinos of Lima included the royal officials Alonso Riquelme and García de Salcedo and Pizarro's secretary Antonio Picado, who was given the encomienda of Huarochirí.

The majority of the original vecinos of the city, however, were men of lower-class origin. One man may perhaps be taken to stand for all of them, though his career in the Indies was longer than that of most. Alonso Martín de Don Benito was born in 1481 in the pueblo of Don Benito in the province of Badajóz.[20] He came out to the West Indies in 1512, spent several years on the island of Española where he received an encomienda, then continued on to Darién soon after it was first settled. Accompanying Balboa on his first crossing of the isthmus, he was one of the founders of the city of Panama, and subsequently participated in Pizarro's early explorations to the south. He left Pizarro, however, to help suppress an Indian uprising in Nicaragua; and there he became one of the founders of the town of León, where he then lived for several years.

The news of the conquest of Peru brought him south again, and in Quito he joined Almagro in time for the latter's negotiations with the interloping conquistador Pedro de Alvarado. After catching up with

Pizarro in Cuzco, he was sent — perhaps because of his past experience
with such matters — to assist in choosing a site for the new city of Lima.
He was rewarded with encomiendas in the Pisco and Lima valleys and
quickly formed a partnership with his brother, Pedro Martín de Sicilia,
who had also received an encomienda in the Pisco valley.[21]

Now in his late fifties, Alonso found himself a Spanish wife and settled down to a more stable existence. Perhaps because of his age, he
managed to avoid any compromising involvement in the civil wars,
unlike his brother, who was a fanatical supporter of Gonzalo Pizarro
and was executed after the latter's defeat in 1548. Alonso died in 1558
without legitimate children, leaving a third of his property to his wife
and the rest to Hernando Alonso, an illegitimate son by an Indian
woman from Central America. This son was later to become a large
landowner in the Cañete valley, and may have inherited some land in
the Pisco valley as well, since we know of a landowner and local official
named Alonso Martín de Don Benito who lived there at the beginning
of the seventeenth century. The widow took the encomiendas to her
second husband, a man named Nuño Rodríguez Barreto, whose descendants would also be landowners in the Pisco valley.[22]

The encomienda provided well for those who became encomenderos, but most Spaniards who came to Peru in the 1530's did not
achieve that status. How, then, did the system provide for the allocation of goods among the Spanish population in general? For the period
after 1550, when a market system began to develop around the mines
and the major cities, the answer to this question is fairly clear; but
before that it is more complicated. Goods were bought and sold in
Peru from the time of the conquest, and there was some circulation of
gold and silver in the form of coins, dust, and bars. But this buying
and selling was limited chiefly to scarce goods of high value, such as
Spanish imports, horses, herds of livestock, or houses. It did not en-
compass the necessities of daily life.[23]

The Incas themselves had not had a market system. Individual communities were encouraged to be as self-sufficient as possible, and what
bartering there was took place mainly on a local level. But most communities produced a surplus which was collected by the Inca rulers
and redistributed among their followers and dependents. After the
conquest this system continued to function. But it was now the encomenderos who collected and redistributed the surplus, with the result
that they possessed a kind of monopoly over the economic life of Span-

ish Peru. They alone had direct access to the surpluses produced by the Indian economy; they alone had the capital necessary to engage in any kind of independent economic activity; they alone had access to significant amounts of Indian labor.*

Most Spaniards were thereby forced to become dependents of the encomenderos. All encomenderos supported and were expected to support large numbers of clients, some of whom formed part of their immediate households, while others operated more independently. They employed servants of many kinds in their large urban residences as well as overseers to manage the encomiendas and numerous ancillary enterprises. They contracted with miners to operate their mines and with merchants to import Spanish goods with their capital. They supported artisans like the tailor Domingo de Destre, who lived in Diego de Agüero's house in Lima for a number of years and had a child by one of his slaves. Finally, they supported military retainers to accompany them when the feudal militia of the post-conquest years was called out to resist invasion or suppress revolt. In a sense, as Lockhart has suggested, encomiendas should be considered as belonging to groups of men rather than to individuals.[24]

In these early years, then, the function of allocating goods among the Spanish population was performed by a system of clientage rather than by a market system. Although the Spaniards engaged in some independent buying and selling, the great houses of the encomenderos were the main centers for distributing common goods. Thus the main concern of the encomendero was less to make a profit than to obtain the goods and services necessary to satisfy large numbers of dependents.

Much of what an encomendero provided for his dependents could be produced locally. His Indians brought agricultural produce — particularly maize on the coast — and cloth. This met the basic requirements of subsistence, but it did not satisfy the desire to enjoy Spanish food. Many encomenderos therefore had their Indians grow wheat, hired men to raise Spanish vegetables and fruits, and built up herds of livestock. They even arranged to supply their households with daily rations of fish. In 1542, for instance, the younger Nicolás de

---

*Churchmen and officials might seem to be outside this system, but in the early years they were usually supported by encomiendas as well.

Ribera formed a partnership with a Spanish fisherman who agreed to provide half an *arroba* (about six pounds) of fish each day if Ribera supplied half the necessary capital plus the labor of six Indians from his encomienda in the lower Rimac valley.[25]

Some goods which the settlers desired, however, still had to be imported: European clothing, wine, and olive oil, for example.[26] Gold or silver was necessary to purchase such goods, which put coastal encomenderos at something of a disadvantage, since the mines were all in the highlands. The only significant source of precious metals on the coast was the Indian burial mounds (*huacas*) which still attract treasure hunters today. But gold and silver could be obtained in other ways. Livestock could be bred for sale — especially horses, whose value in the early years was very high. Another alternative was to provide a service, such as milling flour. Two of the earliest mills in Lima belonged to the encomenderos Pedro Navarro and Jerónimo de Aliaga.[27]

Gold and silver could also be acquired from renting houses and shops in the city. Such real estate dealings would later be one of the principal sources of income for some encomenderos, though in the beginning there cannot have been many who could afford to pay high rents. When Diego de Agüero died in 1544, he already owned six different houses in Lima in addition to the one he lived in; his grandson had as many houses as there were days in the year according to Cobo, and they would have provided him with 80,000 pesos a year in rents had they not been let out on long leases. In 1561, the son of another encomendero was renting out some fourteen different houses, mostly to artisans, for sums which varied between 100 and 450 pesos a year.[28]

Encomenderos held their dependents not only by distributing goods but also by providing services. During the first twenty years after the conquest, Indian labor on the coast was used mainly in construction and domestic service. With their large households, encomenderos required numerous Indians to serve as cooks, janitors, porters, and in other domestic capacities. They probably provided Indian servants for their Spanish dependents as well. Thus at periodic intervals, the curacas of each encomienda were required to send a large contingent of Indians to carry the tribute goods to Lima; these Indians remained in the city until the next tribute payment was due, serving their encomenderos and living on building lots set aside for this purpose by the municipal government.

## The Decline of the Encomienda

This early economic and social pattern began to change in the mid-
1540's. The discovery of new mines—particularly Potosí, in 1545—
helped to stimulate the development of markets in many areas, thus
offering new economic opportunities to those with access to labor. As a
result, encomiendas came increasingly to be valued in terms of their
potential for profit, even when this potential was not fully realized. In
1548 the encomienda of the Chupachos was said to be capable of providing an income of 2,000 pesos a year, "if it were exploited which up
to now has not been the case."[29] Perhaps more important, it was becoming clear that the traditional Indian societies on which the encomenderos depended were changing in ways that decreased their ability
to support the Spanish population. These changes, which occurred
with exceptional rapidity on the coast, were a consequence in the first
place of catastrophic depopulation and, in the second, of profound
political and social disorganization.

First the depopulation. A comparison of the pre-conquest figures
with sixteenth-century Spanish figures for the same areas (table 4) suggests that on the average the tributary population of the central coast
declined in a ratio of about 25:1 between 1525 and 1575 and in a ratio
of about 53:1 between 1525 and 1600 (table 5). Put another way, this
means that the number of tributaries still living in traditional Indian
communities in 1575 was about 4 percent of what it had been before
the conquest; and by the early seventeenth century, this number had
declined to less than 2 percent of the pre-conquest figure. Since the
Spaniards, as we have seen, usually classified a higher proportion of

**Table 4.**   Tributary Population of Central Coast Valleys

| Valleys | Year | | |
|---|---|---|---|
| | c. 1525 | c. 1575 | c. 1600 |
| Chincha | 30,000 | 979 | 316 |
| Lima-Pachacamac | 25,000 | 1,373 | 594 |
| Huarmey-Huaura | 30,000 | 1,089 | 707 |
| Total | 85,000 | 3,441 | 1,617 |

Sources: Molina, "Relación de muchas cosas," p. 67; Vedia, Historiadores primitivos, II, 424; Lizárraga, Descripción breve, p. 44; Cook, "Indian Population,"
pp. 351-353 (encomienda code numbers 61, 101-104, 119-131, 139).

**Table 5.**   Rates of Tributary Decline on the Central Coast

| Valley | 1525-1600 | | 1525-1575 | | 1575-1600 | |
|---|---|---|---|---|---|---|
| | Ratio[a] | Average yearly rate[b] (%) | Ratio | Average yearly rate (%) | Ratio | Average yearly rate (%) |
| Chincha | 95 | 6 | 31 | 7 | 3.1 | 5 |
| Lima-Pachacamac | 42 | 5 | 18 | 6 | 2.3 | 3 |
| Huarmey-Huaura | 42 | 5 | 28 | 7 | 1.5 | 2 |
| Average | 53 | 6 | 25 | 7 | 2.1 | 3 |

[a]Ratios are calculated from the figures given in table 4; denominator = 1.

[b]The average yearly rate is derived from the formula $r = \sqrt[t]{R_t}$ where $R_t$ is the ratio of decline over a specified number of years (t). The percentage rate of decline then equals $\frac{r-1}{r}$

the total population as tributaries than the Incas had done, these ratios may well underestimate the overall decline of the Indian population in these years. We do not have the data necessary to make similar calculations for the northern and southern parts of the coast in the years before 1575, but it seems likely that the population of the south declined about as rapidly as that of the center, while the population of the northern valleys—and particularly of the large Lambayeque complex—declined somewhat more slowly. In all cases, the rates of population decline on the coast seem to have been considerably higher than those in the highlands.

The primary cause of this depopulation was epidemic disease. Having lived in isolation from the Old World, the Indians had no resistance to the diseases carried by Europeans, which were as a result much more devastating. In Peru, smallpox first occurred several years before the Spanish conquest and was probably responsible for the deaths of Huayna Capac and his chosen successor. This epidemic originally struck Mexico in 1520 and subsequently travelled southward through Central America and along the Andes before reaching Peru. It may have killed from a third to a half of the population in the regions it affected, which is consistent with what we know of such epidemics. Moreover, the Indians were fighting not just one new disease, but a whole host of them. Within thirty years of the conquest they had seen at least three more epidemics, possibly of measles, typhus, and of smallpox again.[30]

But the depopulation of the coast cannot be attributed entirely to disease. A quarter-century of political disorder and intermittent warfare, beginning with the Inca civil war and lasting through the suppression of the Hernández Girón revolt in 1554, presumably took its toll, as did exploitation by passing Spaniards. Whether travelling in small detachments or in large armies, the conquerors were accustomed to feed themselves at the expense of the local Indian population and to conscript as many as they needed to serve as carriers. One of the chroniclers — admittedly not an impartial one — tells how Gonzalo Pizarro brought an army to a sierra town early in his rebellion against Blasco Núñez and demanded 10,000 Indians "to carry his clothing and that of his captains and soldiers as well as the artillery and ammunition he had." The curacas, unable to find so large a number, attempted to flee, but Pizarro caught two of them and had them executed. This frightened the curacas of the surrounding territory into assembling 6,000 Indians, including their own wives and daughters, many of them pregnant; most were said to have died of the treatment they received. The story, though probably exaggerated, is not totally apocryphal, and similar abuses doubtless occurred in other towns when armies arrived. Such conscription was also a characteristic feature of the expeditions (*entradas*) sent out after each of the civil wars to get rid of the unemployed soldiers for whom there were no encomiendas, and in spite of government regulations it long continued to be the normal practice for any travelling Spaniard.[31]

Those who criticized the conduct of the Spanish conquistadores often blamed the decline of the Indian population on the encomienda. This point of view, which reinforced the crown's inherent dislike for the institution, found expression in the famous New Laws of 1542, but it was not completely justified. Encomenderos did exploit their Indians for their own purposes, as did most Spaniards in the New World, but their own interest in maintaining the value of their encomiendas for themselves and their heirs set limits on the exploitation. And the encomenderos had a clear interest in preventing others from exploiting their Indians; some important and responsible officials in Peru even believed that the creation of hereditary encomiendas would ultimately be to the benefit of the Indians.[32] Certainly the replacement of encomenderos with *corregidores de indios* was not an improvement from the Indian point of view.

In practice, however, the encomenderos could not protect their Indians effectively enough, either from the armies of the civil wars, from the Spanish transients (*soldados*), or from the mestizos, Negroes, and mulattoes whom the crown was perpetually ordering the viceroys to banish from the Indian towns. In most cases, the encomendero probably found it difficult even to protect them from encomienda employees, whose interest tended to be less than his. Faced with such competition many encomenderos may have decided to take what they could get from their Indians, feeling that otherwise the illicit benefits derived from their encomiendas would merely go to someone else. But the number who provided in their wills that restitution of some kind be made to their Indians suggests that they felt some guilt over this failure to respect their responsibilities. It is perhaps significant that the Indian chronicler Poma de Ayala is less hard on the encomenderos, some of whom he admits are "good Christians and friends of the poor," than on most Spaniards who had frequent contact with the Indians.[33]

Another cause of the depopulation of coastal communities was migration. During the early years of the conquest many Indians migrated to escape from the Spaniards. In Piura, for instance, a visitor in 1535 told how "the few Indians there were have fled to the mountains due to the oppression of the Spaniards, and if they catch someone off the road they kill him." Later on they migrated primarily to the Spanish towns to become artisans or *yanaconas*.* In the early seventeenth century, the Indian population of Lima was drawn from as far away as Chile and Panama, and there were even a few "Indians" from Portuguese Asia.[34]

In 1583 some twenty-five men, about 10 percent of the tributary population of the encomienda of Huaura, were living in or around Lima. Several were serving as yanaconas, one was a shoemaker, and one gained his living by fishing—and these were probably just the recent migrants. Coastal curacas did not have the means to force such emigrants to carry their share of community tribute and labor obligations, and after a time they simply ceased to list them. At the end of the century, men who had lived in the Indian town of El Cercado at Lima for over five years were officially exempted from their obliga-

---

*On the coast during the later sixteenth century, *yanacona* usually meant an agricultural laborer hired by the year.

tions to their native communities, and it is likely that this was little more than a recognition of existing practice. The reasons for this migration were mainly economic. Since Spanish tribute and labor demands were not lowered rapidly enough to keep up with the shrinking population, the burden on individual members of the community tended to increase. At the same time the growth and prosperity of Lima provided new opportunities and sources of income for Indians as well as for Spaniards. A relative shortage of women at home may also have been a factor in the migration. Many of the Huaura emigrants were bachelors—the number of young men was considerably larger than the number of young women—and most of those who were listed as having wives seem to have found them in Lima or one of the surrounding towns.[35]

Although the general causes of depopulation were the same throughout the coastal region, they affected different valleys in different ways. The census figures for the last quarter of the century (table 6) suggest that the valleys of the center and south suffered a more serious decline than those of the north. They also indicate that the most severe depopulation occurred in the valleys around Arequipa, where the magnitude of the decline may have been a consequence of the volcanic eruption which devastated the city and the surrounding area in 1600.[36]

But one cannot assume that the same pattern had prevailed before 1575. It is evident (tables 5 and 6) that the Indian population of the Huaura region declined more slowly than that of most other areas on the coast between 1575 and 1600, but that between 1525 and 1575 its rate of decline had been relatively high. In the Lima area, on the other hand, the rate of depopulation seems to have been unusually low in the earlier period and relatively high during the later one. This would suggest that proximity to Lima helped to protect Indian villages from some of the disruptive forces of the conquest era, especially armies and Spanish travellers. After about 1560, however, local rates of depopulation would have been increasingly affected by the development of the Spanish economy, and since this development occurred most strongly around the main Spanish towns, proximity to Lima served to accelerate the rate of decline.

By the same reasoning, the relatively low rates of decline found in the Huaura area and on the north coast after 1575 probably reflect the distance of these valleys from the main Peruvian centers of demand,

**Table 6.**  Tributary Decline in Selected Coastal Encomiendas, c. 1575-1600

| Encomiendas | Tributary population c. 1575 | Tributary population c.1600 | Ratio of decline |
|---|---|---|---|
| Lambayeque | 1,584 | 1,065 | 1.5 |
| Reque | 650 | 324 | 2.0 |
| Jequetepeque | 896 | 553 | 1.6 |
| Chicama | 955 | 457 | 2.1 |
| Barranca | 268 | 172 | 1.6 |
| Huaura | 391 | 275 | 1.4 |
| Aucallama | 420 | 125 | 3.4 |
| Magdalena | 246 | 89 | 2.8 |
| Surco | 370 | 192 | 1.9 |
| Lunahuaná | 740 | 320 | 2.3 |
| Chincha | 979 | 316 | 3.1 |
| Pisco | 285 | 133 | 2.1 |
| Lurin Ica | 731 | 374 | 2.0 |
| Hanan Ica | 709 | 371 | 1.9 |
| Nazca | 630 | 328 | 1.9 |
| Acarí | 693 | 240 | 2.9 |
| Mages | 303 | 91 | 3.3 |
| Quilca and Vítor | 183 | 56 | 7.4 |
| Caravelí and Atico | 417 | 181 | 2.3 |

*Source:* Cook, "Indian Population," Appendix III.

which were located mainly in the center and south of the country, and which provided the chief stimulus for economic development elsewhere on the coast. But the development of a Spanish economy and rapid depopulation were not always paired in this way. In the Ica and Nazca valleys, depopulation rates were relatively low in spite of the growth of a highly profitable wine industry. The explanation may be that grape cultivation provided new opportunities not only to Spaniards, but also to Indians, who did not have to leave home to take advantage of them. The incentive to emigrate would thus have been lessened, and probably additional Indians were attracted from outside. In Chincha and Aucallama the low level of economic development did not prevent depopulation rates from being very high. Does the fact that both were crown encomiendas perhaps suggest that officials were more efficient about collecting the tribute when it was going to the king instead of to a private encomendero? Certainly the crown, which drove itself into bankruptcy several times during the last quarter of the sixteenth century trying to implement a foreign policy it could not afford, ordinarily exploited its regular sources of income as ruthlessly as possible.[37]

Along with the depopulation of its traditional communities, post-conquest coastal society suffered a growing political disorganization which ultimately left it unable to function adequately. As we have seen, the political structure of the Inca empire was based on a bureaucratic system in which the power of the curacas was limited by the supervisory authority of Inca officials. This tradition had been borrowed by the Incas from the coast; there it played an even more fundamental role, since the continued regulation of irrigation and agriculture was necessary to insure the survival of society itself. Within a few years, however, the Spaniards had brought about the collapse of this bureaucratic system. Having decided to rule through the curacas, who were attached to the encomenderos, they quickly deprived higher officials of all real power, though some of them retained considerable prestige. The curacas therefore tended to become more powerful than they had been under the Incas. As one contemporary picturesquely put it, "each one became in his own dung heap what the Inca had been before in the whole kingdom."[38] But the curacas' new power did not have very stable foundations. It was dependent partly on their ability to get on with their encomenderos, who in the conditions of the sixteenth century were capable of deposing them, and partly on their position within a hierarchical social structure which was gradually being subverted by the appearance of new ways to acquire wealth and power.[39]

The reorganization and consolidation of Indian communities in the later sixteenth century was a logical consequence of the collapse of the traditional political system. As the lawyer Matienzo put it, the founding of new towns or *reducciones* was necessary in order to teach the Indians to govern themselves ("enseñarles la policía humana").[40] But sixteenth-century Spaniards were not democrats. They considered most Indians naturally lazy and thought that, without someone standing over them, they would not work to get their tribute money or even to support themselves; rather they would spend their time drinking maize beer (*chicha*). To the Dominican Reginaldo de Lizárraga in the early seventeenth century—and his opinion was widely shared—drunkenness appeared to be the major cause of Indian depopulation. The Incas, it was thought, had kept laziness and drunkenness under control by forcing the Indians to work and seeing that they did not have much spare time. After their fall the task passed to the curacas, who were more inclined to exploit their subjects than to care for them.[41]

One may question the validity of these Spanish assumptions about Indian behavior, but there is little doubt that some kind of political reorganization was necessary. In the highlands, Spanish policy encouraged many communities to build a new political system, one which was more suited to the conditions of colonial Peru and better able to resist outside pressure. Under this system, which in some areas has lasted down to the present century, leadership was provided by Indian alcaldes (*varayoc*) who exercised authority in accordance with traditional Indian practice. On the coast such reorganization could not save the Indian communities, but it supplied political patterns which were used in the mestizo communities which took their place.[42]

This transformation of coastal society also involved major changes in the system of land tenure. We have seen that the coastal states had regulated the use of water and land, usually on a valley-wide basis and sometimes throughout complexes which included several valleys, and that this practice had continued under the Incas. Within thirty years of the Spanish conquest, however, it had disappeared. The collapse of the traditional bureaucratic structure made it impossible to continue the regulation of irrigation over wide areas, and the allocation of water and land therefore became an essentially local affair. Moreover, as the Indian population declined, less land was needed for its support and less labor was available to maintain the irrigation canals. As a consequence, the old settlements of the coast tended to consolidate themselves into larger towns, which were generally located in the lower reaches of the valleys. The Indians of the Ingenio valley had apparently withdrawn to Nazca before García de Salcedo bought the valley from them in 1546. By 1549 the three colonial Indian towns of the Ica valley had been established. By the early 1550's Surco, Magdalena, and Ate had become the Indian towns of the south side of the Lima valley. And Huaura and Aucallama in the Chancay valley were established in 1551.[43]

This resettlement of the population meant that large amounts of land which would ultimately end up in Spanish possession were effectively abandoned by the coastal Indians, but in the fifties and sixties

Spaniards as yet had relatively little interest in it, except around Lima. Some of this land, including large areas on the north coast, reverted to desert.[44] In other places, where the soil continued to receive some moisture, the abandoned land grew up in various kinds of wild grasses and canes. Elsewhere the ground came to be covered with carob (*algarrobo*) forests. These were most prominent on the north coast, where they were to provide the basis for an important goat-raising industry, and to the south of Ica, where according to Vásquez de Espinosa "there are five leagues of these woods, so thick that the highway is the only way to get through them, and one sees nothing but woods and sky."[45]

Wild growth of this kind provided most of the food for livestock in all the coastal valleys during the sixteenth century as well as hide-outs for the runaway slaves (*cimarrones*) who threatened the lives of travellers and farmers.[46] Such areas would be ever more difficult and expensive to reclaim for cultivation, and thus it became more likely that such reclamation would ultimately be carried out by Spaniards rather than Indians. In later years, Spaniards frequently justified their title to land by citing the expenses of reclamation. One man involved in a dispute over a piece of land in 1559 stated that over the three preceding years he had cleared it, turned it into ploughland, and built a house on it, "in all of which he had spent a sum of money equivalent to the original value of the land, which had previously been useless and unprofitable canebrakes (*cañaverales*)." A man who received a grant in the Chancay valley in 1558 hired a notary to testify that the land involved was all grassland and canebrake and had no irrigation ditches in working order, so that a substantial investment would be necessary before the land could be cultivated.[47]

Accompanying this transformation of Indian coastal society was a major decrease in its overall productivity, which would make it necessary to reconsider the whole economic basis of Spanish colonization in the region. The encomienda system had been established at a time when the Spanish population of the country was still very small. Roughly five hundred encomiendas were granted to vecinos of the towns from Quito to La Plata (Sucre), and any Spaniard who arrived in the country by 1533 and seriously wanted an encomienda probably got one. But as more and more immigrants came, the proportion of the Spanish population holding encomiendas grew progressively smaller. In 1536 about a quarter of the Spaniards were encomenderos, by 1555 only one-sixteenth.[48]

The increase in the number of non-encomenderos created a serious problem. If the system had worked properly, the encomenderos should have taken them on as dependents, but Indian depopulation and the decline in tribute payments greatly cut down on the number they could support. At the same time, with the economic resources of the country largely controlled by the encomenderos and the men who worked for them, there was little opportunity for anyone not protected by some encomendero. It was under these conditions that the class of *soldados* appeared in Peru, where by the 1550's they constituted between 25 and 50 percent of the Spanish population. Unemployed and impoverished, these men wandered about the country living off the Indian population and hoping to win an encomienda or, perhaps more realistically for most, permanent employment in the retinue of an encomendero. They tended to congregate particularly in the region between Cuzco and La Plata, where the authority of the government was least effective. And though poor, they considered themselves conquistadores with as much right to wealth and honor as many of those who had achieved it.[49]

The soldados found their greatest opportunities during the civil wars. By attaching themselves to a leader on the winning side, they might obtain a share of the wealth and privilege from which they had previously been excluded. Their very presence thus served to encourage revolt against those in authority, since they were always ready to enlist in support of any malcontent who seemed to have a chance of success. The royal governors, who early recognized this fact, strove to get rid of as many of the soldados as possible, to "*descargar la tierra.*" This was sometimes accomplished by sending them off on further expeditions of exploration and conquest (*entradas*). But these were wasteful of Indian lives and could in any case only be a temporary expedient, since they almost never discovered the wealth they were seeking. The *Ordenanzas sobre descubrimientos* of 1573 ended the practice by prohibiting most entradas, but a substitute was later found in the Araucanian wars in Chile.[50]

In order to achieve political stability, it was necessary to discover new ways of rewarding these men and changing them into peaceful citizens. The viceroys of the 1550's and 1560's distributed monetary

pensions, obtained by diverting part of the tribute from an encomienda when it was reassigned or by taking it directly from the royal
treasury. The Marqués de Cañete established a salaried viceregal
guard, in large part recruited from the unemployed pretenders to
encomiendas. In spite of royal complaints about the expense, the
guard remained in existence for many years. At the end of the century
it included two companies of one hundred men each, half of whom
were paid 800 pesos a year and half 400 pesos.[51]

These were stopgap measures, however. The root of the problem
was the economic and political hegemony of the encomenderos, and a
real solution could be achieved only if this were broken in order to
provide opportunities to a larger segment of the Spanish population.
Such a reform was encouraged both by humanitarian criticism of the
encomienda and by the official conviction that the wealth and power
of the encomenderos represented a threat to royal authority in Peru.
The trouble was that the crown exercised little real power of its own in
the country and was in no position to impose its will on the encomenderos except by appealing to the revolutionary force of the soldados
themselves.

By the 1550's, however, the encomenderos were no longer as ada-
mantly opposed to reform as they had been earlier. Their encomiendas
had diminished greatly in size and could not provide tribute and labor
on the scale of the 1530's. In many cases the encomenderos were
coming to rely more on the profits of ancillary stock-raising and agricultural enterprises than on the encomiendas themselves. At the same
time, they must have realized that their position was not completely
secure. They represented only a tiny part of the whole Spanish population, and their attempt to monopolize the benefits of the conquest
would be difficult to sustain indefinitely against a growing majority
which included many who were both conscious of the deprivation and
willing to follow any leader who promised to remedy it. Certainly they
had no chance of maintaining their position if they deserted the
crown, thereby forcing it to come to terms with the revolution of the
soldados. Hence, during the years of civil war, the majority of
encomenderos consistently supported the crown. Only in 1544, when
Blasco Núñez Vela threatened them with the immediate and total loss
of their encomiendas under the New Laws, did they desert in large
numbers; and then they quickly reverted to their earlier loyalty once
Gasca assured them that the laws had been suspended. In 1552, when

the government initiated the process of reform with a decree abolishing the right of the encomenderos to the labor of their Indians — and thereby set off a final rebellion in the highlands — most encomenderos limited themselves to sending ineffectual representations to Spain. Though still opposed to change, they would not actively resist it as they had ten years before.

Between 1550 and 1575, then, the government was able to act decisively to restrict the economic and political hegemony of the encomenderos. It terminated their de facto control over the Indian population by creating a whole new network of local officials, the corregidores de indios, who were appointed for limited terms to govern districts known as *corregimientos*. It deprived them of their exclusive right to the labor of their Indians, for which they now had to compete with non-encomenderos. It decreed that tributes were to be assessed and collected by officials instead of by the encomenderos themselves. And in the Spanish towns, it forced them gradually to open up the municipal councils to non-encomenderos. Enforcement was not immediate of course. The encomenderos still had wealth and influence enough to temper the zeal of most officials, and they knew their region and their curacas better than a corregidor could. Thus it was still possible in 1583 for the encomendero of Huaura to force his encomienda Indians to work on his agricultural enterprises in the valley, relying for this purpose on the good offices of the local curaca, who achieved compliance with the whip. In spite of the occasional survival of such practices, however, it is clear that the "tamed" encomiendas of the later sixteenth century were very different from the "feudal" encomiendas of the conquest period.[52]

This reform of the encomienda involved two basic changes in the organization of Spanish-Peruvian society. In the first place, it took the control of the countryside and of the Indian population away from the encomenderos and gave it to the corregidores. This was not as complete a change as one might assume, however. Corregimientos were normally used to reward those with a claim on the government's favor just as the encomiendas had been. Occasionally they were even given to encomenderos. And since the corregidores were not highly paid and the opportunities for adding to their salaries were great, they tended to behave as if they were encomenderos, collecting excessive tribute, developing ancillary enterprises which depended on Indian labor, and engaging in mercantile activities. In 1580 we find the local corregidor using unpaid Indian labor to grow wheat in the Lima valley, much as the encomenderos had done in the 1540's.[53] In many respects one can describe corregimientos as large encomiendas which were granted for limited periods of time.

In the second place, the reform changed the encomienda itself from a license to extort tribute and labor from the Indian population into a pension controlled by the government. And this pension, in the sixteenth century, was a constantly shrinking one. By the turn of the century there were only a few sierra encomiendas which were able to provide an income larger than the salary of an *audiencia* judge in Lima (4,875 pesos), and on the whole coast there were only two encomiendas—both in the Lambayeque complex of valleys—which yielded more than the average salary (1,625 pesos) of a corregidor de indios.[54] But here again the extent of change should not be exaggerated. Few encomenderos seem to have lost their wealth or their position in society because of the reform of the encomienda system. What had happened was simply that the encomienda had gradually ceased to matter. It still provided a little additional income, and the prestige of being an encomendero still meant something in Peru. But it had failed in its original task of supporting the new Peruvian aristocracy, and it had therefore been replaced.

# 3 / The Beginnings of Commercial Agriculture

The classical encomienda of the conquest period was not a productive institution but rather a parasitic one; it enabled the conquistadores to extract goods and services from the conquered Indian population, not, for the most part, to engage in production themselves. But parasitic dependence on Indian society had certain disadvantages. In the first place, the Indians produced few of the goods to which the conquerors thought their new wealth and prestige entitled them. Coastal encomiendas, for instance, could provide plenty of maize and cotton cloth, but little wheat, wine, or olive oil, to say nothing of the luxury goods to which the wealthy of Europe were accustomed. If the Spaniards wanted such things, they would have either to import them or to produce them themselves.

Then too, the importation of goods from Europe required foreign exchange. In Peru, as in the rest of Spanish America, this came primarily from the mining of gold and silver. On the coast, however, where there were few mines, encomenderos had to earn their gold and silver either by investing in commerce or by establishing profit-making enterprises (*grangerías*) to supply Spanish foods for the main centers of Spanish population.

This division of labor, already apparent at Lima in the early 1540's, did not necessarily imply a fundamental change in the organization of Peruvian society. Though they were productive enterprises, the grangerías still depended on labor provided by the Indian communities and were too few in number to offset the dominance of the traditional system of agriculture — and they might have remained in this dependent position. There have been colonial societies — British India and Dutch Java were examples — where a small ruling class managed for many years to satisfy its needs without upsetting traditional patterns of social organization. This was impossible in Peru, however, because of the disastrous population decline of the sixteenth century.

A more important drawback of the dependence entailed by the encomienda system was that any decline in the wealth and productivity of the indigenous society was immediately and directly reflected in the economic position of the ruling class. As we have seen, the Peruvian

encomendero class disappeared before the end of the sixteenth century
because its customary sources of income were not capable of meeting
the demands placed upon them. But it early became clear that individual encomenderos might avoid the fate of their class by diversifying
their sources of income, by using the capital they possessed to establish
new enterprises which were less dependent on the traditional economy
and society. After the discovery of the great silver mines at Potosí in
1545 and the conclusion of the civil wars in 1548, more silver entered
into circulation and the market for Spanish agricultural produce
increased—thereby giving further encouragement to such diversifica-
tion. The opportunities were especially great on the coast, where most
of the Spanish population lived, and it was here that commercial stock
raising and agriculture spread most rapidly during the following years.
But because of the decline of coastal Indian society, it became increasingly difficult for the Spaniards to take advantage of these opportunities within the established framework of the encomienda system. Thus
the new enterprises, which were based on the ownership of land and
organized to function autonomously, had less and less connection with
the encomiendas. No longer able to fill their labor needs from the
Indian communities, the Spaniards gradually turned to the Negro
slave.

## Stock Raising

The earliest Spanish enterprises on the coast were concerned with
stock raising rather than with agriculture. This was due primarily to
the scarcity, and hence the phenomenal value, of Spanish livestock
during the conquest years. Horses, as part of the capital of the expeditions, were particularly expensive. According to Cobo, they were sold
during the early years for prices as high as 3,000 or 4,000 pesos. A
Spaniard writing from Piura in 1534 noted that they were selling for
1,000 to 1,300 pesos there, partly as a result of the increased demand
for them in the conquest of Quito. In Lima, horses could be sold for
more than 1,000 pesos as late as 1537. After 1540 the prices of all
Spanish livestock declined rapidly. But this did not lead to a contrac-
tion of stock-raising activities, since herds continued to multiply irre-
spective of the level of market demand.[1] The horses and pigs which
arrived with Pizarro's expedition in 1531 were the first Spanish animals
to come to Peru. The first goats were imported about 1536, and the

first cattle about 1539. Probably because pigs reproduced most rapidly, Spaniards actively undertook to raise them first. The earliest
recorded transaction involving European animals which had been
raised in Peru seems to have been the sale in 1536 of an unspecified
number of pigs, located in the Cañete valley, for the sum of 1,600
pesos. A contract executed in the next year was probably typical of the
arrangements made by encomenderos for their early stock-raising
enterprises, though most did not bother to formalize them. In this
document two encomenderos from Lima hired a third Spaniard to
manage a drove of pigs which belonged to them, and agreed to provide
four Indians for his assistance. The profits were to be split evenly
among all three.[2]

In spite of the rapid multiplication of animals brought from Spain,
these early enterprises were small-scale operations. In the early 1540's,
for example, Diego de Agüero and Francisco de Ampuero, a Lima
encomendero who had married Pizarro's Indian mistress, established a
partnership which encompassed several different enterprises, stock
raising among them. The two men jointly bought a herd of 31 goats
for the sum of 899 pesos, and a year later added another 14 goats, 103
head of cattle, and 11 calves. In 1546, after Agüero's death, Ampuero
entered into a partnership with another Spaniard to raise horses. Each
man provided 6 mares and a colt, and they jointly put up 150 pesos to
buy a stallion.[3] Another example comes from the Ica valley, where an
inventory of the property of the encomendero Juan de Barrios shows
that in 1546 he was keeping 310 pigs at an inn (tambo).[4]

In the 1550's and 1560's the stock-raising ventures of encomenderos
grew considerably larger. When Diego Pizarro de Olmos died in 1562,
he left about 910 head of cattle, 680 pigs, 178 goats, and 37 horses, all
in the valley of Supe where his encomienda was located. On her marriage in 1568, the daughter and heiress of Pedro de Alconchel owned
500 head of cattle, 300 horses, and 200 goats in the small Mala valley
where she had an encomienda inherited from her father. Antonio
Navarro, the son and heir of the conquistador Pedro Navarro, had
large herds of cattle and horses in the Cañete valley where some of the
Indians of his encomienda were settled; these herds required so much
space that it was necessary to move them elsewhere in 1556 when the
Spanish town of Cañete was founded.[5]

Stock raising on the coast was not restricted to those encomenderos
whose Indians were there also. In 1570 Bernaldo Ruiz, an encomen-

dero in the area of the *pampa de Junín* northeast of Lima, had cattle and horses in the Lurín valley. In 1571 Francisco Velásquez de Talavera owned 1,114 head of cattle (in partnership with another man), 80 horses, and 800 pigs, which he kept during the winter in a place known as the "inn of the partridges" (*tambo de las perdices*) in the lomas of Lachay between the valleys of Huaura and Chancay. Talavera was also raising livestock on his sierra encomienda in the Mantaro valley, where he had some 30,000 sheep, as well as a cloth factory (*obraje*) for weaving their wool into cloth.[6]

Talavera's activities illustrate a significant fact about the early stockraising enterprises in Peru. In the later colonial period, most livestock intended for the Lima market was raised in the sierra, but in the sixteenth century this was not the case. Cattle, horses, pigs, and goats were all raised primarily on the coast by local encomenderos, and even men who had their encomiendas in the sierra, like Ruiz and Talavera, kept most of their livestock on the coast. Only sheep seem never to have done well on the coast. The reasons for this coastal dominance were mainly economic. As long as good pasture land was available there, it was not worthwhile to try to bring livestock down from the sierra. Not until 1582 did the Lima cabildo concern itself about the lack of *cañadas*, the paths by which herds descended from the sierra; these routes would not become of vital importance until the seventeenth century, when greater numbers of livestock were being raised in the sierra, and then brought to the coast to be fattened.[7]

Non-encomenderos — even very poor ones — also became the owners of Spanish livestock. An example was the Portuguese in the Ica valley whose earthly possessions at the time of his death in 1551 consisted of a slave, a horse, and six goats. For some, raising livestock seems to have provided a small supplement to an income earned in another occupation. Thus in 1552, there was a Lima shoemaker with 400 goats, a blacksmith with 200 goats, and a miller with more than 1,000 pigs. Merchants were another group which might have been expected to have capital for investing in livestock, but their preference for more profitable investments usually discouraged them from doing so. Alvaro de Illescas, son of the head of one of Seville's large merchant houses and its representative in Lima, was an exception. He invested in both stock raising and agriculture on the coast, but it is significant that when he first became involved in them he did so over the strong objections of the senior members of his firm.[8]

The stock-raising enterprise with which Illescas was connected was an important one. It was probably established in 1553, though it may have existed in another form for a few years before he became associated with it. He and Francisco de Torres, another merchant, seem to have provided most of the capital, which was invested in 1,472 head of cattle, 3 horses with 2 colts, 30 slaves, equipment for butchering and weighing the meat, and an *estancia* in the Cañete valley. This estancia was not a large cattle ranch, but rather a plot of about 200 acres granted in 1549 to the guardian of Diego de Agüero's son for an inn in the valley.[9]

This business, established primarily to supply meat for the Lima market, was managed by two Spaniards who had previously been running a mill near the city. One of them, Alejos González Gallego, seems to have started out in Lima as a tailor, but during the next forty years he was to become one of the most prominent stockmen in the city: still a partner in the Illescas enterprise in 1569; joint owner, with the encomendero Francisco Velásquez de Talavera, of more than 1,000 head of cattle in 1571; and, eight years after that, still one of the main users of pasture lands belonging to the city on the north side of the Rímac river.[10] In the years between 1553 and 1590, González periodically held the position of *obligado de las carnecerías*, which meant that he was responsible for running the official butchering establishment in Lima and, at least in the beginning, had a monopoly over the sale of meat in the city. In Spanish-American cities, meat was not butchered and sold in privately owned shops, but rather in slaughterhouses (*carnecerías*) under the control of the cabildos, where the weight and quality of the meat could be more closely regulated. The first slaughterhouse in Lima was managed by an inspector-manager (*fiel mayordomo*) and a meat collector (*cobrador de la carne*) who were appointed by the cabildo and supported with fees. After 1549, the cabildo decided to solicit bids from individuals who would undertake the management of the slaughterhouse for a year or more. The person willing to commit himself to supplying the required meat at the lowest price was awarded the contract and became the obligado. In practice, most of the animals slaughtered probably came from the herds of the obligado, although the cabildo did reserve its right to allow others occasionally to butcher some of their own animals.[11]

Like Spanish municipalities, Lima adopted a monopoly system to guarantee an adequate supply of meat at relatively low prices and thus avoid social disturbances. In Spain and during the early years in America, periodic scarcity was always a problem which cities had to face. As late as 1556, the cabildo in Lima could still complain of a shortage of meat. The increase in livestock, however, meant that this preoccupation with scarcity was no longer very relevant. In Lima, the price of an *arrelde* (about four pounds) of beef went down from about two and one half reales in 1550 to about half a real during the 1570's.[12] In this situation the meat monopoly lost most of the advantages it might have possessed, and the privileges of the obligado were cut back, though not abolished. Beginning in the 1570's, those whom the cabildo recognized as stock-raisers could, with its approval, butcher and weigh meat in the slaughterhouse two days a week. In 1594 this was changed to one week out of every month. The meat seems usually to have been sold at the official contract price; but in some cases the seller offered to set the price even lower to encourage the cabildo to give its approval. These changes do not seem to have greatly decreased the value of the contract, since in 1589 González was still bidding for it.[13]

The ownership of livestock was not restricted to Spaniards. Indians in the sierra continued to raise llamas and alpacas as they had done before the conquest, and both they and the Indians of the coast — particularly the curacas — quickly took up the raising of Spanish livestock as well. In the Huaura valley the curaca of the town of Végueta possessed 22 horses, 300 pigs, 500 sheep, and 10 goats at his death in 1562. Thirty-four years later, one of the curacas in the Ica valley left 40 head of cattle, 124 goats, 80-100 pigs, and 100 llamas when he died. Indian communities in the sierra sometimes owned large herds of Spanish livestock, which had in some instances been donated by their encomenderos to gain absolution for earlier exploitation and mistreatment of them. On the coast, Indian communities seem usually not to have owned livestock. Encomenderos who wanted to make restitution to their Indians frequently made their donation in the form of a perpetual rent (*censo*), although in 1561 an encomendero from Piura on the northern coast gave 100 goats to the Indians of his encomienda.[14]

The rapid growth of stock raising on the central coast was to leave virtually no traces in the later system of land tenure. This contrasts sharply with what occurred in Mexico as well as in the Peruvian sierra, where many of the large haciendas originated in grants of land for grazing. To understand why, we must examine more closely the arrangements under which coastal land was used for raising livestock.

According to a decree of Charles V in 1541, all pasture land in Peru, like that in New Spain, was to be held in common. On the coast, there were essentially three types of land which could be included in this category: the abandoned agricultural land in the valley bottoms, cultivated land which provided stubble for grazing after the harvest, and the lomas. In practice, the stubble lands seem to have been relatively unimportant. In 1549, after receiving the royal order which established the regime of common pastures, the Lima cabildo discussed the problem of whether herds of goats belonging to Spaniards should be allowed in Indian lands, but it does not seem to have come to any clear decision. Probably as in Mexico, Spanish livestock was ultimately excluded from Indian lands, which in any case were becoming less extensive. By the 1560's it would have been possible to make use of Spanish farmland in this way, but in practice the stubble was recognized as private property. Thus in 1564 three farmers near Lima could form a partnership to exploit the stubble on their lands by bringing livestock in to feed on it. Probably most landowners were willing to allow animals in their fields after the harvest, but only in return for a small payment. In 1583 one of the complaints of the Indians of Huaura against their encomendero was that he turned his horses loose in their chacras without paying for the privilege.[15]

The abandoned land on the valley bottoms and the seasonal loma pastures both seem to have been more important. The valley lands, overgrown with reeds and wild grasses, could be used during the whole year. The lomas, on the other hand, while often quite extensive, could only be used seasonally and were not completely dependable. Cobo mentions three principal lomas near Lima, one on the *sierra de la arena* north of Ancón (probably the hill marked on modern maps as the *loma de Ancón*), the lomas of Pachacamac, and the lomas of Lachay north of the Chancay valley. There is evidence for a seventeenth-century pattern of transhumant grazing between these lomas and summer pastures higher up in the mountains to the east. This practice probably had begun by the 1560's; or perhaps one should say begun again, since some transhumant grazing seems to have occurred before the conquest.[16]

Most grazing land in valleys farther from Lima remained under the control of the encomenderos, at least until the founding of Spanish towns in several of these valleys in the 1550's. This was probably due less to the efforts of the encomenderos to keep rivals out than to the fact that non-encomenderos who were wealthy enough to own herds of livestock usually preferred to keep them in pastures closer to Lima.

When Spanish-American towns were founded, a certain amount of pasture land was set aside for the general use of the population. The larger part of this land, the *dehesa*, was usually located at some distance from the city, but a small amount next to the town was reserved for the *ejido*, which was roughly analogous to the New England town common. This land, though not intended only as pasture land, came to be used almost entirely for that purpose where it was not usurped by individual landowners. In Lima, the original dehesa was no longer in existence by the 1550's. Thus the Illescas-González enterprise had to pasture its cattle at first in the Cañete valley. When the founding of the town of Cañete in 1556 made it necessary for them to move, the viceroy provided for the establishment of new dehesas for Lima in the valleys of Lurín and Chancay. The Indians cultivating the land which was to form these dehesas were moved to other parts of the two valleys, so that they could continue to cultivate the land without interference from the livestock of the Spaniards. The land set aside for the Chancay dehesa seems to have been taken from the city when the town of Chancay was founded in 1562. In the late 1570's, to make up for this, the viceroy Toledo granted the city more land, located along the shoreline between the mouths of the Rímac and Chillón rivers. In 1579, even before the city had officially taken possession, González was already using it for his cattle.[17]

In few cases do the men who used valley land primarily for grazing seem to have obtained or even claimed legal ownership of it. The granting of sites for livestock ranches (*estancias*) which was of fundamental importance to the development of the hacienda system in Mexico, played a very small role on the Peruvian coast. (The estancias distributed to the early vecinos of Lima were not ranches but grants of agricultural land, analogous to the *caballerías* given to Spanish settlers in Mexico, though at the beginning they seem to have served mainly to provide forage for the horses.) Around Lima, most stock-raising grants appear to have involved land in the lomas.[18] Like the similar grants in Mexico, they did not confer property rights to grazing land, since this would have violated the principle that all pasture lands should be held in common. What they did convey was the right to erect buildings and pens and to prevent anyone else from doing the same within a specified distance. In Mexico this was commonly a league (about two and a half miles); in the Peruvian loma pastures it was generally a quarter of a league. The earliest grants of the Lima cabildo specifically set aside ten solares, equivalent to two and a half of their city blocks, for buildings and pens.[19]

The use of valley land for grazing seems to have created permanent rights of ownership only in the case of some dehesas, and with different results from those found in Mexico. In the Chancay valley, for instance, the land set aside for the dehesa of the Spanish town was considered the common property of the townspeople down to the nineteenth century. In the 1870's, when a local government official tried to take over the land, which was not then being used, the people of the town — now mainly lower-class mestizos — took their case to the law courts and won a favorable decision. Following their success, they divided up the land among themselves, and the old dehesa ended up as one of three surviving areas of smallholding in the valley. In this region, the principle of common ownership seems to have survived in the case of the lomas as well, since the lomas of Lachay continued down to the present century to be used as pastures by livestock owners in the Chancay and Huaura valleys.[20]

What was the effect of the rapid expansion of stock raising on the Indian population of the central coast? In Mexico, Spanish herds were responsible for considerable damage to Indian crops; this is reflected in the numerous remedial measures taken by the viceroys, particularly by Luís de Velasco in the 1550's. On the Peruvian coast, where the problem also existed, the Lima cabildo set fines for animals caught in the maize fields of the Indians. For every horse so discovered the owner had to pay two pesos if the damage occurred during the day, and four pesos if at night. In the case of sheep and pigs, one out of every twenty animals found during the day was taken and one out of every ten at night. In these cases the person who discovered the animals took them to certain pens (*corrales del concejo*), which the cabildo established for this purpose. The animals remained there until the owner came to recover them, at which time the fine was collected. This regulation seems to have accomplished little, since the issue was again under discussion in 1549. Six years later, the curaca of the community of Surco still found it necessary to hire a Spaniard to cure the illnesses of his Indians, capture the slaves who cut down their trees, and seize the cattle which got into their fields.[21] In the ordinances drawn up in 1556 for the town of Cañete, the methods of protecting

Indian crops were much the same as around Lima. Here the owners of cattle responsible for damaging crops had to pay the costs as well as a fine of half a real for each pig, goat, or sheep involved, and one real per head for cattle, horses, or mules. If the animals were discovered at night the fine was doubled. The person who caught the animals and deposited them in the corral del concejo was to receive half the fine. The extent to which Indians could collect damages, when the local justices were also owners of land and livestock in the valley, was of course uncertain.[22]

The effects of Spanish stock raising were sometimes felt in other ways. In 1569, one of the alcaldes of Ica ordered a Spaniard to remove his livestock from the vicinity of the road up the valley, because the dogs he used for herding were attacking the Indians who used the road. Nor was it always the Indians who suffered from the presence of Spanish livestock. In the Cañete valley a herd of cattle got loose in wheat fields belonging to one vecino of the town in 1589, and a lawsuit resulted when none of the Spaniards in the valley were willing to admit that their cattle had been responsible for the damage.[23]

The problems caused by wandering livestock were, however, probably less severe on the Peruvian coast than in other regions. On the irrigated and intensively cultivated soil of the coastal valleys, Indian fields were relatively small and easy to protect, and they tended to be grouped together away from areas of Spanish landholding. Furthermore, many fields seem to have been protected by mud walls. The earliest land titles often mention such walls, and the Jesuit chronicler Cobo tells us that in the middle of the seventeenth century many of them could still be seen, though by that time they were slowly disappearing.[24] In the long run, of course, the gradual expansion of agriculture after the middle of the sixteenth century would force most livestock off the coast into the sierra, thus largely eliminating the depredations.

### Agriculture

The expansion of agriculture, unlike that of stock raising, could not occur in the absence of fairly large markets. Agriculture enterprises required greater and more continuous investment in order to be profitable. A Spaniard therefore would not embark on such projects until there was a reasonable expectation that his produce could be sold.

On the central coast, this essentially meant sold in Lima, which for most of the valleys was the only large population center near enough to be of much significance.

The Lima market did not grow large enough to encourage the development of commercial agriculture for some time after the founding of the city. During the first years of its existence, Lima was a very small place. Since there were only about 2,000 Spaniards in the whole of Peru in 1536, there cannot have been more than a few hundred of them living in Lima; in 1550, when there were approximately 8,000 Spaniards in the whole country, there cannot have been more than 2,000 in Lima. Through most of the 1540's the city remained largely disconnected from the Atlantic trading system, "vegetating" as the Chaunus have put it, like Caracas in the early seventeenth century before Venezuelans discovered the potentialities of cacao. A few Spaniards, mostly encomenderos, had been growing wheat and maize for sale before the end of Gonzalo Pizarro's rebellion, but these ventures were still relatively small and unorganized. Similarly, in Mexico, the absence of a profitable market seems to have discouraged most Spaniards from starting agricultural enterprises before the 1550's. In Lima, this period of dormancy came to an end in the late 1540's under the combined stimulus of the silver poured into the economy from the newly discovered mine at Potosí and the conclusion of Gonzalo Pizarro's rebellion. Significantly, the first land grants to individuals outside the immediate vicinity of the city itself were made in 1549.[25]

The expansion of commercial agriculture on the Peruvian coast depended on the increasing demand for three main products: wheat, wine, and sugar. At the beginning wheat was the most important. In Spanish colonial society it occupied a position analogous to that of maize in Inca society: both were high status foods, whose distribution was more closely controlled by the government than that of other food crops. Further, under the Incas the demand for maize seems to have provided much of the initial impetus for economic and social changes — the appearance of landed estates, for example — while after the conquest it was the demand for wheat which stimulated such changes.[26]

Until about 1540, maize was the staple food of Spaniards as well as of Indians, but the size of the demand did not induce them to produce it for sale. The Indian population was already producing a surplus which came to the city in the form of encomienda tributes and was then redistributed by the encomenderos to their dependents. Thus there was not much of a market for maize. Only where an encomendero could not get enough from his Indians did he become directly involved in growing it. When Francisco Velásquez de Talavera asked the Lima cabildo in 1538 for an extra piece of land near the city so that he could grow maize for his household, it was probably because his encomienda of Checras was located at too high an altitude for the crop to grow well.[27]

Wheat was a different matter. The high price of imported flour provided some incentive for Spaniards to try growing it locally, as they began to do in the late 1530's. The honor of being the first person to grow wheat in Peru was claimed by the wives of several prominent encomenderos. All told roughly the same story. A few grains of the cereal, discovered in a bag of flour or rice, were planted experimentally and turned out to grow especially well.[28] According to Cobo, yields of between fifteen and thirty fanegas of grain for one of seed were normal on the coast in the seventeenth century, and in some valleys considerably higher yields were not unknown. In western Europe, yields of ten to one remained exceptionally high down to the nineteenth century.[29] Wheat production expanded rapidly in the early 1540's, and the price of wheat bread, as fixed by the Lima cabildo, fell. Where a real bought a single pound loaf in 1540, it bought three and a half loaves in 1543 and continued to do so until 1549.[30] This suggests that the introduction of wheat was followed over the next three or four years by a rapid rise in production, but that after 1543 the demand was largely being satisfied and further expansion was limited.

Most of the early wheat-producing enterprises were concentrated in a small area around Lima on the estancias distributed to the early vecinos. In 1534, Charles V had decreed that the vecinos of Peruvian towns were entitled to receive lots (solares) for their houses and gardens (huertas) as well as land for the cultivation of cereals and other crops. The amount of land depended theoretically on rank, the foot soldiers receiving less than the cavalrymen and officers. In practice, however, foot soldiers seem to have insisted on the larger grants (caballerías), as they did in Mexico. Though these land grants were not very accurately measured at the beginning, they seem to have been roughly the same size as those later made at towns like Cañete and Chancay, that is 40 fanegadas* or about 300 acres.[31]

These estancias did not begin to develop into real farms for about ten years after the founding of Lima. At first they served mainly as places where the vecinos could send their slaves and Indian servants to gather wood and fodder for the horses. Some of them must have been producing wheat by the early 1540's, but there is no evidence in the notarial registers to suggest that they had yet developed into stable agricultural enterprises. The planting of wheat started out as a casual activity, undertaken for a single season without much planning or capital. Typically encomenderos had their Indians plant under the supervision of a Spanish overseer, using the traditional tools and methods associated with the cultivation of maize. Similar types of agricultural activity had existed during the early years in Mexico.[32] In the late 1540's, however, these ventures began to change into permanent enterprises which demanded planning, careful management, and considerable capital investment. In the process, they came to be called chacras, like the cultivated fields of the Indians, instead of estancias.

This transition can be observed in a contract from 1546 between Juan de Cáceres, an official who had a small encomienda in the Chillón valley, and a Spaniard named Martínez, whom he hired to manage his chacra near Lima — or more accurately to develop it.[33] Martínez was to plant not only seasonal crops, such as wheat, maize, and beans, but also four or five thousand grape vines. In addition, within the chacra he was to plant a garden (huerta), which would contain several different kinds of fruit trees. The significance of this contract lies not in the planting of wheat and maize, which Cáceres might have had his Indians do previously, but in the planting of fruit trees and grape vines, which could not be harvested the same year they were planted.

*The standard fanegada (fanegada corriente) on the coast was equal to 7.2 acres or 2.9 hectares from the time it was officially established at Lima (1579) as the equivalent in area of a rectangle measuring 144 by 288 varas (a vara equals roughly 33 inches). A slightly larger fanegada (7 ¾ acres) was used in the Cañete valley. (See Cabildos, IX, 77, and Luís de los Heros, Monografía agrícola del valle de Cañete [Lima, 1922], p. 45.) The figures given by Chevalier (Land and Society, pp. 54-56) suggest that Mexican grants were probably smaller. While the Peruvian settlers theoretically received 288 acres or 117 hectares, the Mexican caballería grant given to most settlers was standardized at 106 acres or 43 hectares.

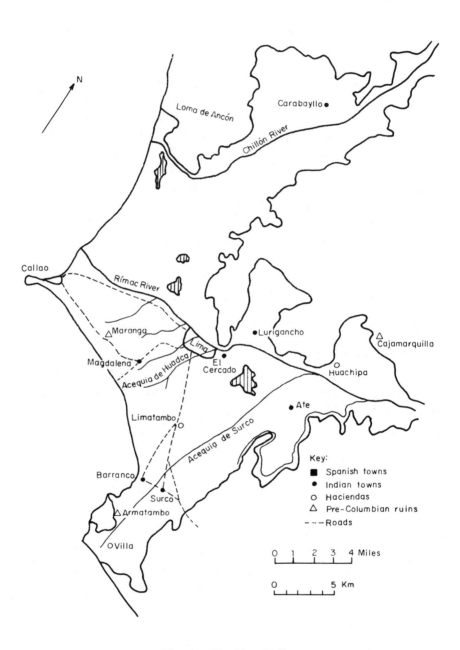

**Map 4.**   The Lima Valley

Also important was the fact that Martínez was hired as a full-time agricultural specialist, obliging himself to live in the chacra for the entire term of the contract.

Throughout the 1540's the encomenderos seem to have possessed an almost complete monopoly of wheat production around Lima. As late as 1549, the cabildo still found it necessary to prohibit them from employing or forming partnerships with the professional bakers in the city, since this practice was preventing others from getting the wheat they needed.[34] In the 1550's and 1560's this monopoly rapidly disappeared. The amount of land occupied by the Spaniards increased as more of their number — mainly notaries, merchants, professionals, and officials — began to develop chacras in the valley. The early estancias had been limited mainly to the area immediately around Lima, but after 1550 chacras began to appear in outlying parts of the valley such as Chuquitanta on the northern edge and Ate and Guanchoguaylas higher up the river.

This expansion reflected changes in the economic and political situation. The end of Gonzalo Pizarro's rebellion and the influx of silver from Potosí at the end of the war seem to have stimulated an increased demand for wheat. The cabildo had to raise the fixed price of bread by 40 percent in May and June of 1549, so that a real bought only 2½ pounds rather than 3½, as it had since 1543. The price remained at this higher level for two years but was then reduced, presumably because the supply of wheat had again increased.[35]

At this time also, the crown renewed its attack on the privileges of the encomenderos. Their virtual monopoly over the labor of the majority of Indians who still followed their traditional way of life was legally abolished in 1549, though Gasca, afraid of the consequences of the decree, refrained from publishing it. And in 1552, when the audiencia tried to implement the order, the attempt set off a rebellion in the sierra which forced its suspension. Nevertheless, the privileged position of the encomenderos was clearly eroded during the 1550's. Indian labor came to be allocated through a draft system (the *mita*) taken over from the Incas, and it was available to many Spaniards who were not encomenderos. In addition, the number of African slaves brought into Lima rose sharply after 1549, when the slave trade resumed after Gonzalo Pizarro's rebellion, and many were bought by non-encomenderos. The price of slaves rose also, evidence of an increasing demand for labor.[36]

The encomenderos, then, were no longer the only people in Lima with wealth and influence. The emergence of an economically and politically significant group of non-encomenderos (there was too much variety within it for it to be called a class) was common to all of Peru, but it occurred most rapidly in Lima. Even before the 1550's, Lima contained many Spaniards whose incomes were not directly derived from encomiendas; indeed their presence decisively affected the outcome of the civil wars.[37] After 1550, with the decline of the encomendero monopoly, these men could begin to establish chacras of their own.

One of these new chacras is described in a 1552 contract between its owners and the man hired to manage it. It contained an already established vineyard and garden as well as a herd of 150 goats, which provided meat and milk to be sold in Lima. In addition, it was supposed to produce wheat, maize, beans, and melons.[38] There were two important differences between this chacra and the earlier Cáceres one. While the latter had been cultivated by encomienda Indians, the former had a permanent labor force of four African slaves, though the owners promised six or seven Indians to help with the weeding.* The owners had also invested in equipment and draft animals for cultivating the chacra: four oxen, several ploughs, three horses, and a cart used to carry produce to the city. A similar chacra which was sold the same year contained four oxen and a cart, valued together at 350 pesos, and four slaves (two of them old) valued at 650 pesos. The two elderly slaves must have had little value, since the average price of a slave at the time was roughly 300 pesos.[39]

Another chacra, located fifteen miles up the Rímac valley from Lima, covered about 190 acres in 1574.[40] About 70 acres were in wheat, 10 in beans, 2 in maize, and a small amount in barley. Within the chacra were also a vineyard, a garden, a house for the overseer, and a herd of 125 goats. The labor force of three slaves had six oxen and seventeen horses to assist them. In addition to the farming implements and tools, including sickles, hoes, axes, and hammers, the chacra had a wine press, twelve earthen jars for storing wine, and a small millstone.

---

*It is not specifically stated that Cáceres did not have slaves or oxen, but one can assume that he did not: if they had been present, they would have been too valuable not to mention in the contract.

Like the encomenderos, most non-encomenderos did not manage their chacras in person. Many of them hired overseers who were on salary or else received a share of the produce. Salaries for these men in the 1550's seem to have been in the vicinity of 200 pesos a year. An overseer who was paid in produce generally received a quarter of the crop, and often a specified amount of money or food in addition. Cáceres' overseer received one-fourth of the crop and fifty pesos. In the early 1550's, another overseer received one-fifth of the wheat, maize, and beans, plus one-third of the melons and one-fourth of the increase of the herd of goats for which he was responsible. For sustenance he was given eight pigs and twelve fanegas of wheat.[41]

In some cases the owner of a chacra entered into a more equal partnership with his overseer. In an agreement from 1572, one of the partners agreed to supply a chacra, a free Indian laborer (*yanacona*), and a drafted Indian laborer (*mitayo*), while the other provided a slave, a second yanacona, and his own services to manage the chacra. The profits were to be split evenly between the two. In a few cases, the two partners agreed to divide the chacra between them when the term of the partnership was over. In 1571, Juan de Turín and Miguél Díaz jointly purchased a chacra about ten miles up the river from Lima. In an agreement drawn up the next year, Díaz agreed to supply the working capital for the enterprise (1,500 pesos) while Turín agreed to manage it. After the four-year term of the partnership was completed, the property was to be divided between the two men. But Díaz, who died in 1574, complained in his will that Turín had not reported to him on his management of the chacra, and in 1575 his heirs ceded their rights to Turín, presumably receiving some compensation in return.[42]

Many smaller chacras were run with little if any supervision by one or more of the owner's slaves, who either lived in the city and commuted, or more often lived on the chacra itself. Another arrangement was to rent the chacra or the land for one, either in exchange for a share of the produce or for a fixed sum of money. Thus we find one farmer in the Lima valley selling off his slaves and farming implements, along with some unharvested wheat, all of which were in a chacra which did not belong to him. Renters were often black freedmen living in Lima. The will of one of these men, drawn up in 1560, shows that in partnership with another man (probably black also) he owned a quantity of wheat, barley, maize, and melons, all growing in a chacra apparently rented from a Spaniard. A brother, also free, had a similar arrangement in another chacra. The two brothers had done well enough from their agricultural activities during the preceding years to buy a house in the city together for the sum of 200 pesos.[43]

A few Spaniards ran their own chacras, and were known as *labradores*, a name applied also to Spanish overseers and renters. Many of them, particularly in the 1550's and 1560's, had started out as overseers and had eventually made themselves independent. Others seem to have had more wealth and status when they started. Juan de Turín, for instance, provided about half of the more than 6,000 pesos needed to buy the chacra he managed. Similarly, Rodrigo Díaz, a labrador who bought up several chacras on the north bank of the Rímac in the 1580's, was able to provide his daughters with dowries of 10,000 pesos apiece and to establish his son as a prominent member of the landowning aristocracy in the valley.[44]

Outside the Lima valley the rise of wheat farming was slower, though it followed a similar pattern. At first the encomenderos did not engage in agriculture themselves, expecting the Indians to supply what they needed as part of their tribute. But while the Indians could grow large amounts of maize, attempts to get them to grow wheat on their own were not very successful.[45] Many encomenderos therefore instructed their overseers to organize the production of tribute crops themselves, using fields located near the center of the encomienda and tribute labor provided by the Indians. In a contract from 1547, for instance, the stated duties of the overseer of the encomienda of Coayllo and Calango were to "serve and reside" in the towns of the encomienda, to supervise the planting of wheat and maize, and to watch over the encomendero's cattle, horses, and pigs. His payment for these services was to be one-sixth of the wheat and maize he sent to Lima.[46] These agricultural activities, then, were casual ones, organized from year to year. They required little capital, since the Indians employed their traditional methods and tools, and they seldom involved the legal ownership of land until later on, since the encomenderos had access to all the land they needed anyway.

To some extent, such casual activities continued to exist alongside the more highly organized agricultural enterprises which developed later. In the 1580's, the encomendero of Huaura was still illegally compelling his Indians to provide labor for planting and harvesting, both on land which he owned and on land which he had never bothered to claim. It was mainly the corregidores, however, who continued to engage in this kind of activity. In 1580, for instance, the corregidor of Cañete was accused in his *residencia*\* of using Indian labor to plant wheat in Indian lands without paying for either the labor or the land. His method was the traditional one of turning the occasion into a fiesta, providing large amounts of food and maize beer (*chicha*). It is worth noting that this violation occurred within fifteen miles of Lima during the administration of the reforming viceroy Toledo.[47]

More stable agricultural enterprises began to develop outside the Lima area in the late 1540's and early 1550's. The first sign of change was a sudden interest on the part of some encomenderos in acquiring legal title to land outside the valley of Lima. Toward the end of 1548, Ruy Barba Cabeza de Vaca received from the cabildo a grant (*merced*) of about 175 acres of land in the Chancay valley where he had a small encomienda. Jerónimo de Aliaga, who also had a small encomienda in the valley, strongly opposed this grant. Nine months later Barba informed the cabildo that he had a second grant of land — probably from Gasca — but he did not specify the size. These grants set off a wave of requests for others. Early in 1550, the cabildo gave about 210 acres each in the Chancay valley to Hernando de Montenegro and Diego Pizarro de Olmos, encomenderos whose Indians were farther to the north. Several days later, one of the alcaldes was sent to the valley to make sure that these grants did not involve land needed by the Indians. When his report was later discussed in the Lima cabildo, three of the members, who had also requested land in the valley and thus had a personal interest in the matter, had to be requested to leave.[48]

Land in the Chancay valley, which was the closest of the large valleys to Lima, would naturally have been in greater demand than elsewhere, but grants were made in other valleys as well. In 1549, Gasca gave land to Pedro de Alconchel in the Mala valley where he had an encomienda; other grants went to Nicolás de Ribera in the Ica

---

\*The residencia of an official took place at the end of his tour of duty, when a man with judicial powers (often his successor in the office) was sent to hear complaints against him, to redress any wrongs he had committed, and to fine him for any failure to exercise his office in accordance with the laws and regulations governing it.

valley and to Jerónimo de Silva in the Cañete valley. Silva was not an encomendero in his own right, but was acting as the guardian of Diego de Agüero, the son of the conquistador, who was. Separate chacras in the Cañete valley belonging to Agüero and to Alonso Martín de Don Benito may also have been established at about this time, since they were already in existence when the town of Cañete was founded in 1556.[49]

The arrival of the viceroy Don Antonio de Mendoza in 1551 seems to have put an end to coastal land grants from the cabildo of Lima. Because they were awarded over a period of little more than two years, except in the valley of Lima itself, these grants were of much less importance than those of the cabildo of Mexico City. Mendoza himself made few if any grants of land, and after his death in 1552 rebellions in Upper Peru and in Cuzco left the audiencia, which had taken over the government of the country, with little time to consider them. One Spaniard who did receive a grant during these years was Francisco Camacho, a resident of Lima previously engaged in agriculture close to the city, who was given land next to Ruy Barba's in the Chancay valley. It is not clear exactly when this grant was made, but when Camacho hired an overseer for his new chacra in 1554, its boundaries had not yet been established.[50]

It was the viceroy Cañete (1556-1560) who first put the granting of land to Spaniards on a systematic basis. Records have survived of a number of his grants to individuals, particularly in the valleys of Lima, Chancay, Pativilca, and Ica; and there were undoubtedly others for which the documentation has disappeared. Moreover, the founding of new agricultural towns, which was initiated by Cañete, involved the granting of land to many Spaniards. Most of Cañete's grants, whether individual or collective, seem to have been made to men who did not have encomiendas—another indication that the agricultural monopoly of the encomenderos in the valleys had come to an end.[51]

Obtaining a land grant from the Lima cabildo, the audiencia, or the viceroy was not the only means of getting legal title to land in the 1550's. Land could also be purchased from curacas. In 1553, for example, a Spaniard named Luís Dávalos de Ayala bought a chacra from a curaca in the Huaura valley for the sum of 800 pesos. This curaca may have been the one who in 1562 listed among his possessions some twenty different chacras, the largest of which was about 140 acres. Dávalos, like Camacho, is an early example of a relatively wealthy non-encomendero who became an agricultural entrepreneur. In 1552, he owned at least one chacra in the valley of Lima, where he hired a Spaniard, at the large salary of 250 pesos a year, to manage certain "chacras and estancias" in which he had slaves and oxen. In the same year he sold 330 goats, which he had in a chacra near the city, for the sum of 1,340 gold pesos. He subsequently obtained more land in the Pativilca valley, and in the seventeenth century his descendants owned a large hacienda there.[52]

Most of these early chacras concentrated on the production of food crops, particularly wheat, for the Lima market. But there were also a few agricultural enterprises which produced sugar before 1550. The largest and earliest of these belonged to the encomendero of Nazca, García de Salcedo, and was located in the valley of Collao, later known to Spaniards as the Ingenio valley. In 1546, this entire valley was purchased from two curacas by one Pedro Gutiérrez, probably a dependent of Salcedo's and the man who later succeeded him as encomendero. The price was 200 pesos de oro, 300 pigs, and two cows with their offspring. Gutiérrez immediately resold the land to Salcedo for 1,500 pesos which he said he had already received. Presumably he was acting for Salcedo the whole time. The deed indicates that sugar cane was already growing in the valley. It had been introduced experimentally a few years earlier, perhaps from the northern coast and ultimately from Mexico, where Cortés had been growing it since 1528 or 1529. The initiative for the enterprise may have come from Salcedo's wife Beatriz, who had come to Peru as a morisco slave.* She was a resourceful woman who managed many of her husband's business interests for him and was one of those who claimed to have introduced the cultivation of wheat in Peru.[53]

Sometime after 1546 Salcedo built a sugar mill (*ingenio*) in the valley. Around it he developed an enterprise which, according to the seventeenth-century writer Vásquez de Espinosa, employed some three hundred African slaves and five hundred Indians. Such a large number of slaves is improbable, and a better idea of the truth is probably given by the statement of a sixteenth-century chronicler that the

---

*Moriscos were Moslems converted to Christianity, often by force; in Castile they were generally considered more industrious and enterprising than the Old Christians.

army of the rebel chieftain Francisco Hernández Girón carried off about forty from the place in 1554. This was still a large number for an agricultural enterprise in the 1550's. There was another early ingenio in the Acarí valley farther south, which belonged to the encomendero there, Pedro de Mendoza. In 1547 he hired a Spanish artisan to make some caldrons for boiling down the sugar. There may have been still other mills, for Cieza de León tells us there were many "plantations of sugar cane" in the coastal valleys, though the sugar was only processed "in some places."[54] The economy of this part of Peru, however, was to be based on wine rather than sugar. Already by 1554, Salcedo had planted grape vines and olive trees, since Girón's men were able to carry off quantities of wine and oil as well as preserves made from sugar. When the overseer of the enterprise hired an artisan in the early 1560's to make six caldrons for boiling down the cane sap, the early settlers of Ica were beginning to plant the vines that would within a few years make the valley the main center of Peruvian wine production. At the end of the sixteenth century the ingenio was only a memory perpetuated in the name of the valley where it had once existed.[55]

## From Encomienda to Hacienda

Most of the new agricultural enterprises which began to appear on the coast during the 1540's started out in association with encomiendas, developing only during the second half of the century into independent farms called chacras, and later haciendas. But what role did the encomienda itself play in this process? Was it, as has been suggested, an early version of the hacienda, a kind of large estate which was characteristic of the conquest period? Or was the hacienda a fundamentally new institution, which owed little to the encomienda?[56]

On the Peruvian coast, both views would appear to have some validity. As we have seen, the encomienda and the hacienda functioned in basically different ways: the former to extract goods produced by the Indian population, and the latter to organize the production of goods required by the Spaniards. Encomiendas usually involved much wider areas and larger populations than haciendas did. Few of the large coastal valleys contained more than two or three encomiendas, but later on they were likely to have at least fifteen or twenty haciendas. And the encomiendas contained thousands of tributaries, while even in the eighteenth century coastal haciendas could consider themselves fortunate if they had more than a few hundred laborers. In addition, there was a considerable lapse of time between the failure of the coastal encomienda system and the appearance of the hacienda system which took its place. The encomienda system had lost most of its economic importance by the early 1560's, but at this time agricultural land on the coast was still largely in Indian hands. Before the hacienda system could be consolidated, most of this land would have to be transferred to Spanish ownership.

Nevertheless, it is clear that individual encomenderos played an important part in the evolution of the coastal hacienda system. There were many who founded large haciendas, though these were not always near their encomiendas and were sometimes built up after the possession of an encomienda had ceased to mean much in economic terms. In the Chancay valley, for instance, there were at least three haciendas founded by encomenderos: Palpa, established by the Dominicans who had originally held the encomienda of Aucallama; Torre Blanca, established in the 1550's by Ruy Barba Cabeza de Vaca next to his encomienda town of Zupillán; and Cuyo, founded in the 1590's by Francisco de Cárdenas, whose encomienda of Checras was in the highlands to the east. Though Jerónimo de Aliaga also had some Indians in the valley, he did not build up an hacienda there but concentrated his efforts in the Lima valley and the Callejón de Huaylas. Similarly in the Huaura valley, Juan Bayón de Campomanes and Sancho de Ribera, both of whom had Indians in the valley, established the haciendas of Vilcahuaura and Cuyo; but in both instances the land was acquired only after 1570. A third hacienda (Ingenio), mentioned in the eighteenth century by Juan and Ulloa, was founded by Juan Fernández de Heredia, encomendero of Cajatambo to the northeast.[57]

South of Lima the situation was very similar. García de Salcedo had his sugar plantation in the Ingenio valley before 1550. Pedro de Alconchel, the encomendero of Chilca and Mala, had built up an estate of almost 1,000 acres with a tambo, mill, and wine chacra in the Mala valley before his death in the 1560's. His earliest grant of land in the valley had been made by Gasca in 1549.[58] Both Diego de Agüero (Lunahuaná) and Alonso Martín de Don Benito (Huarco) had chacras in the Cañete valley in the 1550's. Agüero's survived to become Hacienda Hualcara; Martín's probably developed into an hacienda also, since we know that his son, Hernando Alonso, was one of the large landowners in the valley during the latter part of the century.

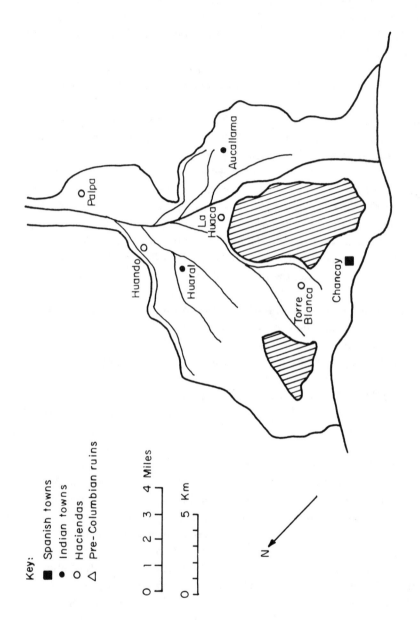

Key:

■ Spanish towns
● Indian towns
○ Haciendas
△ Pre-Columbian ruins

Map 5.   The Chancay Valley

Antonio Navarro (Coayllo and Calango) possessed a large stock-raising enterprise in the Cañete valley in the early 1550's, but he did not acquire much land and his herds were forced out when the town of Cañete was founded in 1556.[59] Nuño Rodriguez (Humay), Pedro de Zárate (Pisco), and Juan Dávalos de Ribera (Lurin Ica) all founded haciendas in the Pisco valley, probably after 1570. Surprisingly, the encomenderos of the Ica valley do not seem to have established large haciendas there. Both the Riberas and the Barrios acquired some land in the valley, but their seventeenth-century descendants would have their haciendas elsewhere, the former in Pisco and the latter in Chincha.[60]

The evidence therefore suggests that on the Peruvian coast there was little institutional connection between the encomienda and the hacienda. The two represented fundamentally different approaches to the problem of how to organize the country and support the Spanish population, and it was the economic failure of the one which led to the ultimate success of the other. On the other hand, the encomenderos as individuals played an extremely important role in the development of the hacienda system. Faced with declining incomes and growing political pressure, they were forced to depend ever more heavily on the earnings of their ancillary enterprises. As a result, they expanded these enterprises and gradually loosened their encomienda ties, thus creating the first chacras and haciendas and setting an example which would soon be followed by those without encomiendas.

# 4 / The Age of the Gentleman-Farmer

The rise of the hacienda system is often treated as a variation on an old Iberian theme, a development which reflected the culture and traditions of the Spanish settlers. This is not unreasonable. Extreme concentration of landholding was characteristic of both Spain and her American colonies. In both regions the rise of large estates occurred following a conquest: in the Spanish case it came after the Christian conquest of the Moslem kingdoms of the south in the thirteenth century. Furthermore, it is logical to assume that the colonists who created the hacienda system were influenced by the aristocratic ideals and norms which permeated the society in which they had been raised, and that when given the opportunity, they would naturally try to build up large estates like those of the Spanish nobility. Nevertheless, closer observation shows that the social and economic circumstances which encouraged the rise of great estates in the two regions were quite different.

In Spain the reasons for the rise of the great latifundia were as much military and political as economic. Having greatly increased the size of their dominions in the course of the thirteenth century, the rulers of Castile found themselves lacking enough Christian settlers to occupy and defend the conquered territories. They were therefore compelled to turn much of the task of defense over to the nobility, the military orders, and the Church, and to reward them with huge expanses of land. A new and more powerful nobility was thus created, which continued to dominate the kingdom until the reign of Ferdinand and Isabella, and which succeeded in preserving most of its economic privileges down to the nineteenth century.[1]

In Peru, the situation was very different. By the 1550's the monarchy had established effective political control over most of the country, and there was no military threat to speak of, once Manco's rebellion had been suppressed. The chief problem facing the viceroys was an excess rather than a scarcity of settlers. Under these circumstances the crown, then engaged in cutting back the wealth and power of the encomendero aristocracy, had neither the need nor the intention of granting vast expanses of land to individuals. Thus Peruvian estates were seldom created out of a single large grant, but rather through the combination of relatively modest grants and purchases.

Far from favoring the rise of large estates on the coast, the crown and its representatives seem to have hoped that the settlers would become gentleman-farmers, using Indian or slave labor to produce agricultural goods for local and regional markets. To encourage this outcome, the viceroys set out to found new towns in which the vecinos were to be farmers rather than encomenderos. The distribution of land to the Spaniards who settled in these towns did not give rise to large estates but rather to a system of chacras which survived until the consolidation of the hacienda system at the beginning of the seventeenth century. Indeed, in the south, and to some extent around Lima, chacras have remained the most common type of agricultural enterprise on the coast, though they are now called small haciendas or *fundos.**

### The System of Chacras

In the 1550's and 1560's, the most serious political and social problem facing the men responsible for the government of Peru was that of the soldados, the turbulent and dissatisfied Spanish immigrants whom the encomienda system had proved incapable of supporting. Much of the policy of the viceregal government during this period can be explained in terms of the need to settle these men down and turn them into peaceable citizens.

For the soldados themselves, the problem involved the rewards (*mercedes*) to which they were entitled in return for the services (*servicios*) done for the king in conquering and settling the country.[2] But while the concepts of servicio and merced had been appropriate to a place and an era in which kings and their vassals were bound by close personal ties, they played a subversive role in post-conquest Peru, encouraging many participants in the conquest to expect more substantial rewards than the rulers of the country were able to provide. From Francisco Pizarro on, the governors of Peru were plagued by the pretensions of men who thought themselves inadequately rewarded for

---

*The distinction between a chacra and an hacienda has never been a sharp one. Chacras were essentially small haciendas, but the line which divided them from large haciendas was vague. In this book coastal farms of 50 fanegadas (359 acres) or less are generally described as "chacras" and farms of more than 50 fanegadas as "haciendas."

the great services they deemed themselves to have performed. Thus on the eve of his execution, Gonzalo Pizarro could take pleasure in the sight of his victorious rival, Gasca, besieged by the pretenders who had once pursued him; and Gasca himself admitted that the struggle with his "friends" was worse than the previous one with his enemies.[3] The effect of the situation was to keep the country constantly on the verge of rebellion; the viceroys had either to reduce the pretensions or to find ways of satisfying them.

Though Gasca was probably the most astute politician of all the men who governed Peru in the colonial period, he found himself totally unable to solve this problem. In the end, he simply gave up, convinced that only his departure from Peru would deprive the pretenders of their hopes for the distribution of more encomiendas and force them to find other means of support. This was to play for time in the hope that the problem would solve itself, but in 1549 there was probably not much else that could be done. When the Viceroy Cañete arrived on the northern coast seven years later, he wrote to Spain of being met by hordes of pretenders, "102 kinds of people, some vecinos, whom they call encomenderos, and other gentlemen soldados who have participated in these rebellions." He decided to proceed to Lima by sea, rather than by land as was usually done, preferring the long and difficult voyage against the wind and current to the prospect of facing similar crowds all the way to the capital.[4]

Cañete acted more firmly than Gasca had been able to do, however. He summarily executed several men who had joined Girón's rebellion and subsequently changed sides. He also offered small mercedes to some of the pretenders; when these were indignantly rejected as inadequate, the men were shipped to Spain where he said the king could reward them. According to Garcilaso, his reasoning was that

it will take them a year to get to Spain, a year to do their business, and a year to get back. And even if they bring letters in their favor I can settle them by kissing the letters and placing them on my head, and saying that I obey the instructions but that they cannot be executed. And by the time they have gone back for letters of confirmation and reached here with them, three more years will have gone by: that makes six in all, and heaven knows where we shall be by then![5]

Though such tactics got rid of the worst troublemakers, they did little about the economic situation which had produced the soldados in the first place by depriving many Spaniards of the chance to make a satisfactory income. Thus the viceroys also found it necessary to create incomes out of government funds, using the money either to make new jobs or to pay pensions. Cañete's viceregal guard was perhaps the best example of this practice, but there were many others, as a list of salaries and pensions drawn up in the 1560's indicates.[6] One old supporter of Almagro, for instance, was at that time receiving a pension of 1,000 pesos a year granted by Cañete; he was described as a pretender to "more mercedes and another life" (that is, for the right to bequeath the pension to his heir). Jerónimo Zurbano, whom we will later meet as the founder of the town of Cañete, was receiving three separate incomes. Cañete had given him a pension of 3,000 pesos a year besides appointing him governor (*alcaide*) of the Inca fortress of Huarco at a salary of 1,200 pesos. Subsequently he was given an encomienda in the region of La Paz as well. According to the compiler of the list, Zurbano never performed the duties connected with his Huarco post and was replaced by another vecino of the town of Cañete, a nephew of an official who came out with Nieva, at a salary of 800 pesos. Nevertheless, Zurbano was still receiving his salary at the time the list was drawn up.

The number of jobs and pensions the viceroys could create was limited, however, and the crown did not help matters with its frequent orders to reduce the amounts paid out in pensions and salaries. Cañete's viceregal guard, created to provide for some of the more deserving soldados, had originally included seventy pikemen, fifty halberdiers, and thirty harquebusiers, and when Nieva came out in 1561, he had orders to reduce the units to ten, four, and twenty, respectively. He found it impossible to go this far, however, and left them at forty, twenty-four, and twenty, "because there are many here who have served in a manner deserving of some reward, and this seems to be one way of paying them."[7]

Furthermore, the crown was often tempted to get people off its hands by sending them out to Peru, frequently ordering the viceroy to provide them with pensions or jobs. Toledo, who believed that the desire of Spaniards for encomiendas, pensions, and offices remained even in the 1570's the most serious obstacle to social and political stability, noted that the king had been warned many times, both by his predecessors and by himself, of the damage caused by this practice, and of the danger in which it placed the country. Even when immigrants did not have to be provided with an income, they could create problems. Nieva complained that he was always being told to get rid of the vagabonds who wandered about the country, yet the Spanish authorities allowed many who lacked any means of supporting themselves to come to Peru. Without property or the income from an office, he commented, the only thing they could occupy themselves with in the colony was rebellion.[8]

In the 1550's, the beginnings of agricultural development on the coast enabled the viceroys to reward some of those who had claims on them with grants of land. As we have seen, some encomenderos had obtained land grants in the late 1540's, and a few non-encomenderos soon thereafter. Such individual grants became more frequent after the arrival of Cañete in 1556, but their impact was limited for two reasons. First, Cañete was quite conscientious about refusing to give away Indian community land, restricting himself to Inca or cult land, and to abandoned land which had not been cultivated for many years.[9] Thus the number of such grants tended to remain small. Second, land grants could produce income only when the recipients possessed the resources to develop them by clearing the land, repairing the irrigation ditches, and establishing agricultural enterprises on them. Since many of the people the viceroys had to take care of did not possess such resources, they had little interest in the prospect of becoming landowners.

Land grants proved to offer a satisfactory way of settling down poor Spaniards only when used in conjunction with the founding of small agricultural towns (Cañete and Santa, 1556; Camaná, 1557; Chancay, 1562; Ica and Saña, 1563). In the valleys where these towns were established, the Indians were concentrated in one or two sections where they were guaranteed enough land for their needs. The remaining land was then distributed among the Spanish vecinos. This appears to have been done fairly honestly, and the Indians were probably left with more land than they could exploit with the resources available to them. To meet the need for labor, the vecinos were assigned Indians drafted under the mita system. In Cañete they were also provided with cash grants: 300 pesos apiece "for oxen, some cattle, and other things needed for their work."[10]

The founding of these new towns did not go unopposed. Encomenderos looked unfavorably on the idea of having Spanish towns in the valleys where their Indians lived. Their opposition, however, was no longer as effective as it would have been earlier. Antonio Navarro later claimed that he had lost more than 3,000 pesos a year because of the founding of the town of Cañete. At the time, the viceroy had taken his opposition seriously enough to buy him off with two small encomiendas. Similarly, in 1562, Nieva wrote to the king that the foundation of the town of Chancay had been opposed by the members of the Lima cabildo, who feared its effect on wheat prices; the leader of the opposition was Ruy Barba, "who, with the excuse that he owned some land there, had occupied and usurped most of the best land in the valley."[11]

The encomenderos were joined in their opposition by some clergymen and officials. In 1582, Francisco Falcón, one of the outstanding defenders of Indian rights in sixteenth-century Peru, argued before the third provincial council of the Church in Lima that "no more Spanish towns should be founded in these kingdoms [i.e., Peru] than are necessary to support and back up the preachers of the gospel, nor should Spaniards be permitted to live in them for any other reason . . . and that those which have been established without this necessity should be abandoned."[12] The crown must have felt some sympathy for this position. Nieva's justification of the foundation of Ica in 1563 has a distinctly defensive tone, and an order to abandon Chancay seems actually to have been issued by the crown, although it was not carried out. Two additional towns, however, which Nieva had planned for the Pisco and Chincha valleys, were not established at this time, and Toledo's suggestion that more such towns be founded seems to have met with no response.[13]

Perhaps because of this opposition, the viceroys placed many of the early towns in valleys where the Indian population was relatively small, so that the effects of giving land to the Spanish settlers were not so overwhelming. The original vecinos of Cañete, as we have seen, found only about seventy Indian households in the valley when they arrived. Similarly, Cieza de León tells us that the population of the Santa valley had already declined to some four hundred households by the late 1540's, several years before the town of Santa was established there; at this time, he says, the Chincha valley still contained five thousand Indian households.[14] Ica, on the other hand, was founded in one of the most heavily populated valleys on the coast. As Nieva reported, however, the vecinos were given only enough land for a house and a garden and had to buy whatever else they needed from the Indians. At Cañete in 1556 such a requirement could not have worked; but by 1563 Spaniards were coming to realize that small pieces of land could be used quite profitably to grow wine grapes. There is in fact some evidence that they had already begun to settle in the valley, and presumably to buy land from the Indians, even before the town itself was founded.[15]

The establishment of these towns was entrusted to men of some importance in the country. Jerónimo Zurbano, the founder of Cañete, was a seaman from Bilbao who had been second-in-command of a fleet which was in the harbor at Lima when the viceroy Blasco Núñez Vela was seized to be sent back to Spain. Refusing to have anything to do with these proceedings, Zurbano had taken the ship he commanded to Panama and had subsequently retired to Spain when Gonzalo Pizarro's supporters gained control of the isthmus. After the founding of Cañete, he was given an encomienda in the district of La Paz, where he became a vecino. Jerónimo Luís de Cabrera, the founder of Ica, was a younger son of a nobleman from Seville. Having married the widow of the conquistador Garcilaso de la Vega, he became corregidor of Potosí and later governor of Tucumán, where he was responsible for founding the Argentine city of Córdoba.[16]

Founding a town was basically a job for these men, and though they received grants of land, most of them did not intend to settle permanently. Cabrera decided to sell all his property in the Ica valley only five years after the town was founded; it seems that his intentions were not entirely carried out, since his widow and children still owned a little land there in 1583. Zurbano's land in the Cañete valley was still in the possession of his heirs in the 1590's, but he appears to have left its exploitation to others. His widow was renting part of it in 1573 to a merchant in Lima for forty-five fanegas of wheat a year. Little is known of the founder of Chancay, Luís Flores, but he too seems to have sold his lands in the valley fairly quickly. Along with the lands belonging to several other vecinos, they became part of the large Jesuit hacienda of La Huaca.[17]

The first step in the founding of a town was choosing a site. This was usually done by the founder with the advice of a few men familiar with the valley where it was to be located. Zurbano, for example, was advised by three men who had previously lived in the valley and who were to become vecinos of the town.[18] The sites chosen were always toward the lower end of the valley, closer to the ocean, on which produce could be shipped to Lima. Such a location also meant that the vecinos were less likely to deprive the Indians of the water they needed for irrigation, since the latter, at a higher elevation, received their water first.

Cañete, Chancay, and Ica were all built around inns (*tambos*) which had been established earlier, and around which small Spanish settlements had already begun to grow up. In valleys where no Spanish towns were founded until much later, these tambos tended to become the main centers of Spanish settlement, like the village in the Chincha valley known as the *Tambo de los españoles* (modern Tambo de Mora). In some cases, the Spanish tambos had themselves been built on the sites of older Inca tambos. This seems to have been true of both Tambo de Mora and Cañete, where the Spaniards founded their town on the site of an old Indian town which contained a tambo.[19]

The new towns were seldom very large. Cañete started out with twenty-five vecinos, Santa and Chancay with about twenty each; Ica was the largest with about forty. Most of these men were far from wealthy. As we have seen, the original vecinos of Cañete were so poor that the viceroy had to provide them with capital to get started. Such outright gifts were not made again, and may have elicited some criticism from the crown, since Nieva later remarked pointedly in a letter that Ica had been founded at no expense to the treasury.[20]

The instructions given to Zurbano specified that the founders of Cañete should be married persons who were competent farmers and intended to live in the town. These instructions seem to have been followed fairly closely. Most of the original vecinos were men whose names appear only in connection with the town. Even the leading citizens were not very prominent. One was a conquistador who had come to Peru with Almagro and gone on with him to Chile. He probably fought on the wrong side in the early civil wars, which would explain why he did not have an encomienda. Another was probably the illegitimate son of the encomendero Alonso Martín de Don Benito. One man was the nephew of a high government official. This anonymity of the vecinos of Cañete contrasts with the situation in Chancay later on, where a number of the original vecinos were prominent residents of Lima and probably had no intention of actually living in the town.[21]

The procedure of distributing lands among the vecinos seems to have been similar in all the new towns. Each man was entitled to one house lot, a small piece of land for a garden close to the town, and a somewhat larger amount of farmland. Solares were rectangular, and their size was fixed by the viceroy in his instructions to the founder. In

Cañete they were about 150 by 300 feet, and in Chancay about 150 by 200. The preferred gridiron plan was probably not followed in Cañete, since the town was established on the site of the existing Indian settlement of Huanca. Witnesses later testified that even the houses of the Indians had been distributed among the vecinos. In Cañete, Zurbano was told to set aside a total of about eight acres of land next to the town for the gardens of the vecinos. In Chancay, the vecinos were each given one block (*cuadra*) of land for their gardens; if these blocks were the same size as those in the town itself, they would have been slightly less than three acres. The vecinos of Ica do not seem to have received any separate land for gardens, which had to be planted in the lots granted for their houses.[22]

In addition to solares and land for gardens, the vecinos of most of the new towns were entitled to a grant of forty fanegadas (about 300 acres) of land in which they could establish chacras.[23] This rule was made after the first distribution of land at Cañete, apparently because confusion and argument had resulted from a lack of standardization, leading some of the vecinos to appeal to the viceroy to clarify how much land each person should receive. When Chancay was founded, it was understood from the beginning that each vecino was to be given forty fanegadas.[24]

The process of land distribution at the founding of Cañete can be described in some detail.[25] First, however, we must take note of certain geographical features of the valley (see map 6). At the time of the conquest, the irrigated lands of the Cañete valley, located largely on the north side of the river, received their water from four long irrigation canals, which the Spaniards were to call the acequias of Huanca, Chome, and Hualcara, and the Acequia Imperial. These canals are still in use today. The highest of them, the Acequia Imperial, had ceased to operate by 1556, leaving the irrigated area of the valley considerably smaller than it had been. This area was further reduced when a landslide blocked the Acequia de Hualcara where it passed around the Cerro de Montalbán, a hill in the middle of the valley. This canal was subsequently known as the "broken acequia" (*acequia quebrada*) and gave its name to the modern hacienda La Quebrada, which is located in this part of the valley. Neither it nor the Acequia Imperial would be successfully repaired until the end of the eighteenth century.[26]

The Indian descendants of the pre-Inca population of the valley had

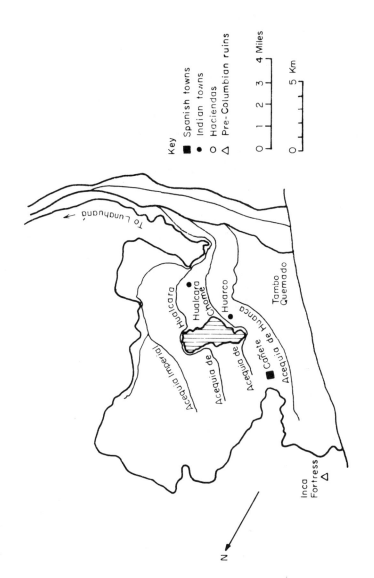

**Map 6.** The Cañete Valley

been assigned after the conquest to Alonso Martín de Don Benito. Most of them lived in the town of Huarco, though there was also a small group of fishermen living in the northwest corner of the valley.[27] Several immigrant groups were also present in 1556. Indians from Coayllo to the north had established the town of Huanca in an abandoned section of the valley following the Inca conquest. Similarly, there were Indians on the south bank of the river from Lunahuaná and Chincha.[28]

When the Spanish settlers arrived in 1556, they established their new town at Huanca, moving the Indians east of the Chome canal, where they were assigned land. The Huarco Indians were left with the land bordered by the Chome and Huanca canals, the Cerro de Montalbán, and the river. The remaining land, excluding an estancia which belonged to Diego de Agüero (later Hacienda Hualcara) and two grants previously made to Alonso Martín de Don Benito and Andrés de Quincoces, was available for distribution among the settlers. When the lower section of the Hualcara canal was blocked several years later, depriving the Huanca Indians of water, these arrangements had to be changed. Both groups of Indians were moved into the corner of the valley east of the upper Hualcara canal (Rinconada de Hualcara), where they received land which had originally been distributed to Spaniards. The latter were probably compensated with the land given up by the Huarco Indians. Huarco itself became a secondary center of Spanish population in the valley, and when Cañete was destroyed in the great earthquake of 1687, the town fathers decided to rebuild there instead of on the original site.[29]

The initial distribution of lands to the vecinos of the new town took place over a period of about eleven months, between December 1556 and November 1557. First of all, certain lands were set aside for dehesas close to the shore in the northern part of the valley and next to the river. Then, the parts of the valley within which lands would be assigned to Indians and to Spaniards were delineated. Most of the grants made to the original vecinos were in the area to the north of the Cerro de Montalbán, although the larger grants given to Zurbano as the founder, and to a few others, were closer to the river. A small amount of land was reserved for men who might settle in the town later, but much of it was close to the river and the shore where the soil was not as good as along the canals. The Cañete cabildo continued until 1560 to distribute this poorer land to new vecinos, of whom there would be about ten more; but much of it had still not been brought under cultivation at the end of the century. A few plots were given at the orders of the viceroy to men who almost certainly did not become vecinos. The chief constable (*alguacil mayor*) of Lima, for instance, received a grant of thirty fanegadas. The viceroy also ordered varying amounts of land given to the wives of two vecinos and to the daughters of several more.[30]

The distribution of land to the original twenty-five vecinos was made by lot—most of them receiving their allotments in two, three, or even four separate pieces. The assortment given to a vecino named Luís Pérez was fairly typical: 78 acres along the Huanca canal, 101 acres along the Chome canal, and 132 acres along the Hualcara canal. Most of the grants were rectangular—the second of Pérez's plots, for instance, was measured at 212 by 550 *brazas*\* (about 1,300 by 3,300 feet)—probably because the canals irrigating this section of the valley ran nearly parallel to each other; recent aerial photographs suggest that long rectangular fields are still characteristic of the valley. This practice of giving the vecinos their land in several pieces was probably common to most of these early towns, though it is seldom well documented outside of Cañete; only at Chancay is there clear evidence that the vecinos were assigned land in more than one place.[31]

For the exploitation of their land the vecinos required Indian labor. This had to be provided by the government, since the Spaniards who settled these towns could not afford to pay wages which would have guaranteed them an adequate supply. To meet this need, Indian tributaries were drafted from nearby encomiendas for limited periods of time (usually six months) under the system known as the mita. At Chancay, for example, one hundred Indians from coastal encomiendas were assigned to serve during the summer months; one hundred more were brought from sierra encomiendas to the east during the winter, when the climate was considered least unhealthy for them. Since there were about twenty vecinos, each one would presumably have had the use of five Indians at a time, if they were distributed evenly. The Spaniards were required to pay each Indian the wage of one *tomín* (about one real) a day and to provide their food.[32]

The proliferation of Spanish landholding in the coastal valleys

---

\*Since the Cañete fanegada was roughly 7¾ acres, a braza would have been about 6 feet, which approximates the modern value of 5½ feet.

during the 1550's and 1560's, then, was primarily a consequence of the
need to provide economic opportunities for those conquerors and
settlers who did not consider themselves suitably rewarded for their
services under the encomienda system. Land took on particular
importance in this context for several reasons. First, the alternative
rewards which the viceroys and governors could offer, such as pensions
and offices, were too few in number to meet the demand. Secondly,
the ending of the encomenderos' monopoly made available the Indian
labor with which the settlers could grow cash crops on the land they
received. Finally, the increasing demand for farm products had
created a significant market for such crops.

Under these circumstances it is probable that whatever policies the
viceroys might adopt, coastal land was likely to be occupied by Spaniards at a fairly rapid rate, either with or without the sanction of the
law. This was especially true since, as we have seen, there were considerable amounts of land which the Indians had in effect abandoned.
The viceroys tried to control this process of occupation instead of
resisting it. They decided it was possible to transform the turbulent
soldados who plagued the country into prosperous gentleman-farmers,
and from about 1550 they were willing to make moderate grants of
land to individuals on request. But even this solution to the problem
was inadequate, partly because of the poverty of many of the potential
recipients of such grants, and partly because of the caution necessary
in abrogating Indian rights to appropriated land. It therefore proved
simpler and more successful in the long run to settle Spaniards collec-
tively rather than individually, founding agricultural towns whose
cabildos took responsibility for the distribution of land and labor to
individuals. This policy received its share of criticism, from both encomenderos and humanitarians. But it is difficult to believe that the
alternative—the perpetuation of Indian rights to most land and the
strict limitation of Spanish settlement—could have been effectively
enforced.

### The Decline of the Chacra

The viceregal policy of establishing agricultural towns and providing poor Spaniards with modest land grants might logically have
been expected to result in an agricultural system based on medium-
sized farms, something like the one which existed in the British North

American colonies. Such a system did not develop in most of the coastal valleys, however. Even in valleys like Cañete, Santa, and Chancay, where chacras predominated in the 1560's, the future proved to lie with the larger hacienda.

The success of haciendas in areas where chacras had previously established themselves is difficult to explain. We have usually thought of haciendas as relatively unproductive enterprises which could advantageously be replaced by smaller and more efficient family farms. But if smaller farms tend to be more efficient than larger estates, why did agricultural expansion lead to the replacement of chacras with haciendas in the sixteenth and seventeenth centuries? One possible answer is that Spaniards wanted land for the prestige it gave them rather than for the profit that could be made from it. This has some truth in it, but as an explanation of the hacienda it is not completely adequate. If the desire for prestige had been the main reason why Spaniards wanted to acquire land, nearly all Spaniards would have become landowners. But in fact, large haciendas arose because relatively few Spaniards were able to make an adequate income as farmers.

The main reason for the failure of the chacras was that their owners seldom had the capital necessary to engage successfully in commercial agriculture. Most of the original vecinos of Cañete, as we have seen, were too poor even to buy the oxen and equipment they needed. And profits were too low to allow for much reinvestment. Though the demand for agricultural products in Lima and the mining areas might be growing, it was still not large in absolute terms. Nor was it regular. The cabildo of Lima periodically sent men to purchase wheat in the valleys between Barranca and Chincha for the city. This might seem to indicate a high level of demand, but in fact such trips occurred only in periods of scarcity and were intended to keep wheat prices in the city from rising. In this they seem to have been generally successful. Prices tended to remain so low that farmers in the valleys north of Lima found it more profitable to grind their wheat into flour and ship it to Panama. As a result, when the cabildo wanted to buy wheat in these valleys, it had to restrain them forcibly from exporting it to the north.[33]

In the face of these economic difficulties, it was difficult for the small farmers favored by the early viceroys to survive. This can best be shown in the Cañete valley, for which documents drawn up by a town

notary and the landowner Hernando Alonso list all the original land
grants of the 1550's and indicate the owners of each piece of land in
1593.[34] Both lists show that very few of the original grants to the
vecinos of the town were still in the hands of their descendants
thirty-seven years later, and most of those lands either lacked water —
several pieces were on the *acequia quebrada* — or were otherwise uncul-
tivable. Of the men present in 1556, only two — the founder Jerónimo
Zurbano and Hernando Alonso — clearly had descendants among the
larger landowners of the valley in 1593, though two or three more may
have done so and several had daughters married to large landowners.
Only half the family names which appear on the list of the original
twenty-five vecinos can be found on the list of those who settled their
titles to these same lands in 1593, and some of this repetition was
probably coincidence. The names of most of the original vecinos were
common ones, and one cannot assume that a González or a Sánchez on
the 1593 list was descended from an earlier González or Sánchez.
The contrast with the colonial towns of New England, where the
original family names tended to reappear generation after generation,
is marked.[35]

By 1593, many of the early Cañete land grants had been sold, often
in fragments. Eight of the original nineteen grants made below the
Huanca canal, for instance, had been split into at least two pieces;
below the Chome canal the corresponding figure was eight out of
twenty-one. Some of these fragments were as small as three acres. By
means of these sales, much of the Spanish-owned land of the Cañete
valley was transferred from the twenty-five or thirty settlers who came
in the 1550's to a group of about ten larger landowners, primarily
made up of more recent immigrants to the valley, though it also
included the descendants of two encomenderos. Most of these men
were not yet hacendados in the strict sense, since their holdings were
scattered in different parts of the valley. The exception to this rule was
Diego de Agüero, whose purchases around his early estancia make it
apparent that he was already the master of a fairly unified estate.
Others were soon to follow his example, however, and by the 1630's
haciendas were well established in the valley.

The replacement of chacras by haciendas was a characteristic phenomenon on the Peruvian coast. In the Chancay valley, many of the
early chacras were absorbed into the large Hacienda La Huaca built
up by Juan Martínez Rengifo, and several more of the nine or ten

haciendas which existed in the valley by the 1590's must have been built up in much the same way. The evidence from Santa suggests a similar pattern. Only in the wine-producing valleys of the south do we find a tendency for chacras to multiply without growing or being absorbed into larger estates.[36]

One consequence of this process of consolidation was the appearance of a substantial group of Spanish settlers who possessed little land of their own. In Cañete, for instance, sixteen out of the forty-one individuals listed in 1593 as owners of the land distributed at the founding of the town possessed so little of it that they paid less than 25 pesos to settle their title with the crown; on the same list the nine largest proprietors paid sums ranging from 150 to 450 pesos. A visita of Santa made this same year found that only about half the Spanish families living in the town owned a significant amount of land in the valley. The heads of the other households were merchants, innkeepers, bakers, carpenters, and small gardeners, rather than farmers.[37]

By the end of the sixteenth century, then, the small gentleman-farmers whom the viceroys had tried to help were gradually disappearing from most of the coastal valleys. The reason seems to have been that many chacras were simply not capable of providing their owners with an acceptable income. In the last quarter of the sixteenth century, a Spaniard living in Lima and supporting himself as an artisan or merchant was probably able to earn at least 400 pesos a year, as did the lowest-paid members of the viceregal guard. To make a comparable income from wheat farming, a man would probably have had to produce between 500 and 1,000 fanegas (750-1,500 bushels), since wheat sold for one to four pesos a fanega in Lima and for less elsewhere. But in fact, few chacras produced this much except in the immediate vicinity of Lima, and even there harvests of 200 or 300 fanegas seem to have been common. And given the limited size of the market, expanding production was risky, since it might bring lower prices.[38]

A second difficulty confronting the owners of chacras was the acute shortage of labor which prevailed on the coast in the latter part of the century. As we have seen, the small farmers of the 1550's and 1560's had relied mainly on the labor of Indians brought from nearby encomiendas under the mita system. They could not continue to do so after 1570, because there were no longer enough coastal Indians to go around. It might have proved possible to fill the gap with Indians brought down from the highlands, but in practice humanitarian opposition and competing demands for labor made this difficult. Coastal landowners thus found it harder and harder to obtain the labor they needed. A case from the end of the century gives some idea of the problem. In 1596, ten Indians from an encomienda in the Huarmey valley were assigned to work on an hacienda in the neighboring Huaura valley. The local corregidor, who apparently needed Indian labor for enterprises of his own, failed to send them until several years later, when he received a court order to do so. By that time a new census had determined that the population was 30 percent smaller, so that only seven mitayos, rather than the promised ten, could be sent.[39]

To make matters worse, reforms enacted in the 1570's took the power to allot mita laborers away from local officials and restricted it to the viceroys, thus giving the wealthier and more influential landowners a considerable advantage in obtaining Indian labor, particularly if they lived in Lima. By the middle of the seventeenth century, the remaining Indians were assigned mainly to the largest landowners, for tending livestock. In 1651, for instance, a group of thirteen sent to the Chancay valley was divided up among four landowners; these included a son of the Marqués de Guadalcázar, a descendant of the encomendero Ruy Barba, and the Jesuit College of San Pablo in Lima.[40]

Well before the end of the sixteenth century, then, the mita proved unable to satisfy the labor needs of coastal farmers. In the valley of Mexico, by comparison, such a collapse did not occur until the 1620's, when it was brought about by depopulation and the increasing diversion of Indian labor to construct drainage works. Elsewhere in Mexico, dependence on drafted Indian labor lasted even longer. On the Cortés sugar plantation near Cuernavaca, encomienda Indians continued to perform much of the work until late in the seventeenth century, in spite of the fact that the draft system had officially been abolished long before.[41]

Throughout Spanish America, depopulation and the decline of draft systems like the mita brought a change in the methods used to obtain Indian labor, making it necessary for Spaniards to rely on the "free" labor of Indian peons or sharecroppers. On the Peruvian coast, however, the possibility of attracting such "free" Indian labor was small. Agricultural workers existed, but they were few in number and could demand relatively high wages. By the end of the sixteenth century, some were earning fifty or sixty pesos a year, and fifty years later we hear of short-term laborers who made as much as six reales a day.[42] Sharecropping would become important as the coastal population recovered during the eighteenth and nineteenth centuries, but it was less common before that. There was one hacienda near Lima which was "renting" part of its land to Indians in 1615, but the notarial registers give the impression that black sharecroppers were more common in the valley than Indian ones.[43] It is evident that before the end of the sixteenth century successful agricultural enterprises on the coast had come to rely primarily on the labor of slaves imported from Africa. About the year 1600, the Lima valley had a black population of 40,000 or 50,000, mainly working on the chacras around the city; its Indian communities at this time contained fewer than 600 adult males eligible for the mita (of whom only one seventh could be drafted at a time). The Ica and Pisco valleys were each said to have 10,000 slaves, while their Indian communities contained about 700 and 200 adult males respectively.[44]

For the smaller Spanish landowners of the coast, the shift to slave labor was difficult. They might be able to afford the tomín a day paid a mitayo during the sixteenth century, but the 300-600 pesos needed to buy a good adult slave was another matter.[45] In effect, dependence on slave labor increased the initial cost of buying or setting up a chacra (or hacienda) by up to 100 percent. This was already true in the Lima valley in the 1550's, as the notarial records consistently show. In 1552, we read of a chacra near Chuquitanta which was sold for the sum of 1,700 pesos: 700 for the chacra itself and the grain planted in it, 650 for four slaves, two of whom were no longer of working age, and 350 for four oxen and a cart. And slaves continued to represent a large proportion of the value of chacras and haciendas, both in the Lima valley and elsewhere. In 1639, for instance, the eleven adult slaves who worked on one wine chacra near Ica must have been worth at least one quarter of the 20,000 pesos for which it was sold in that year. And two years later, the seventy-five adult slaves on the hacienda of Vilcahuaura in the Huaura valley probably accounted for close to half of the 76,000 pesos for which it was sold.[46]

Since most Spaniards did not possess the capital to invest on this scale, they could not afford the labor necessary to make their lands productive. Perhaps for this reason some tried raising their own slaves.

At the beginning of the seventeenth century, a councilman (*regidor*) of the new town of Huaura listed six slaves in his will; of these one was a man, two were women, and three were children. About the same time, one of his neighbors had eight slaves: one man, three women and four children. The demographic pattern suggested by these figures was strikingly different from that found on the larger haciendas, where the slave population averaged over 80 percent male and there were relatively few children.[47]

There were two areas where agricultural profits were high enough to enable chacra owners to buy the slaves they needed. One was the valley of Lima itself, where farmers benefited from their proximity to the best market on the coast for grains and other food crops. The other was the southern part of the coast, particularly the area around Ica, whose prosperity was based on the export of wine, not only to Lima, but throughout most of the viceroyalty of Peru and even as far as Central America. Wine was the traditional alcoholic beverage of Mediterranean Europe, and the demand for local varieties was high, since imported wine was very expensive. But the number of good wine-producing areas in Spanish America was limited. The highland regions were generally too cold, and the lowland regions too hot and humid. The best wine-producing areas eventually turned out to be in peripheral regions like Chile and California, which did not begin producing on a large scale until much later. The Peruvian coast, with its dry temperate climate, was thus one of the few areas suited to wine production which was also close to major centers of Spanish population. But wine did not prove equally profitable in all the coastal valleys. It was early recognized that the best wines were made in the valleys from Pisco to the south. The others always produced a little, even in the far north, but they were never able to compete successfully. The southern valleys thus came to possess a kind of informal monopoly of wine production which would have important consequences for their development.

Because of this monopoly, the Spaniards who settled the Ica valley in the 1560's soon found that it was much more profitable to plant grapevines than wheat or other grains. A man who planted a vineyard of fifteen or twenty acres with 1,500 or 2,000 vines was capable after several years of getting 1,200-2,000 gallons (300-500 *arrobas*) of wine a year. In Lima, this wine could be sold for six or seven pesos an arroba in the 1570's and for nine or ten in the 1590's; or it could be sold in Ica

itself for three to five pesos an arroba. Thus a man with only a few
fanegadas of land might make 1,000 pesos or more, and with less effort
than would have been required for growing wheat.[48]

Wine was well suited to production on a small scale. Grapevines
needed four to six years to reach maturity, and they required a good
deal of individual attention—easier to provide on a small chacra than
on a large estate. In this respect they resembled the small tobacco
farms described in Fernando Ortiz's *Cuban Counterpoint*. In contrast
to the overseers around Lima, who were paid salaries or received a
portion of the crop, overseers in Ica often became partners in the
enterprises for which they worked and might ultimately become landowners themselves. In such a partnership one man usually provided
the capital, land, and labor, and the other agreed to plant a vineyard
and manage it. When the contract ran out, the vineyard would be split,
with a third of it going to the overseer, or perhaps half if he had contributed a share of the capital.[49] It is not surprising, then, that small
chacras persisted as the main type of agricultural enterprise in the Ica
area. A sampling of the notarial registers of the town from the late
sixteenth and early seventeenth centuries suggests that the majority of
chacras in the Ica valley were smaller than ten fanegadas or seventy-
two acres (see table 7). And though some larger estates did grow up in
the valley, the early pattern of land tenure has largely survived, as one
can observe in modern maps and aerial photographs.

The success of the chacras was even more striking in the case of the
Ingenio valley south of Ica.[50] García de Salcedo had purchased the
entire valley in 1546 from the curacas of his encomienda of Nazca,
subsequently developing it into a large sugar estate which was sold
several years after his death to his successor as encomendero, Pedro
Gutiérrez. Apparently unable to pay the whole price himself,
Gutiérrez formed a partnership with Diego Maldonado, one of the
original vecinos of Cuzco. Under this arrangement, the land in the
valley was held in common by the two men instead of being divided
up. Matters were further complicated when Maldonado proceeded to
entail his as yet indeterminate share of the valley. At this point the
valley was still unified, and the entail apparently made any division of
the land even more unlikely than it had been before. Nevertheless, it
was not long before the first alienations occurred. When Gutiérrez
married his daughter to one Diego Núñez de Paredes, he gave the
couple a third of his share of the land, or one-sixth of the valley, which

**Table 7.**   Spanish Landholding in the Ica Valley

| Date | Size (in fanegadas) | Description |
|------|---------------------|-------------|
| 1577 | 6 | viña: 3,000 plants |
| 1583 | 1½ | |
| 1583 | 2½ | viña: 15,000 plants |
| 1583 | 2 | |
| 1583 | 2 | "montuosos" |
| 1583 | under 2 | viña: about 8,000 plants |
| 1583 | 1½-2 | |
| 1583 | 2 | viña: to be planted |
| 1583 | 1 | |
| 1588 | 2 | viña: 1,500 plants |
| 1589 | 15[a] | |
| 1594 | 4 + | viña |
| 1599 | 4 | viña: over 12,000 plants |
| 1600 | 28[a] | viña |
| 1602 | 26[a] | viña |
| 1611 | 7 | |
| 1618 | 9 + | viña |
| 1618 | 6 + | "alfarfar y tierras" |
| 1618 | 6½ | |
| 1639 | 48[b] | |
| 1650 | 4-5[c] | viña: 4,000 plants |
| 1652 | 8 | |
| 1658 | 6 | |

*Sources:* ANP, Notarios de Ica, Leg. 2, 3, and 9 (1577-1599) and Títulos, cc. 60, 85, 133, 134, 148, 156, 173, 178, 280, and 385 (1594, 1600-1658).

[a]Bought from a cacique.
[b]Previously owned by an encomendero.
[c]Size measured in 1605.

was subtracted from the lands of the partnership, presumably with Maldonado's agreement. This land, partially planted with grapevines, was passed on to the next generation, and some pieces of it were subsequently sold.

In the meantime Gutiérrez, like many Spaniards, had gone into debt and established a *censo* over his remaining third of the valley.*

*The *censo* or rent-charge originally appeared in sixteenth-century Europe as a device for loaning money at interest without violating the traditional prohibition against usury. It also served as a means of providing a secure monetary income or of paying for religious services, particularly after death. Most censos were reaeemable at will (*censos al quitar*) or perpetual (*censos*

After his death in the 1580's, this land was awarded to certain of his
creditors, who sold it to a vecino of Arequipa, Pedro Rodríguez de
Santillán. By this time the expansion of the wine industry had created
a considerable demand for small pieces of land; thus Santillán and his
heirs began to subdivide and sell off what they had. The titles have
survived for one piece, which was sold to an official from Lima in 1602
and planted with grapevines. It was later resold to a notary with the
audiencia, who in turn sold it to Juan Francisco Arias Maldonado, the
grandson of Gutiérrez' partner and now the owner of the entailed half
of the valley. Instead of adding the vineyard to his own estate,
however, Maldonado sold it in 1619 to the Jesuit college in Cuzco for
12,850 pesos.

With his entailed estate, Maldonado was in something of a predica-
ment. Economically it made sense to break up the estate into smaller
chacras to take advantage of the wine boom, but the entail prevented
him from selling parts of it as Santillán had done. Renting was not a
satisfactory alternative because of the slow maturation and long life of
the vines. Few prospective winegrowers would be willing to invest the
time and capital needed to start a vineyard without more security of
tenure than renting could give them. Nor could Maldonado offer part
of the chacra in remuneration as other landowners sometimes did. His
solution was to request permission from the audiencia to break the
entail by exchanging individual pieces of land for perpetual censos.
This was granted, probably because it was obviously in the long-term
financial interest of the Maldonado estate, and in 1647 the entailed
half of the valley was split up into ten chacras pledged to pay censos of
70-110 pesos a year.[51] In a similar case from the beginning of the
seventeenth century, the lands and vineyard of the encomendero Nuño
Rodríguez Barreto in Humay were divided up among his heirs, who
had found it impossible to sell the whole estate for a satisfactory
price.[52]

Small Spanish landowners were not the only ones to benefit from the
opportunities provided by the wine industry. Indian curacas, who con-

---

perpetuos), and their interest rates were set by the crown for all Spanish dominions. In the later
sixteenth century, interest was limited to 1/14 of the principal a year (7.14%), but this limit was
lowered in 1614 to 1/20 (5%), primarily to ease the burden of payments on the higher nobility in
Spain. In Spanish America, the censo served mainly as a kind of mortgage to facilitate the purchase of land and as a device which made it possible for religious corporations or clergymen to
convert land or capital assets into regular income.

trolled large amounts of land and could divert some of the labor traditionally owed by their subjects into the planting and tending of grapevines, were among the largest wine producers in the Ica valley. Don
Fernando Anicama, curaca of San Juan, for instance, owned nine
different wine chacras when he died in 1571. Apparently influenced by
the same fears and guilt feelings which led many Spaniards to leave
property to Indians they had mistreated, he ordered in his will that the
income from these chacras, which must have been substantial, be paid
to the poor among his Indian subjects. Another curaca, Don Diego
Sulca Changalla, owned a number of wine chacras, one in partnership
with a Spaniard named Rodríguez who lived in Ica. The size of this
chacra is suggested by the fact that in January 1583 Rodríguez was
able to obtain an advance of 3,000 pesos for wine from the next
harvest, which would not be ready for more than six months.[53]

Nor were the curacas the only Indians to take up the production of
wine. Indian commoners did so on a large scale as well, though their
individual holdings were much smaller. In 1577, the viceroy Toledo
ordered that some hoya lands north of Ica be sold, because the Indian
owners had been moved to the Pisco valley, and it was considered
unwise to allow them to keep lands at such a distance from their
homes. At the time, the Indians were using these lands to grow grapes,
an activity which they had taken up about ten years previously. In
order to compensate individual Indians for the land, a list of their
names was drawn up giving the number of vines each had and the
amount of wine they usually produced. Almost one hundred growers
were mentioned, of whom the largest, with more than two hundred
vines, sold about forty arrobas of wine a year. More than half those
listed produced ten or more arrobas a year, probably selling the new
wine immediately after the harvest to local Spaniards for a peso or two
per arroba as Indians in the Ica valley usually did. For many of them
wine production must have represented a substantial source of income,
comparable to the wages of Indians who worked as agricultural
laborers around Lima (8-20 pesos a year).[54]

The only other crop which enjoyed relatively widespread success on
the coast was sugarcane. Though generally more profitable than
wheat, it was never as lucrative as wine, as is evident from the fact that
sugar haciendas seldom appeared where wine chacras were successful.
Unlike wine, sugar could be produced competitively in most of the
coastal valleys and even in some of the warmer sierra valleys—those of

Abancay and Andahuaylas, for example. Hence no single region enjoyed a monopoly of production and the corresponding profits. It is difficult to understand how colonial Spanish Americans consumed enough sugar to support an industry; but the fact is that they did eat astonishing quantities of sweets, as Father Cobo observed in the seventeenth century. This was perhaps a case of conspicuous consumption, fastening on sugar in the absence of other traditional luxuries. À century later the Czech miner, Thaddeus Haenke, noted that the consumption of sweets had declined and that people were spending their money on furniture and coaches instead.[55] The demand for sugar stimulated the development of haciendas which required many slaves. By the 1650's, for instance, San Jacinto (Nepeña valley) and Vilcahuaura (Huaura valley) were both operating with more than eighty slaves apiece; at the end of the eighteenth century there was a sugar hacienda near Barranca which had 672.[56] To be profitable, however, sugar planting required large amounts of capital, and it was therefore a feasible undertaking only for Spaniards who were fairly rich to begin with. Thus the number of sugar haciendas was always limited; while sugar could be grown in most of the irrigated lands of the coast, there were seldom more than one or two sugar haciendas in any valley. On the other hand, the sugar haciendas of the seventeenth century were more highly developed and better organized than most agricultural enterprises on the coast; many of them belonged to the Jesuits, who took legitimate pride in the efficiency with which they were run. They therefore provided the model which was followed in the nineteenth century, when an increased demand for Peruvian sugar and cotton brought about the modernization of the coastal hacienda system.[57]

For Spanish farmers whose land was not in one of the good wine-producing valleys, and who did not have the capital to take up sugar planting, the opportunities to be found in commercial agriculture were limited. Most of them marketed cereals, vegetables, fruit, and sometimes a little wine, but not in sufficient quantity to bring much profit. Only in the Chancay valley was a new source of prosperity discovered in the fattening of pigs to supply the Lima market with lard (used as a substitute for olive oil); and even there it was too late to save most of the small Spanish farmers in the valley.[58] Forced to practice something very close to subsistence agriculture, they had sold their land and departed, tempted by the greater opportunities to be found in Lima and the southern valleys. Thus Chancay, Santa, and Cañete remained poor and backward by comparison with the towns of the south, and even Trujillo declined. At the beginning of the seventeenth century Lizárraga lamented the disappearance of the easy liberality which had been practiced by the early vecinos of the city, attributing it to the poverty of their descendants and to the fact that a once considerable trade with Lima had greatly fallen off.[59]

This general pattern would not change much until after independence. Some late eighteenth-century statistics (see table 8) on the value of goods produced and the size of the Spanish population in each of the coastal provinces (*partidos*) show the southern provinces to be the most productive and prosperous, as they had been two centuries earlier. The northern provinces appear as the least productive, excepting Chancay with its lard business, and Lambayeque, whose prosperity came from manufacturing. The case of Lambayeque is especially interesting. Since the end of the sixteenth century its main exports had been cotton cloth, soap (made from goat's fat), and leather goods made by Indian artisans. This reflects a pattern which predated the conquest. Cieza de León says that the Indians of this region carried on considerable trade both locally and with the sierra, and he particularly mentions the extensive fields of cotton, from which they made

**Table 8.**  Productivity and Spanish Population on the Coast, c. 1790

| Provinces | Annual value of goods produced (1,000 pesos) | Spanish population |
|---|---|---|
| Piura | 73 | 2,874 |
| Lambayeque | 308 | 2,299 |
| Trujillo | 32 | 1,434 |
| Santa | - | 279 |
| Chancay | 465 | 969 |
| El Cercado de Lima | 50[a] | 18,219 |
| Cañete | 35 | 465 |
| Ica | 589 | 2,158[b] |
| Camaná | 300 | 5,105 |
| Arequipa | 639 | 22,687 |
| Moquegua | 70 | 5,596 |
| Arica | 161 | 1,585 |

Source: Haenke, *Descripción del Perú*.

[a]This figure does not include goods produced in the city of Lima itself.
[b]Haenke gives a figure of 20,158, which is presumably a misprint.

cloth. The prosperity of Lambayeque thus rested not on the expansion of Spanish agriculture but on the survival of a relatively large Indian population (compared to the rest of the coast) which was able to adapt its traditional economic patterns to colonial circumstances.[60] The population figures for the coastal provinces tend to confirm the economic picture. In 1795, about 56 percent of the Spanish population of the coast was concentrated in the five southern provinces, even though the region had considerably less than half the cultivated land. If we exclude Lima, more than 80 percent of the Spanish population lived in the southern provinces. Few Spaniards wanted to live in the poor valleys north of Cañete when they could live better in Lima or in the more prosperous valleys of the south.

This contrast between rich valleys and poor valleys and its implications for the survival or disappearance of chacras is fundamental to an understanding of the development of the coastal hacienda system. Its consequences are indeed still visible on the ground, in spite of the inroads of modernization. Aerial photographs of valleys like Huaura and Chincha, where agriculture was not very profitable and where the early chacras were largely incorporated into haciendas, show a sharp line of demarcation between the indigenous zones of small-scale agriculture and the Spanish zones of estate agriculture. In valleys like Ica or Lima, which were more prosperous at the end of the sixteenth century, the division between Spanish and indigenous zones is much less sharp, partly because more small or medium-sized holdings survived, partly because Spaniards were more likely to acquire land within indigenous zones, and partly because the Indians were more rapidly hispanicized, becoming commercial farmers themselves. In the light of this evidence, then, it appears that the development of the hacienda system on the coast followed no single basic pattern, but rather two: one which was characteristic of valleys where agriculture was profitable, and one which was characteristic of valleys where it was not.

# 5 / The Consolidation of the Hacienda System

When Francisco de Toledo arrived in Peru in 1569, the change from a conquest society based on the encomienda and the traditional community to a colonial society based on the hacienda was far from complete on the coast. Spanish chacras were scattered through the valleys and particularly around Lima, but there was as yet nothing that could be described as an hacienda system. The few larger estates that existed were usually called *heredades;* the word "hacienda" itself would not come into general use until the end of the century.

In the present chapter we will examine two aspects of the consolidation of the hacienda system: the fixing of Spanish attitudes concerning the role of the hacienda within the social system and the acquisition of rights to land and water. Before 1569 few wealthy Spaniards except for the encomenderos had thought that the possession of a large landed estate was necessary to assure their position in society. By the middle of the next century, on the other hand, landownership had clearly become the principal basis for determining aristocratic status. In 1569, Spaniards still owned relatively little land on the coast. Only in the Lima valley and perhaps in that of Cañete had they gained possession of as much as half of the available land. By the middle of the seventeenth century, in contrast, most of this land had been transferred to Spanish possession and belonged to the haciendas, except perhaps on the northern coast. With regard to water, there was no system at all for allocating it among those who needed it in 1569. While this lack was not completely remedied by 1650, we will see that a beginning had been made.

## The Hacendados and Their Motives

The hacienda system of the southern coast was the creation of a prosperous rural gentry who supported themselves through the production of wine. They lived in the numerous small valleys between Pisco and the Chilean border, often on their chacras in the countryside. Since they were seldom important enough to have their accomplishments remembered, we know relatively little about them except as their activities are documented in the many volumes of deeds, contracts, and wills laboriously recorded by the notaries of Ica and other towns.

As a representative of this class of small hacendados, we may take Baltasar de los Reyes Esquível. He was an immigrant from Spain who first appears in 1574 as the owner of a chacra outside the walls of El Cercado at Lima. In the 1580's, he seems to have sold this chacra and moved to Ica, where he bought a wine chacra in the Chavalina district, a house in the town, and about 340 acres of land elsewhere in the valley. At his death in 1639, Esquível had apparently sold the house in town and was living in one he had built on the chacra. He owned 400 or 500 acres of land, fourteen slaves, and a team of forty mules. His son was a prior of the merchant guild (*consulado*) in Lima, and he had three grown daughters, two married locally and the third a nun in the convent of the Encarnación in Lima.[1]

Men like Esquível seem to have been interested in acquiring wine chacras primarily because of the income they provided. As the notarial registers consistently show, the value of chacras was measured less by the amount of land they occupied — many bills of sale left this figure out altogether — than by the number of grapevines they contained. Thus they tended to remain relatively small. In fact few really large estates ever grew up in the Ica valley. Even prominent vecinos of Lima were content with rather small haciendas around Ica, provided they were profitable. At the beginning of the seventeenth century, for instance, Doña Grimanesa de Mogrovejo — widow of the governor of Chile, Don Francisco de Quiñones, and sister of the sainted Archbishop of Lima, Toribio de Mogrovejo — bought a wine chacra in the Ica valley which occupied only about 200 acres of land. Though hardly a large estate, this chacra was considered an important hacienda and remained in the possession of the Quiñones family down to the end of the seventeenth century, when it was sold to the Count of Villaseñor.[2]

To the north of Pisco the situation was quite different. There were a few small hacendados, men like Pedro de San Martín, a vecino of Chancay from the 1560's, who bought some land which had belonged to the Indians of Ruy Barba's encomienda and developed it into an hacienda of about 500 acres which still belonged to his heirs in 1643.[3] But the northern valleys, except for that of Lima, were typically dominated by large landowners, men who come closer to our idea of an hacendado and whose estates often covered several thousand acres.

Some of these men were encomenderos or their descendants. Others were officials, men like Juan Martínez Rengifo, who built up the large hacienda La Huaca in the Chancay valley (which included the present-day haciendas of La Huaca and Jesús del Valle) and subsequently donated it to the Jesuit college in Lima.

Rengifo's activities are especially interesting. He was a lawyer who arrived in Peru about 1560, taking up a minor post with the audiencia in Lima. Subsequently he was promoted to prosecutor (*fiscal*) of the court and married the daughter of one of the judges.[4] In the 1570's Rengifo became a close advisor to the viceroy Toledo, who appointed him the official protector of the Indians for the area which fell within the jurisdiction of the Lima audiencia, with responsibility for administering the land and property of the Indian communities. He held this position for about ten years, and seems to have used it to some advantage in building up one of his haciendas. Rengifo began to accumulate land soon after his arrival in Peru. In 1562, he and a brother received grants of forty fanegadas of land each as founding vecinos of the town of Chancay. Though Rengifo continued to live in Lima, leaving the brother to manage the Chancay enterprise, he provided money to buy more land, so that during the next twenty years an estate of nearly 4,000 acres was built up. Several years later he persuaded Toledo to give him 2,000 acres in the Condor section of the Pisco valley — an exceptionally large land grant on the coast. He also acquired a chacra near the town of Ate in the Lima valley and an estate of some 1,600 acres at Huachipa, nine miles up the river.

Another interesting case was that of Francisco de Soto, who settled in Cañete about 1573, probably as the town's notary. He married the daughter of one of the original vecinos, who provided the couple with a wine chacra, 240 acres of land, three Negro slaves, and some livestock. Making good use of the dowry and of his notarial position, Soto soon became one of the leading landowners in the valley. By 1590, he owned several thousand acres, including several wine chacras which together were said to produce 1,000 arrobas a year, an olive grove, a huerta, 3,000 head of cattle, and ten slaves. He and his wife possessed clothing and furniture valued at 10,000 pesos. He was handling the sale of tribute produce from the encomienda of Lunahuaná, and had some 4,000 pesos of debts owed to him. With his position thus established, he was able to survive an acrimonious lawsuit with his wife's

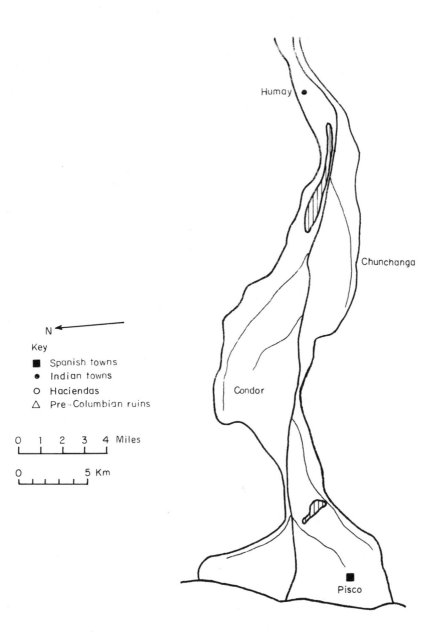

Humay

Chunchanga

N

Key
■ Spanish towns
● Indian towns
○ Haciendas
△ Pre-Columbian ruins

0   1   2   3   4  Miles

0           5  Km

Condor

Pisco

**Map 7.** The Pisco Valley

family when she died childless in 1590 and later to marry a niece of one of the audiencia judges in Lima.[5]

There is a fascinating inventory from the Jesuit hacienda in the Chancay valley, dating from the first quarter of the seventeenth century.[6] At this time — a number of years after Rengifo had given the hacienda to them — the Jesuits were beginning to convert to sugar production. They had a couple of small sugar mills (*trapiches*), which were powered by horses, and about thirty-five acres planted in cane. In other respects, except for a new house and a chapel, the hacienda had probably not changed very much since it had belonged to Rengifo. It had a vineyard with 12,000 plants, a dilapidated wine cellar with a wooden winepress and a large number of earthen jugs, both old and new, for storing wine. In addition it had a small olive grove, a garden with a wide variety of fruit trees, a small field of alfalfa, and a resident labor force of sixteen slaves. There were also large herds of livestock: 549 head of cattle, which they planned to expand to 800, about 1,500 pigs, and more than 150 mules.

What strikes one about this estate is the small scale of the commercial side in comparison with the large amount of land which belonged to it. Of the 4,000 or so acres that the hacienda possessed, only a few hundred — less than 10 percent of the total — seem to have been cultivated. In a sense, it was not so much an hacienda as a chacra, similar to those of the Lima valley, which was surrounded by acres of land used only for grazing livestock. The inventory, in fact, specifically calls it a chacra. What we know of other haciendas in the valleys north of Pisco suggests that this pattern was fairly typical.

It is therefore not entirely accurate to say that the early hacendados of these valleys — the Agüeros, the Rengifos, the Sotos — were basically agricultural entrepreneurs, men concerned primarily with productivity and profits. Though they developed their haciendas to produce marketable crops, they also endowed them with large amounts of land whose acquisition had little to do with economics. Rengifo's 6,000 acres in Chancay and Pisco cannot even be explained as a speculative investment. Though land prices did tend to rise in the course of the sixteenth century, he clearly had no interest in selling his property, and none of his major acquisitions were in fact sold until after his death. Yet had he wanted to, he could undoubtedly have made a substantial profit by subdividing and selling off his Pisco land, much as Maldonado was to do a little later.

Such extensive purchases of land should probably be seen as a form of consumption rather than a type of investment. By building up or purchasing a large estate a man was acquiring a position in the aristocracy, not a source of income. Even in eighteenth-century Mexico, as Brading has shown, the profits of most haciendas were low in comparison with the inflated sums needed to purchase them. Ironically, this meant that those who purchased their way into the landed aristocracy were usually unable to guarantee that their descendants would remain in it for more than a few generations.[7] The contrast with the southern coast, where agriculture was more profitable, is striking. There land was purchased as an investment which could be expected to yield a satisfactory return. As a result more Spaniards were in competition for the available land, which in turn tended to keep down the size of landholdings. Thus in the valleys north of Pisco, the growth of large haciendas seems directly related to the low level of agricultural profits, which by making land a poor investment kept most of it in the hands of men who did not want it primarily for economic reasons.

## The Acquisition of Land

The development of commercial agriculture on the coast involved the replacement of the traditional Indian system of land tenure with a radically different Spanish one. This was not a matter of the outright theft of Indian lands, as it has sometimes been portrayed. On the whole, the Spaniards seem to have shown as much respect for Indian land rights as the Pilgrims and Puritans did in New England.

The pre-conquest societies of the Andes had recognized three basic types of land: community land (which on the coast was regulated by the state), cult land, and state or office land. While accepting this system, the Spaniards tended to misinterpret it. They believed, for example, that the curacas had possessed large private landholdings, even entailed estates. This, however, was not the case. The lands of the curacas traditionally pertained to the office (*cacicazgo*) and not to the individual who filled it, as the subordinate chiefs (*principales*) of Carabayllo complained in 1575, when their curaca tried to sell some of his land.[8] As we shall see, the effect of this misunderstanding was to create a new category of privately owned Indian land.

Inca state and cult land, which had passed to the crown after the

conquest, was available to Spaniards through land grants, but it did
not amount to very much. In most of the country it was the community
lands which were by far the most extensive. Indian ownership of these,
however, was explicitly recognized by the government and the courts,
and was protected well enough to make any transfer of land to Spanish
ownership both complicated and risky for the recipient. Thus the
misconception of the nature of the curacas' landholdings provided a
loophole of considerable importance. As depopulation reduced the
Indians' need for land and their ability to use it productively, the
curacas found it possible to claim community lands as their personal
property and to sell them as such to Spaniards. Such action might even
prove necessary to meet Spanish demands for tribute.[9]

Sixteenth-century Spaniards were able to acquire land on the
Peruvian coast in three principal ways: by getting a land grant from
the local representatives of the crown; by purchasing it from individual
Indian owners (or later from Spanish owners); by purchasing it from
an Indian community or, later, from the crown. The granting of land
was primarily a prerogative of the viceroys, though the cabildos of the
main Spanish towns also made some grants. The early viceroys seem to
have taken quite seriously the requirement that only Inca lands or cult
lands be given away. Later viceroys added the category of *baldías* or
*vacas,* lands which had been physically abandoned by their traditional
cultivators and had therefore reverted to the crown. The identification
of baldías was difficult, however. Indian communities might remember traditional claims long after they had ceased to utilize such lands,
and the grants usually stated explicitly that they were valid only insofar
as they did not prejudice the existing rights of third parties.[10]

An example will illustrate the procedures and difficulties involved in
obtaining land grants. In 1559 Diego de Porras Sagredo, a vecino of
Lima, petitioned the viceroy Cañete for a grant of about seven
hundred acres of land close to the southern edge of the valley of Lima,
in an area where he claimed there was no cultivation and no
functioning irrigation canal. The viceroy sent out a representative to
take a look. His report stated that the land had not been cultivated for
many years and that repairing the canal and getting water to the area
would require much work, which would, incidentally, be of great
benefit to those who had land and chacras nearby. Porras received the
grant, but he apparently did not consider his title completely secure,

for in 1575 he agreed to give one hundred sheep and two oxen to the community of Surco in return for a renunciation of its traditional rights to his land.[11]

Spaniards also acquired Indian land by purchase from individuals, usually the curacas or other members of the traditional nobility, though in the latter part of the century Indian commoners also appeared as private landowners, particularly around Lima and in the south. These lands were considered to have been inherited from ancestors who had owned them before the conquest, and legal ownership under Spanish law was therefore proved by presenting witnesses who could testify that the land in question had indeed been inherited from such ancestors. The word "own" had different connotations to Indians and Spaniards, however, and "inherited" landholdings frequently increased through the addition of unused community land.

In the beginning, few limitations were placed on the right of Indians to alienate their private landholdings. As the demand for land increased, however, the process became more complicated. By the 1570's the viceregal government had concluded that it was its duty to insure that Spaniards, with their greater sophistication and familiarity with the law, would not have the opportunity to cheat the Indians out of land they needed. To this end, all Indians, including the curacas, were treated as minors before the law, able to sell land only with the permission of local officials. Even this procedure seemed inadequate when large amounts of land were involved; in such cases the officials required that the land be sold at public auction, which supposedly insured a fairer price. An Indian who sought permission to sell land had first to present a petition stating the reasons for selling, and to find witnesses to declare that the statements in his petition were true. In some cases, local Spanish farmers (labradores) were brought in to establish a fair price for the land, or to testify to the fairness of a price already agreed upon.[12]

A typical transaction of this nature occurred in 1602, when one of the curacas of Magdalena in the Rímac valley requested permission to sell two fanegadas of land on the road between Magdalena and Lima. He stated that he had been jailed for debts owed to several Spaniards in the city which he could not pay without selling the land. In any case, he added, he could not make any profit out of it because the travellers who used the road periodically damaged the crops he planted there.

The permission was given, and the land was sold to a Spanish farmer in the valley for 650 pesos: 250 in cash and the remainder in the form of a censo of 28½ pesos a year.[13]

Although these requirements undoubtedly made it more difficult to purchase Indian land, there were usually ways of getting around them. This was especially true outside of the Lima area, where the local protector of the Indians, if there was one, was likely to be just another Spanish landowner. On the other hand, such restrictions did not always work to the advantage of the Indians. Particularly around Lima and Ica, where Indians were more involved in the Spanish economy and learned early how to exploit lands they could not cultivate themselves, such protection could turn out to be an irritating and costly nuisance. In 1582, for example, one of the curacas of Carabayllo complained that the protector of the Indians had ruled that he could rent twenty fanegadas of his land only by going through a public auction "as if they were *bienes de difuntos* [property left by a man who died intestate with no known heirs] or I a minor and incompetent." He had been renting out this land for several years, spoke good Spanish, and knew perfectly well what was good for him. "In effect," he commented, "this is to deprive me of the liberty which his majesty wants us Indians, as his free vassals like all other Spaniards, to have."[14]

Private Indian landholdings also passed into Spanish possession through marriage. Coastal curacas were often willing for their daughters to marry Spaniards, provided their status was not too low, since this placed their descendants in the ranks of the Spanish landowning class. For the Spaniards, on the other hand, the curacas and their families were part of an indigenous "nobility" with whom one could intermarry without losing status. Such marriages usually involved the transfer of land, which constituted much of the curacas' wealth. Late in the sixteenth century, for instance, when the curaca of Lurin Ica, Don Alonso Huamán Aquixe, married his daughter to a grandson of the encomendero Pedro Gutiérrez, he gave the couple part of a large and valuable wine chacra which they subsequently sold to the Jesuits. After Aquixe's death, his widow also married a Spaniard, bringing him the rest of this same chacra.[15] There was also the case of Pedro de Olea, a Spanish farmer who first appears in 1574 as an overseer on a chacra in the Huaura valley, receiving the meager salary of 160 pesos a year. One of the curacas in the valley gave him 700 acres of land, which he later sold to the encomendero of Cajatambo, Juan Fernández de Heredia. At the time of the sale, Olea said that he had legally inherited the land from the curaca's widow, which suggests that he had married her.[16]

Indian lands were sometimes acquired by direct purchase from Indian communities — though only occasionally prior to 1570. Salcedo had purchased the Ingenio valley from the Indians of Nazca, represented by their curacas, as early as 1546, and some Spaniards may have bought community land at the time Ica was founded. The status of such purchases under Spanish law was uncertain, however, because it was not clear who had the right to make the sales. Salcedo's heirs, for instance, found themselves embroiled in a lawsuit in the 1550's when the Nazca Indians claimed they had been defrauded; they were ultimately forced to put up another 1,300 pesos plus a herd of one thousand llamas.[17]

After 1570, with the Indians' need for land obviously decreasing, such sales became more frequent. They were not carried out freely, however, but under the close supervision of the viceregal government. Requests for the sale of community land were presented by the curacas to the protector of the Indians in Lima and had to receive final approval from the viceroy himself. Only then was a public auction announced and written bids received for a period of several months, at the end of which the land was sold to the highest bidder. The purchaser seldom paid cash but committed himself to pay a censo of 7.14 percent of the price each year into the Indians' community treasury.[18]

A case from the Lima valley may serve as an illustration. In 1576 Don Alonso Chumbi, the curaca of Naña about nine miles up the river from Lima, petitioned for the sale of approximately 1,100 acres of community land at Huachipa, so that the proceeds could be used to assist his Indian subjects in the payment of their tribute. These Indians had previously been moved to the town of Lurigancho farther down the river, and the Huachipa land was said to be too far away for them to cultivate easily. The argument in favor of selling was further elaborated by two Spanish witnesses: the encomendero of Naña, Francisco de Ampuero, and the local priest. According to both men the Indians lived too far away from the Huachipa land to prevent the crops from being damaged by travellers and livestock who used the road up the valley. Toledo approved the petition and ordered that some of the proceeds be used to pay the Lurigancho Indians for land taken from them and assigned to the Indians of Naña. In the ensuing auction the bidding was kept open for the unusually long period of ten months because the offers were considered too low. The land was finally sold to Melchor de Cadahalso Salazar for a censo of 437 pesos a year. Three years later the land and the obligation to pay the censo were assumed by the protector of the Indians, Rengifo, who was Cadahalso's brother-in-law.[19]

In the 1590's a shift in royal policy brought about a change in the disposition and sale of Indian community lands. Excess community lands were now treated as vacant lands (*baldías*) and passed to the crown. At the same time, the crown recognized an obligation to guarantee each community enough land for its needs. Though in the long run this provided a certain protection for communities which might have found it difficult to preserve their land, in the short run it meant that land would now be sold for the benefit of the crown rather than for that of the communities. Sales of baldías were thereafter carried out by *visitadores de tierras,* high-ranking officials who periodically toured the country to inspect Spanish titles, to collect payment (*composición*) when they were inadequate, and to auction off crown lands.

The methods of acquiring land differed from region to region. Around Ica, land grants seem to have had little importance. Some land in the valley was purchased from Indian communities and curacas. The original vecinos bought land in the districts of San Martín and Chavalina (map 8). These purchases probably involved community land and may have been made by the town for distribution among the individual vecinos. Higher up the valley, most of the land seems to have been claimed and sold off by the curacas. In 1594, for instance, the visitador Alonso Maldonado de Torres discovered several large pieces of community land which had recently been sold by the curaca Don Juan Anicama. Such sales seem to have left little abandoned land for the crown to claim, and Maldonado found little to sell in 1594.[20]

The largest share of the land which passed into Spanish possession around Ica was purchased from individual Indians. By the 1590's Spaniards appear to have bought land in most sections of the valley, where their chacras were interspersed among those of the Indians. The sixteenth-century notarial registers contain numerous references to chacras and small pieces of land purchased from individual Indians, usually but not always curacas or other members of the Indian nobil-

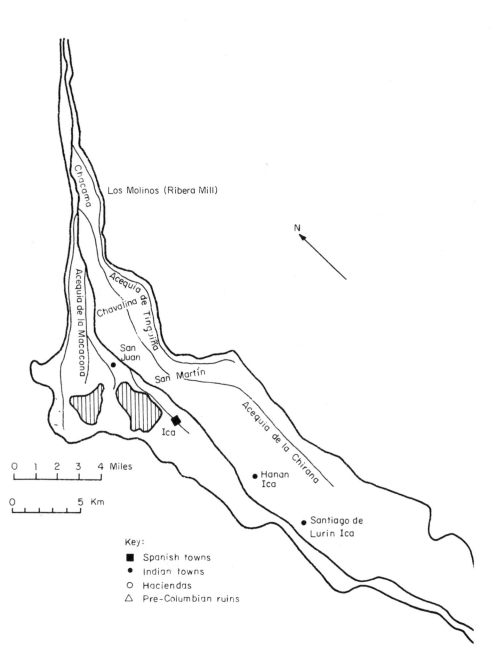

**Map 8.** The Ica Valley

ity. In 1569, for instance, a widow named Catalina Gomez purchased a small piece of land from an Indian for the sum of 14 pesos. The description of the boundaries makes it clear that this land was completely surrounded by her chacra, which one may presume had been built up through the purchase of other small pieces of Indian land.[21] While most common in the south, the sale of small plots of land was well known around Lima also. A new inspection of land titles was ordered for the valley in 1640 on the grounds that the Indians were selling or giving away the community lands assigned them in 1594, enabling Spaniards to develop new chacras out of land which was legally the crown's.[22]

Outside of the Lima area and the south, small individual purchases of land seem to have been less frequent. The grandson of the conquistador Juan de Barrios built up a 1,200 acre hacienda in the Chincha valley during the first three decades of the seventeenth century by piecing together seventeen individual purchases, most of less than 100 acres; but this seems exceptional and may reflect the customs of Ica, where he had lived.[23] Land grants were more common, particularly the grants made to the vecinos of coastal towns like Cañete and Chancay. In the north, however, the most important mechanism for transferring land to Spanish possession was the auctioning of community lands. From the 1590's down to the 1640's the visitadores sold off large blocks of Indian land, which almost always went into large estates; indeed, some haciendas acquired all their land by this means.

The contrast between the prosperous southern valleys and the backward northern ones appears less significant when our perspective is widened to include the densely populated highland areas of Middle America and the Andes, where Spanish appropriation of land was poorly controlled and chaotic.[24] In coastal Peru the process of appropriation was more orderly, partly because the Indians, with their tradition of irrigated agriculture, were able to remember and secure recognition of their rights to land in spite of the demographic and social collapse, and partly because the density of the Spanish population increased the demand for land. Under these circumstances Indian land tended to be sold long before the viceroys realized it was available for granting. Furthermore, since viceregal grants were valid only insofar as they did not affect the rights of third parties (which included Indians), there was always a chance that they would ultimately turn

out to be worthless or at the very least far more expensive than antici-
pated. The danger was not so much that the Indians might try to
reclaim such lands as that they might sell their rights to other Spaniards. The risk was all the greater because the investigations carried out
before making a grant were seldom thorough. At least one case is
documented in which the same viceroy granted a single piece of land
to two different Spaniards.[25]

A case from the early seventeenth century provides an illustration of
the difficulties which might face a person whose title to land depended
on a viceregal land grant. In the 1590's Graviel Solano de Figueroa, a
prominent churchman in Lima who had recently served as a visitador
de tierras in the sierra, asked the viceroy Cañete for a land grant on the
coast, claiming to have spent a substantial amount of his own money in
the performance of his official duties. He first suggested a piece of land
in the Mala valley which he believed was unclaimed. This land had in
fact been sold, so Solano asked instead for a tract of about 700 acres in
the Condor section of the Pisco valley. It was determined to be without
an owner and was granted to him.

Solano made no attempt to develop his land, and at his death in
1600 he left it to a hospital in Lima, which likewise did little with it. In
1617 the hospital in turn sold it to Don Juan de la Cueva, a prominent
vecino of Lima and a member of the military order of Calatrava, for a
censo of 425 pesos a year (5% of 8,500 pesos). At this point a group of
landowners in the Pisco valley asserted that this land had been set aside
in 1594 as common pasture and woodland for the residents of the
valley. This competing claim involved Cueva and his heirs in a lawsuit
which dragged on for fifteen years. Cueva's widow ultimately forced
the hospital to take back the land on the grounds that their title to it
had been unclear (incierta), and in 1635 the hospital resold it to one of
the protesting landowners for the same price Cueva had agreed to
almost twenty years earlier. It is uncertain who lost the most in this
case. The Cuevas presumably had heavy legal expenses which ultimately brought them nothing. The hospital, on the other hand, must
have lost most of the payments on the censo for a period of eighteen
years.[26]

The Peruvian coast also experienced little of the land grabbing
which was and continued to be common in other regions of Spanish
America. Coastal haciendas seem to have owed relatively little to the

seventeenth-century title settlements, which in Mexico enabled Spaniards to obtain legal title to usurped land by means of a modest payment (*composición*) to the crown.[27] The owners of the hacienda of
Vilcahuaura, for instance, had to settle for only about 500 of its 1,500
acres; and the 500 acres probably included land purchased from Indians or even granted by the viceroys, but for which the title had never
been confirmed by the crown itself. At the time of the first title settlements in 1593, the son of Nicolás de Ribera had adequate title to all
1,032 acres of his hacienda in Chunchanga (Pisco valley), which was
made up of a small chacra purchased from a curaca and about 900
acres bought in an auction of community lands. In the 1640's, the same
hacienda was found to contain only 968 acres, but since 143 of the
original 1,032 acres had been sold to another Spaniard, there were 79
acres of *demasías* (land held in excess of the amount specified in the
titles). Such cases were more typical than that of Alonso Vidal
Gallardo, who in 1618 had acceptable titles for only 287 of his 523
acres in the Chincha valley, and who seems to have been reluctant to
appear before the visitador.[28]

On the whole, then, relatively little land seems to have been transferred to Spaniards in this way, for reasons which the Solano case
makes fairly clear. Good land in the coastal valleys was in considerable
demand by the beginning of the seventeenth century, and hacendados
who wanted to hold on to it were well advised to pay something in
order to obtain satisfactory title. For this reason the land which was
occupied without proper title probably tended to be marginal and of
less value. In this respect the situation on the coast seems to have
resembled that found in the valleys of Puebla and Atlixco in Mexico,
where the presence of a large number of Spanish farmers keeping an
eye on each other meant that irregular titles were the exception rather
than the rule. Chevalier tells us that the farmers of Atlixco protested
against title settlements in their region, claiming they were justified
only where the cheapness of land encouraged hacendados to usurp
uncleared fields without worrying about who owned them. The
farmers of Cañete could have made the same argument; in 1593 they
had to pay out more than 4,000 pesos in settlement for the approximately 7,000 acres which had been distributed, on viceregal orders, to
the original vecinos of the town.[29]

In the wealthier agricultural regions, then, title settlement seems to
have acted as a kind of land tax levied in proportion to the size and

value of landholdings. Its weakness was not that it led to the loss of Indian land but rather that it was assessed only once and therefore too heavily on each piece of land. On the Peruvian coast, the settlements probably hindered the usurpation of Indian land. While Indians had earlier been forced to provide witnesses who could testify to their ownership of land, after 1593 officials and judges could refer to the complete lists of landholdings, both Spanish and Indian, which were drawn up by the visitadores. Title settlement was not required of the Indians, of course, but their lands were listed so that they could be recognized promptly as crown property if they should cease to be cultivated. Although these lists have survived only in small fragments, contemporary references to them make it clear that they constituted a fairly complete and accurate land register, with measurements checked by the surveying staff which accompanied the visitadores. The very existence of such records must have made illegal occupation of Indian land less likely and probably had a good deal to do with its orderly transfer to Spaniards.[30]

If Indian land was better protected on the Peruvian coast than elsewhere in Spanish America, however, this was not simply because the records of title settlements made it easier for Spanish officials to enforce the law. The fundamental reasons were demographic. In the first place, the presence of especially large numbers of Spaniards competing with one another for the available land tended to raise its value and substantially increase the risk of using illegal means to build up an estate. Secondly, the rapid decline of the coastal Indian population meant that Indians could not be expected to provide most of the labor needed by the Spaniards. The primary motive for land grabbing in the highland regions of Middle America and the Andes — to deprive the Indians of the means of supporting themselves, thus forcing them to work on the haciendas — was therefore missing. On the coast the number of Indian agricultural laborers remained small, and they were always better off than the downtrodden peons of the highlands; in later years, many of them would even achieve a certain prosperity as tenant farmers.[31] But though coastal Indians may not have been driven off their land deliberately, there were economic pressures which tended to produce a similar result. Systematically deprived through the operation of the tribute system of the capital which might have made it possible for them to exploit the surplus land left after the great epidemics, the Indians found they could derive economic benefit from this land only by selling or renting it. Since Spaniards — at least some of them — had or could obtain the capital necessary to put such land under cultivation, most of it ended up in their hands.

## The Allocation of Water

The changes in the traditional system of irrigation associated with the consolidation of the hacienda system on the coast were less orderly than those affecting the land system. The control of land has always been less important on the coast than the control of water; the extent of cultivation was determined in the colonial period, as it still is, by the supply of water rather than by the availability of land. Struggles over water therefore tended to be more frequent and more violent than struggles over land.

In addition, the problem of regulating the use of water was more complex and difficult than that of regulating land distribution. Land remained in one place, and Spaniards were capable of measuring it fairly accurately. Once the size and boundaries of a particular field had been established with reference to local landmarks, one could safely presume that they would remain the same for some time. Irrigation water, on the other hand, was constantly in motion, the rate of its flow fluctuated with the seasons, and once it had passed through the canals and fields it was irretrievably gone. Spaniards would not learn how to measure its flow with complete accuracy until hydraulics developed as a science in the eighteenth century.

The coastal Indians had possessed a surprisingly effective system for allocating water, which survived the coming of the Spaniards by ten or fifteen years, though conquest and depopulation ultimately led to its collapse. Ambrosio Cerdán y Pontero, an eighteenth-century audiencia judge and the author of a detailed account of the irrigation system in the Lima valley, tells us that in the early years the vecinos of the city were allotted water by the "primitive chiefs" who managed the system, and Cieza de León's description of Peru in the 1540's suggests that in many of the coastal valleys the traditional arrangements were still working at that time.[32]

Although the traditional irrigation systems eventually ceased to function as they had before the conquest, many of their basic principles and techniques were incorporated into the colonial irrigation systems. Cerdán, for instance, describes the techniques used for measuring water in the eighteenth century as dating from "the remotest times."[33] These principles were strikingly different from those which governed the traditional Moslem irrigation systems found in southeastern Spain. While the Peruvians created a bureaucracy to measure and regulate the flow of water by means of sluice gates (tomas), the Moslems built tongues of masonry to divide the water into proportional parts, making measurement unnecessary. And while the Peruvians directed water wherever it was needed at a particular time by opening and shutting the tomas—Cieza de León, for instance, describes the experience of pitching camp for the night next to a flowing canal only to find suddenly that the water had been diverted elsewhere—the Moslems allowed the water to flow continuously through the whole canal system.[34]

The assimilation of these indigenous principles took many years, however, and the collapse of the old irrigation systems was therefore followed by a period in which there was no effective way of regulating the use of water at all. The sluice gates, whose operation had been carefully supervised before the conquest, ceased to be watched, enabling Spaniards to take as much water as they wanted. Then, as the number of Spanish landowners increased, the distribution of water tended to become a matter of custom; and when disputes arose, customary rights to water were converted into property rights by means of the decisions of judges. In cases where abandoned canals had to be restored, custom gave all the water they carried to those who participated in the project, leaving Spaniards who took up land in the area later on to depend on the excess water (demasías) which flowed through the original chacras. Rights to water thus became preferential rights, worth more to upstream farmers than to those downstream. Traces of this pattern survived for many years. Even at the end of the eighteenth century, Cerdán could complain about the "tomas libres" of the upper Rímac valley, which were able to divert unlimited amounts of water during the daytime hours, essentially because regulating them was too difficult and expensive.[35]

This uneven distribution of water was not a problem in the 1550's and 1560's, since there was plenty of water for all without resorting to complicated allocation schemes. The minute books of the Lima cabildo suggest that, up to the 1570's at least, the city fathers were far more concerned with how to dispose of excess water which collected in the roads or formed ponds and swamps than with making sure that everyone got enough water.[36] The need for allocation would arise only when the growth of the Spanish agricultural economy increased the demand for water to the point that some farmers could not get enough and disputes became more and more frequent. Thus in 1577 Toledo cited the multiplication of fights and lawsuits (*rencillas y cuchilladas y atrevimientos y muertos y muchos pleitos*) as the main reason he found it necessary to legislate on irrigation in the Lima valley.[37]

By the mid-1550's it was already necessary in Lima to ease the burden of irrigation disputes on the city magistrates by creating the municipal office of water judge (*juez de aguas*), a step later copied by most of the coastal towns. While this provided a way of settling individual disputes, it did not do much about the underlying problems. In the absence of adequate knowledge of how much water there was and how much landowners needed, the water judges had little choice but to base their decisions on the customary rights which had been established when water was less in demand. And since they came from the oligarchy of Spanish landowners, they did little — as Toledo commented — to prevent the Indians from being unfairly treated in the allocation of water.[38]

The problems facing a water judge are well illustrated in a case from the 1580's in the Lima valley, involving five chacras which had grown up along the small Magdalena canal immediately to the west of the city. The first of these dated from the original distribution of Spanish land and belonged during the 1550's to Don Pedro Portocarrero, one of the few genuine noblemen among the Peruvian conquistadores.* It was quite probably Portocarrero himself who opened the canal and established preferential rights to its water. In any case, by the 1580's there were four more chacras below Portocarrero's, relying on the excess water which flowed from his chacra, and since several of these were growing wheat commercially, the supply of water no longer seemed adequate.

In 1582, Don Pedro de Santillán, a prominent vecino of Lima who had recently bought the fourth chacra and was probably just starting to develop it, brought suit claiming that he could not get enough water because the farmers above him were not letting it through. When the

---

*This chacra was included in the property over which Portocarrero and his wife established a censo in 1557 (Real audiencia: procedimientos civiles, leg. 5 [Núñez v. Saavedra]). The boundary description given at that time suggests that it may have been the one later called Breña, located next to the city between the roads to Magdalena and Pachacamac (see map 4).

judge ordered that the excess water from the Portocarrero chacra be divided equally among the chacras lower down, the decision was appealed by two of the owners on the grounds that a previous judge had specifically given permission for them to divert all this water for themselves. The audiencia probably decided in favor of Santillán, since it was clearly recognized by this time that prior claims to unmeasured amounts of irrigation water could not be indefinitely sustained. This would not have been a complete solution, however, since the Portocarrero chacra, which was not a party to the dispute, presumably continued to take all the water it wanted.[39]

In view of the importance of irrigation on the coast, it is not surprising that the viceroys soon intervened with the intention of reforming the system. In 1577, Toledo drew up his *Ordenanzas de aguas* for Lima which established the basic lines of a centralized irrigation system under viceregal control. His goal was clearly stated: that each chacra be given the amount of water it needs as determined by reason and calculation ("que se le dé á cada chácara por cuenta y razón el agua que hubiere menester"). There were to be no absolute property rights in water, whose use was to be regulated in accordance with traditional techniques borrowed from the indigenous irrigation system. All canals were to be kept clean and dressed (i.e., properly levelled and aligned) "so that each one can take the water it needs." Each canal and each chacra was to have a sluice gate to control the amount of water which could flow into it; meddling with them was prohibited under severe penalties. Toledo's system required a specific unit of measurement; though not mentioned, it was probably the *riego,* which was used in later years. According to Cerdán, this measure was defined in the Lima valley as the amount of water per unit of time which flowed through a square opening one-sixth of a *vara* (about 5½ inches) on each side. The measurement was carried out by means of ancient rule-of-thumb techniques which were accurate enough for their purpose, at least during the dry season, which was the only time it really mattered. The enforcement of Toledo's ordinances was to be the responsibility of the water judges in the valley, who continued to be chosen in the Lima cabildo by virtue of a royal decree of 1568. They were theoretically to be subordinate officials of the executive branch—Toledo refers to them as "ejecutores"—working under the direction of a superintendent appointed by the viceroy.[40]

Toledo's ordinances were only a blueprint, however, and were not fully implemented for many years. In the Lima valley itself, it was not until 1617 that a "bloody riot" at the head of the Surco canal forced the viceroy Esquilache, who had personally rushed to the scene, to do something about the allocation of water. An official in the audiencia was then assigned the task of systematically dividing the waters of the Rímac among the principal canals, specifying the number of riegos for each (or in two cases the proportion of the water) and the dimensions of the opening in each sluice gate. The systematic allocation of water among individual landowners was not achieved until the second half of the century. On the Surco canal it dated from 1655, on the Huatica (Huadca) canal from 1661, and on the Ate canal from 1692. And none of this could be described as permanent regulation, but only as temporary interference which served to keep disputes from getting completely out of hand. There was no permanent department of the viceregal government to deal with irrigation until 1777. Before that time, as Cerdán explains, irrigation affairs had been "divided up among the senior officials according to the will or disposition of the viceroys."[41] The fact of the matter was that the government simply could not afford a system of water regulation which would function continuously and effectively enough to overcome the inclination of Spanish landowners to do as they pleased. Thus in spite of Toledo's ordinances, control of irrigation remained largely in the hands of the landowners and their representatives, the local water judges.

In the absence of an effective centralized system of irrigation, it was difficult for officials to protect Indian rights to water as well as they protected Indian rights to land. Nevertheless, they seem to have tried. One method was to reserve land around the heads (*cabeceras*) of rivers or irrigation canals for Indian communities located downstream. In 1594, for instance, the visitador Alonso Maldonado de Torres set aside most of the land in the upper end of the Ica valley (above the modern town of Los Molinos) for the Indian communities of the lower valley. In order to do this he had to take back some land which had previously been sold to Spaniards, because it was "en cabecera de agua," where experience showed that the planting of Spanish vineyards resulted in the loss of Indian crops downstream. Nor was this an isolated case. We have records of judicial proceedings from 1603 in which several vecinos of Ica had to surrender vineyards which threatened the water supply of Indians located below them.[42]

Only in the Ica valley, with its large Spanish population, do the

Indians seem to have been seriously threatened with the loss of essential water before the end of the sixteenth century. Elsewhere the danger was less immediate, and extreme protective measures were unusual. In the valleys of Lima, Chancay, and Huaura, most upriver land was auctioned off to Spaniards during the last quarter of the century. Even in Ica, the land reserved by Maldonado for the Indians seems to have passed into Spanish hands by the middle of the seventeenth century, perhaps because other methods of protecting Indian water rights had proved more economical: as land appreciated in value, keeping it out of Spanish hands became increasingly costly. In the long run, the policy of reserving upstream lands was probably most successful when applied to major irrigation canals rather than to whole rivers. The survival of large zones of indigenous landholdings around such Indian towns as Huacho and Chincha Alta may be attributed in part to the fact that their canals originated fairly high up on their respective rivers and flowed almost entirely through Indian lands.

A more important method of safeguarding Indian water was to require Spaniards and Indians to irrigate at different times: the former on workdays from dawn to dusk and the latter on Sundays and holidays and at night. The separation of daytime and nighttime irrigators first appears in Toledo's ordinances in 1577, which decreed that all Spaniards should shut their sluice gates at night so that the Indians could take the water they needed. The custom still prevails in many valleys though there is no longer much racial basis for it. This rule seems to have grown out of existing practice, for in the early years Spaniards customarily worked their lands only during the day when they could get mita labor. The Indians of Huacho, for instance, complained in 1583 that they were left no time or water to cultivate their own lands except at night and on Sunday. Thus the rule probably had little immediate effect, but it provided a basis for protecting Indian water later on, since it was undoubtedly easier to prevent Spaniards from taking any water at certain times than to limit the amount they took all the time.[43] It ultimately enabled the colonial government to stabilize the distribution of water between the Spaniards and the Indians, giving the latter a limited right to water which could be defended, and preventing the former from appropriating unlimited amounts of water. As in the case of land, however, the continued decline of the Indian population, combined with the expansion of Spanish agriculture, created pressure to reallocate Indian water to Spaniards and made it necessary to develop legal methods for transferring water rights.

In the course of the seventeenth century much of the water reserved to the Indians under Toledo's ordinances and similar laws was legally transferred to Spanish landowners. This seems to have occurred in three principal ways. First, when Indian lands were sold to Spaniards they often carried water rights with them; thus an hacienda built up of small plots purchased from Indians was likely to take its water at night instead of during the day. Secondly, water rights might be transferred by viceregal decree. In 1616, for instance, the viceroy Esquilache took from the Indians of Surco their right to irrigate on Friday and Saturday nights and gave it to four Spaniards who owned chacras nearby. The stated reason was that, since the population of the town had decreased by three-quarters since the conquest, the Indians no longer needed all the water Toledo had set aside for them. Finally, water rights might be transferred by means of private agreements, usually made with official approval, between Indians and Spaniards. In the middle of the seventeenth century, the Indians of Surco made such an agreement with two neighboring haciendas owned by the Jesuit and Mercedarian establishments in Lima, giving them each eight riegos in return for a commitment to send men to watch the upstream sluice gates when necessary.[44]

As the result of such transfers, the use of water came to be regulated on the basis of a system of turns. On the Surco canal, for instance, one group of landowners (the daytime Spaniards) irrigated on weekdays; another (the nighttime Spaniards) irrigated Monday through Thursday nights; a third group of Spaniards irrigated on Friday and Saturday nights; finally, the Indians of Surco irrigated Sunday nights. The right to irrigate during the day on Sundays and holidays alternated among the last three groups. This pattern, which had developed before the end of the seventeenth century, survived with little change into the twentieth.[45]

The consolidation of the hacienda system with respect to water was therefore a less legal and orderly process than its consolidation with respect to land. While land was most commonly purchased, water was frequently appropriated without much legal sanction, and down to the later years of the sixteenth century such appropriations became permanent. The separation of daytime and nighttime irrigators made it easier to guarantee the Indians enough water to meet their needs, but it also confirmed Spaniards in the possession of a good deal of water to which they had little traditional claim. This was probably inevitable. The viceregal administration in Peru possessed neither the knowledge nor the resources to maintain centralized irrigation systems of the type that had existed before the conquest. But without such systems, there was no effective way to limit the use of water. In contrast with its systematic regulation and taxation of land on the coast, then, the government's policy with regard to irrigation dictated intervention only when necessary to prevent conflicts among Spaniards from getting out of control and to guarantee the Indian communities the small amount of water they needed for survival.

# Conclusion

The hacienda system developed on the Peruvian coast in response to social and economic changes which took place during the century after the conquest. Of these changes, three were of primary importance: (1) the growth of the Spanish population, which was stimulated initially by the news of Cajamarca and later by the attractions of the coastal climate and new economic opportunities; (2) the rapid decline of the Indian population in the disastrous epidemics of the sixteenth century, and later as a result of the pressures generated by economic development; (3) the rise of agrarian markets to supply the needs of a sizeable Spanish urban population.

In combination with one another, these changes brought about a gradual shift from indirect or encomienda-like to direct or hacienda-like patterns of economic exploitation. The conquerors had been attracted to Peru in the first place by the wealth of traditional Andean society, and their primary goal had been to gain control of this wealth for themselves. For this purpose they used the encomienda, an institution which served to divert existing surpluses of goods and labor into their own hands. Encomiendas often came to have profit-making enterprises associated with them, but their basic function was to redistribute wealth, not to create it. They were therefore dependent on an Indian society whose capacity for producing wealth declined drastically along with its population. Concurrently the number of Spaniards continued to grow, with the result that the encomiendas were soon unable to support enough of them to insure social and political stability. The resulting discontent of the soldados threatened the authority of the crown, but at the same time it enabled the colonial bureaucracy to do away with the encomienda system altogether. The alternative to living off the tribute and labor provided by Indian communities was to establish new income-producing enterprises which were not so dependent on Indian society. From the beginning, haciendas depended on the existence of markets for their products and, except in the rare cases where their products were exportable, they developed only within range of substantial towns — usually administrative centers, mining towns, or major ports — which contained a wealthy Spanish population. The geographical spread varied according to the size of the town and the nature of the particular product; in the case of wheat it was narrow, but for sugar, livestock, and especially for wine it was much wider.

On the Peruvian coast, stock-raising enterprises began to appear in the late 1530's; agricultural enterprises known as chacras first developed in the 1540's around Lima, spreading to other valleys after 1550. The earliest chacras were established by local encomenderos who found themselves forced to develop supplementary sources of income as a result of the steady decline in their tributes. Originally they depended on Indian labor, but soon they began using Negro slaves instead; by the end of the sixteenth century their enterprises had become almost independent of traditional Indian society. These chacras were clearly haciendas in our sense, though small ones. They continued to be found around Lima and in the wine-producing valleys of the south, where agricultural profits were high, but in the valleys north of Lima they tended to be replaced by large haciendas. The evolution of the hacienda system, then, was one aspect of the gradual transformation of coastal society. It was not, however, an inevitable consequence of the Spanish conquest. We know there were some places—the Lambayeque region and many highland areas in Peru, for instance, or the Oaxaca valley in Mexico—where in spite of the existence of a few haciendas, indirect patterns of exploitation continued to predominate, delaying the appearance of an hacienda system until much later.[1] Spanish wealth continued to be extracted mainly from Indian society. In Lambayeque it came from the manufacture of cotton cloth, leather goods, and soap, and in Oaxaca it came from the cochineal dye which was exported to Europe by way of Mexico City. In the Peruvian sierra, Indians sold their surplus labor to the mines for silver in order to satisfy the demands of local corregidores who doubled as merchants.

Similar patterns of economic exploitation grew up, at a somewhat later date, in the Old-World colonial empires of the British, the Dutch, and the French. British India, for instance, was governed by district officers who resembled the corregidores de indios, though they were better paid and better supervised; the same was true of most of Southeast Asia and Africa. It was only in southern Africa and Algeria that a significant colonial landowning class emerged. The contrast with Spanish America was probably due to the absence of catastrophic depopulation and to the low level of European immigration. Conversely then, it seems likely that without the massive depopulation and heavy immigration of the sixteenth century, the Spanish-American hacienda system would not have developed when it did.

This does not mean, of course, that the pre-conquest heritage of the Spaniards can be ignored. The attitudes and actions of the conquistadores clearly show the influence of the military and aristocratic ideals of the Iberian reconquest. Such ideals were not always attainable, however, in the New World. As Lockhart has shown, most Spanish settlers were not aristocrats and the myth of their unwillingness to perform any kind of manual labor has little basis in fact.[2] Many of the first generation of settlers practiced the trades they had learned in Spain; it was presumably better to be a tailor with an income than an unemployed soldado. Though artisans might have preferred to be encomenderos, their chances of getting one of the limited number of encomiendas were usually remote.

Similar conditions prevailed for the encomenderos themselves. They may have wanted to emulate the Castilian aristocracy by turning their encomiendas into vast estates for the benefit of their heirs, but they were in fact unable to achieve this goal, seeing their encomiendas converted instead to mere pensions. For them the possession of an hacienda became an incomplete way of preserving the wealth and status which was theirs under the encomienda system. In early colonial Peru there was nothing particularly aristocratic about owning land; most chacras and haciendas were established for the thoroughly practical purpose of supplying their owners with income. Thus the typical Spanish landowner on the coast was not the large hacendado of the northern valleys, but the owner of a small wine chacra in the prosperous south. Indeed, the largest and most aristocratic haciendas grew up in the northern valleys precisely because commercial agriculture was less profitable there, so that fewer Spaniards came to settle and there was less competition for land. In this sense the growth of large estates should be considered not so much the fulfillment of a universal Spanish dream as testimony that this dream was beyond the reach of all but a few.

How did patterns of change on the coast compare with those found elsewhere in Spanish America? We do not know enough about the economic and social development of most regions to suggest more than tentative answers to the question. In most rural areas of the New

World, Spaniards seem to have faced similar choices when it came to supporting themselves. They used encomiendas or other indirect systems of economic exploitation where the local Indian society was strong and wealthy enough. Otherwise they relied on various types of haciendas, including chacras, plantations, manorial haciendas, and ranches. Though each of these alternatives owed something to Spanish attitudes and models, they can best be understood in terms of the local conditions they faced: the productivity of Indian society, the number of Spanish immigrants, the level of agricultural prices, the cost of labor. In the end their degree of success or failure was determined by their relative ability to provide for the economic needs of the Spanish population.

Of the basic alternatives, the encomienda was almost always the first to appear. It was feasible only in areas where there was a fairly dense and settled Indian population. Since Spanish colonization during the early years was generally confined to such areas, the encomienda was a nearly universal phenomenon. Two basic types may be identified. The large, semi-feudal encomienda was characteristic of Mexico and the Andean region (including the Peruvian coast). It was based on the preservation of traditional forms of organization, the extraction of tribute and labor, and the redistribution of wealth among non-encomenderos through a system of clientage.

The small encomienda, on the other hand, appeared in areas where the population was less dense than in the Inca and Aztec regions — the West Indies, Central America, Chile — and where the traditional political structure was simpler. Such encomiendas contained fewer Indians, provided less income, and supported few Spaniards other than the encomendero himself. From the Spanish point of view, they were most satisfactory in areas where the Indians could be set to mining gold. In most of Spanish America, the encomienda systems of the early years collapsed as a result of the massive depopulation which took place following the conquest. The effects of the decline were most devastating in the small encomiendas, which soon ceased to be worth exploiting. This in turn sometimes led to the departure of much of the Spanish population, as in Española, where the western part of the island was largely abandoned after 1520.[3] In all cases decline brought about a process of retrenchment in which those Spaniards who remained tried to provide for themselves as best they could. Thus, at the end of the sixteenth century, much of the Spanish population of

Central America abandoned the towns, where they could no longer afford to live, and moved out to small farms in the countryside which provided barely enough to sustain them. The more heavily populated areas of Mexico and Peru were less drastically affected. The Indian population declined less rapidly and completely (though the Peruvian coast was an exception), and enough silver continued to flow in to generate new economic opportunities and sources of income. In a few cases this made possible the survival of indirect patterns of economic exploitation, but more often it served instead to ease the transition to some kind of hacienda system.

The chacra or small hacienda, under whatever name it was known locally, became the principal type of Spanish hacienda in areas where the market for agricultural produce was especially good. A band of chacras, which might grow quite large under favorable economic conditions, sprang up around most towns in the Indies to supply them with provisions. Chacras were numerous in the Cochabamba valley (Bolivia), which supplied much of the wheat consumed at Potosí. In Mexico they were concentrated around the capital, in the Puebla and Atlixco valleys on the way to Vera Cruz, and in the Bajío on the road to the mining areas of the North. The chacras of the Peruvian south coast were perhaps exceptional in their heavy concentration on wine, but in their exploitation of profitable markets — both in Lima and in the mining areas of the southern sierra — they were typical. In the valleys north of Lima, on the other hand, and in much of Central America, chacras were little more than subsistence farms which tended to disappear into large estates.[4] Where economic conditions were unsuitable for chacras, larger haciendas appeared. These might take the form of plantations, which depended on slave labor, or manorial haciendas, which used local Indian labor, or ranches.

The plantation imported slaves because it was typically located in an area where the local Indian population was not large enough to provide the labor it needed.[5] But since the acquisition of slaves was expensive, plantations needed large amounts of capital to get started. Such capital was forthcoming only where exceptionally high profits could be expected. Most plantations which developed in the New World before the nineteenth century therefore grew tropical produce of various kinds, principally sugar, which they exported to European markets. Except for Venezuela and the West-Indian islands, most of Spanish America was too remote to participate in this export trade, and plantations of the West-Indian type were limited in number. Most regions possessed a scattering of less developed plantations, usually producing sugar for sale in nearby Spanish towns. The Peruvian coast probably had the largest group of plantations outside the Eastern Caribbean, but they remained backward by West-Indian standards until the late nineteenth-century boom in sugar and cotton exports.

The manorial hacienda, in contrast with the plantation, usually developed in areas where the local Indian population remained dense enough to provide the Spaniards with adequate labor. This was the case, for instance, in the highland regions of Middle America and the Andes in the seventeenth century, and in a somewhat different form in eighteenth-century Chile, where the Indian population had been largely replaced by a mestizo one. Manorial haciendas produced for a market; but since their markets were small and unreliable, they were compelled to protect themselves from gluts by producing below capacity.[6] Their owners acquired large amounts of land not because they intended to cultivate it, but because the monopolization of land conveyed certain indirect benefits, increasing their power in local affairs, forcing local Indians to provide the hacienda with cheap labor, and discouraging competition from other Spaniards. We should perhaps view the manorial hacienda, then, as a marginal type whose most distinctive characteristics were adaptations to insure survival in an inhospitable economic climate.

In one sense ranching was also a marginal activity. Plantations and manorial haciendas were often ranches in part, cultivating only a fraction of their land and leaving the rest for grazing. For them, pasture land was frequently agricultural land they could not afford to cultivate. But ranching could also be a specialized economic activity with relatively good markets, as in northern Mexico where cattle ranches provided meat for the mines, in the parts of Mexico and the Andes where sheep ranches furnished wool to local textile factories, and in the Piura region in Peru where ranches supplied goats for the soap-makers and leather-workers of Lambayeque.

Ranches generally had low operating expenses: the animals were simply left to feed and reproduce by themselves; transport expenses were minimal, because the animals could carry themselves to market; the small amount of labor that was needed could generally be obtained without consuming scarce capital; and of course herds continued to grow regardless of market conditions. Ranches therefore had less need to make the kind of adjustments characteristic of manorial haciendas.

The largest and most important ranching areas were found where the traditional Indian population was nomadic and hostile. For the sixteenth and seventeenth centuries the best example was northern Mexico; in Brazil, the dry interior of the northeast followed a similar pattern.[7] Somewhat later, extensive ranching areas appeared in the Orinoco valley and around the shores of the Río de la Plata. In all these regions frontier conditions prevailed at first and Indian raiders presented a continual threat to life and property. The government was therefore more willing to countenance the feudal patterns it rejected elsewhere, conceding generous privileges explicitly or implicitly to men who could organize and pay for the defense of territory on their own. These conditions resembled those found in fourteenth-century Andalusia, and it is therefore not surprising that of all haciendas, the north-Mexican ranches were the ones most like the great sheep-raising latifundia of the south of Spain.

The Spaniards were not the only European settlers in the New World confronted with the problem of how to support themselves in an alien land, and their solutions to this problem were not unique. Brazil also had its plantations and ranches, as well as its chacras, which typically sold provisions to the plantations which used their own land for sugarcane. The English and French in the West Indies had plantations for sugarcane, and chacras mostly for tobacco. One basic difference must be emphasized, however. The Portuguese, English, and French colonies were never dependent on local Indian societies in the way the Spanish society of conquest had been. In the non-Spanish areas, colonial societies emerged only after the possibility of using indirect systems of economic exploitation had passed, and their economic foundations had to be built up from the bottom. It was only in Spanish America that colonial societies grew up on economic foundations which already existed, and it was only there that these foundations had to be reconstructed when the Indians could no longer support them.

Appendix, Notes, Bibliography, Glossary, Index

# Appendix / A Land Grant in the Chancay Valley (1558)

I, Don Hurtado de Mendoza, Marqués de Cañete, guarda mayor of the city of Cuenca, Viceroy and Captain General of these kingdoms and provinces of Peru for His Majesty, having issued a decree at the request of Juan García ordering Fray Agustín Juárez of the Dominican order to inspect a piece of land in the Chancay valley located below the section of Huaral at the foot of a hill around some mud walls which Mateo Guerra once used for certain of his cattle, and also to inspect other lands in the said valley of Chancay, which is sometimes called Huaral; and Fray Agustín having reported that in response to the said decree he had inspected the land and made inquiry of certain chiefs and other Indians and ascertained that in the said valley of Chancay there are three pieces of land, one which is said to have belonged to the Inca, one to the sun, and the third to Yaucaguallan, mayordomo of the Inca; and that these lands are bounded at the top and on the river side by lands belonging to the Indians of Chancay in the encomiendas of Jerónimo de Aliaga and Ruy Barba, on the third side by large canebrakes [cañaverales] and a swamp [ciénaga] from which much water drains, and at the bottom by some hills which extend to the canebrakes next to the river; and that the said lands also share a boundary with land lying next to the river which belongs to Don Felipe, curaca of the encomienda which belongs to the crown; and that since few Indians are left in the said encomiendas, the said lands can neither be cultivated nor exploited; and having made inquiry and verified certain things contained in the said decree on the basis of this report, I hereby grant to the said Juan García in the name of His Majesty twenty fanegadas of land in one of the said three pieces of land which belonged to the sun or the Inca or the mayordomo of the Inca in the said valley of Chancay, starting from the lower part and going up the valley as the said Juan García will indicate, in order that he may possess and use this land as his own, insofar as this is not prejudicial to the Indians or their lands and irrigation ditches, nor in violation of the rights of any other third party. And as soon as the said Juan García requests it, I order Francisco Camacho, resident in the section of the

valley called Pasamayo, to go and look at the piece of land hereby
granted, and in the said part of the valley to designate, measure, and
set up boundary markers around the said twenty fanegadas, following
the standards of measurement customarily used in this city of Lima,
and to put him in possession of this land, and after this to order the
justices of His Majesty to aid him and not permit him to be despoiled
of it without first being heard in court. Done in Lima on the twenty-
eighth of September 1558 by order of His Excellency. [signed] Juan
Múñoz Rico.

## Act of Possession

Then the said Señor Francisco Camacho said that he was ready to
fulfill the said decree as His Excellency ordered, and he went with two
witnesses and the said Juan García to a piece of land, which was the
one mentioned in the decree as having belonged to the Inca. This land
is bounded on one side by an old acequia which comes from the main
acequia to Supillán in Barba's encomienda, on the second side by a
canebrake and swamp running toward the river, on the third side by
some mountains of a reddish color, two on each side with a loma and
dry valley [quebrada] of white sand in the middle, and on the fourth
side by the said main acequia of Supillán. Close to the road to
Supillán, the said main acequia intersects with another acequia which
runs out of it next to two pacay trees; they made a cross on one of these
trees and cut a piece out of the other. Then, using a rope which was
the length of the side of a block in the city of Lima, they began to
measure from the said acequia at the intersection and pacay trees. At a
distance of six lengths of the rope they came to some old walls and
corrals, below which were the canebrake and swamp, and here they
made three crosses. From there they went on, measuring a little less
than seven lengths of the rope, until they arrived near the red mountains where the loma is and also some old walled enclosures [cercados]
in the middle of the red mountains opposite the loma, and here they
made three crosses in another wall and erected a stone boundary
marker. From there they went on another six lengths of the rope until
they ran into the main acequia, and they made three crosses on some
walls near the said acequia and erected another boundary marker.
From there they went on a short seven lengths of the rope, which
brought them back to the above-mentioned pacay trees and

intersection. Then the said Francisco Camacho declared that within these boundaries were contained the twenty fanegadas of land which His Excellency had granted to the said Juan García. To all this Anton Texeda and Pedro Díaz were witnesses, and the said Francisco Camacho signed with his rubric before me, Melchor de Ocaña, notary.

And then the said Francisco Camacho declared that in fulfillment of the said decree and in accordance with it, he took the said Juan García by the hand and placed him inside the boundaries of the said land, saying that he was giving and gave him possession of it; and the said Juan García, standing inside, said that he was taking and took possession of the said twenty fanegadas of land; and in sign of possession he walked through it from end to end, tearing up clumps of earth, cutting branches off the trees with his sword, and performing other acts of possession openly, quietly, and peacefully, without contradiction from any person. He requested this document in testimony, and the said Francisco Camacho ordered it given him for the protection of his rights, having signed it with his name before the said witnesses Anton Texeda and Pedro Díaz. [signed] Francisco Camacho. Passed before me, Melchor de Ocaña, notary.

On the said day and month of the said year, in order to support his rights, the said Juan García asked me, the said notary, to give written testimony before the same witnesses that the above-mentioned land showed no signs of recent cultivation [*no había camellones hecho*], but was all untilled and covered with reeds and wild grass [*cañaverales y gramadales*], and that it contained no functioning irrigation canal, one which had existed there being totally destroyed [*quebrado*] so that a large amount of money would be necessary to repair it before it could carry water. And I, the said notary, in fulfillment of the above, certify that I saw the above-mentioned land with my own eyes, and that it contained a canebrake of moderate thickness and a piece of land heavily overgrown with wild grass. I certify also that I saw two canals, both broken down in many places; and that these canals do not seem to have carried water for many years, because they do not contain any plant life except for some cane shoots and are very dry; and that many laborers would be necessary to repair these canals so that they could carry water. And I further certify that in the said land there is nowhere any sign of recent cultivation, all of it being flat and overgrown with wild grass, canes, thickets [*matorrales*] and many pacay trees. In testi-

mony of this, at the request of the said Juan García, I gave the present
on the third day of October 1558 and sign it with my name.

[Melchor de Ocaña]*

---

*BNP A345.

# Notes

References to archival documents are given by legajo (leg.), cuaderno (c. or cc.), and folio (f. or ff.), or by sala, estante (est.), and anaquel (ana.). The following abbreviations are also used:

| | |
|---|---|
| AA | Archivo Arzobispal de Lima |
| AH | Archivo Histórico del Ministerio de Hacienda |
| AHNC | Archivo Histórico Nacional del Cuzco |
| ANP | Archivo Nacional del Perú |
| BAE | Biblioteca de Autores Españoles |
| BNP | Biblioteca Nacional del Perú |
| CDIA | *Colección de documentos inéditos . . . . de América y Oceanía* |
| CDIHE | *Colección de documentos inéditos para la historia de España* |
| CDIU | *Colección de documentos inéditos . . . . de ultramar* |
| CLDP | Urteaga and Romero, eds., *Colección de libros y documentos referentes a la historia del Perú* |
| HAHR | *Hispanic American Historical Review* |
| RANP | *Revista del Archivo Nacional del Perú* |

*Introduction*

1. For a theoretical introduction, see Robert Redfield, *Peasant Society and Culture* (Chicago, University of Chicago Press, 1956).

2. Bloch's book is available in English translation by Janet Sondheimer as *French Rural History: An Essay on Its Basic Characteristics* (London, 1966). For an introduction to the work of the demographic historians, see Peter Laslett, *The World We Have Lost: England before the Industrial Age* (London, Methuen, 1965).

3. The most important exceptions, works on which I have relied heavily, are François Chevalier's *Land and Society in Colonial Mexico: The Great Hacienda*, ed. Lesley B. Simpson and trans. Alvin Eustis (Berkeley and Los Angeles, 1963) and Charles Gibson, *The Aztecs under Spanish Rule: A History of the Indians of the Valley of Mexico, 1519-1810* (Stanford, 1964). I have also borrowed much from the anthropologist Eric R. Wolf, whose *Sons of the Shaking Earth* (Chicago, 1959) is an excellent historical study of the Indians of Middle America, and from Woodrow Borah and his associates at the University of California, who have added much to our knowledge of the economic and demographic history of Mexico.

4. Gilberto Freyre, *Casa-grande e senzala* (Rio de Janeiro, 1933); trans. Samuel Putnam: *The Masters and the Slaves: A Study in the Development of Brazilian Civilization* (New York, Knopf, 1956).

*Chapter 1: Coastal Society before the Spanish Conquest*

1. On the Peru current and its effects, see Preston E. James, *Latin America* (3rd ed., New York, 1959), pp. 190-193, and Glenn T. Trewartha, *The Earth's Problem Climates* (Madison, 1961), pp. 23-31.

2. Bernabé Cobo, *Obras* (2 vols., Madrid, 1964), I, 87-90.

3. Frederic Engel, *Geografía humana prehistórica y agricultura precolumbina de la quebrada de Chilca* (Lima, 1966), pp. 21-22, 59-63; Jeffrey R. Parsons, "The Archaeological Significance of *Mahamaes* Cultivation on the Coast of Peru," *American Antiquity*, 33 (1968), 80-85.

4. Herbert Addison, *Land, Water and Food: A Topical Commentary on the Past, Present and Future of Irrigation, Land Reclamation, and the Food Supplies They Yield* (2nd ed., London, Chapman and Hall, 1961), p. 19.

5. Tenney Frank, ed., *An Economic Survey of Ancient Rome* (5 vols., Baltimore, 1933-1940), II, 7; Paul Kosok, *Life, Land and Water in Ancient Peru* (New York, 1965), p. 34.

6. See the maps on the end papers of ibid.

7. Ibid., p. 147.

8. This paragraph is based primarily on the account in Edward P. Lanning, *Peru before the Incas* (Englewood Cliffs, N.J., 1967), chs. 4-8.

9. Garcilaso de la Vega, el Inca, *Royal Commentaries of the Incas and General History of Peru* (2 vols., Austin, Texas, 1966), I, 42.

10. Bartolomé de las Casas, *Obras escogidas*, ed. Juan Pérez de Tudela Bueso, BAE, 95, 96, 105, 106, 110 (5 vols., Madrid, 1957-1961), IV, 415.

11. Karl A. Wittfogel, *Oriental Despotism: A Comparative Study of Total Power* (New Haven, 1957), p. 3.

12. Ibid., pp. 87-100 and 280-291.

13. Thomas F. Glick, *Irrigation and Society in Medieval Valencia* (Cambridge, Mass., 1970), pp. 4-5, 30-44, 198-206.

14. E.R. Leach, "Hydraulic Society in Ceylon," *Past and Present*, no. 15 (April 1959), p. 11; D.G.E. Hall, *A History of South-East Asia* (2nd ed., London, Macmillan, 1964), p. 68.

15. See William McNeill, *The Rise of the West: A History of the Human Community* (Chicago, University of Chicago Press, 1963), pp. 30-32.

16. Wittfogel, *Oriental Despotism*, pp. 165-166.

17. As Clifford Gertz comments (*Agricultural Involution: The Processes of Ecological Change in Indonesia* [Berkeley and Los Angeles, 1968], pp. 28-37): "Under premodern conditions gradual perfection of irrigation techniques is perhaps the major way to raise productivity not only per hectare but per man. To develop further water works already in being is often more profitable than to construct new ones at the established technical level."

18. Kosok, *Life, Land and Water*, chs. 16 and 17; Cristóbal de Molina, "Relación de muchas cosas acaecidas en al Perú," in Francisco Esteve Barba, ed., *Crónicas peruanas de interés indígena*, BAE, 204 (Madrid, 1968), p. 67; Lanning, *Peru*, pp. 120-121, 151-153; Dorothy Menzel, "The Inca Occupation of the South Coast of Peru," *Southwestern Journal of Anthropology*, 15 (1959), 125-142; Dorothy Menzel and John H. Rowe, "The Role of Chincha in Late Pre-Spanish Peru," *Ñawpa Pacha*, 4 (1966), 63-77.

19. Lanning, *Peru*, p. 152; Garcilaso, *Royal Commentaries*, I, 379; Cobo, *Obras*, II, 301.

20. Molina, "Relación de muchas cosas," p. 67. Don Gonzalo's name appears in the Lima notary books on several occasions around 1560; the documents show him selling pieces of land and entering into a partnership with a Spaniard to grow wine grapes (ANP, Derecho indígena, c. 23; ANP, Notarios, Ambrosio de Moscoso [1554-66], cc. 12, 17); Estete's statement is in his account of Hernando Pizarro's journey to Pachacamac, which is included in Francisco de Jérez, "Verdadera relación de la conquista del Perú," CLDP, ser. 1, V, 89.

21. Julian Steward, ed., *Handbook of South American Indians* (7 vols., Washington, 1946-1959), II, 167 (hereafter cited as *Handbook*); John H. Rowe, "The Kingdom of Chimor," *Acta Americana,* 6 (1949), 39.

22. Much of the terminology used here is borrowed from Max Weber, who discusses these types of societies in *The Theory of Social and Economic Organization,* ed. Talcott Parsons (New York, 1947), pp. 324-386.

23. Rowe, "Kingdom of Chimor," pp. 47, 55; María Rostworowski de Diez Canseco, *Curacas y sucesiones: Costa norte* (Lima, 1961).

24. Rowe, "Kingdom of Chimor," p. 45.

25. Rostworowski, *Curacas y sucesiones,* pp. 101-106.

26. Iñigo Ortiz de Zúñiga, *Visita de la provincia de León de Húanuco en 1562,* ed. John V. Murra (2 vols., Huánuco, 1967-1972), I, 36, 46; John V. Murra, "On Inca Political Structure," in *Systems of Political Control and Bureaucracy in Human Societies,* ed. Vernon F. Ray, *Proceedings* of the 1958 Annual Spring Meeting of the American Ethnological Society (Seattle, 1958), pp. 30-41; Cristóbal de Castro and Diego de Ortega Morejón, "Relación y declaración del modo que este valle de Chincha y sus comarcanos se governavan antes que oviese yngas y despues que las ubo . . . ," *Quellen zur Kulturgeschichte des präkolumbischen Amerika,* ed. Hermann Trimborn (Stuttgart, [1936]), pp. 239-240.

27. Rowe, "Kingdom of Chimor," pp. 45-46.

28. Marcos Jiménez de la Espada, ed., *Relaciones geográficas de Indias: Peru* (3 vols.; Madrid, 1965), II, 43; Sally F. Moore, *Power and Property in Inca Peru* (Morningside Heights, N.Y., 1958), pp. 18, 28.

29. John H. Rowe, "Inca Culture at the Time of the Spanish Conquest," in *Handbook,* II, 265-266.

30. Ibid., p. 43; Murra, "Inca Political Structure," p. 31.

31. Miguel Cabello Balboa, *Miscelánea antártica: Una historia del Perú antiguo* (Lima, 1951), pp. 319, 332; Garcilaso, *Royal Commentaries,* I, 351-354, 381-383; Pedro de Cieza de León, *El señorío de los Incas,* ed. Carlos Araníbar and Pierre Duviols (Lima, 1967), pp. 194-199; Rowe, "Kingdom of Chimor," p. 44.

32. Cieza de León, *Señorío,* pp. 200-202, and *La crónica del Perú,* in Enrique Vedia, ed., *Historiadores primitivos de Indias,* BAE, 22, 26 (2 vols., 1852-1853; reprint, Madrid, 1946-1947), II, 422-423; Domingo Angulo, ed., "Don Andrés Hurtado de Mendoza y la fundación de la villa de Cañete," *Revista Histórica,* 7 (1921-1925), 43-44 (hereafter cited as Angulo, "Fundación de Cañete").

33. Menzel and Rowe, "Role of Chincha," pp. 67-68; Garcilaso, *Royal Commentaries,* I, 383.

34. Ibid., p. 352; Kosok, *Life, Land and Water,* p. 82.

35. Jérez, "Verdadera relación," p. 89; Rowe, "Kingdom of Chimor," pp. 45, 55.

36. Menzel and Rowe, "Role of Chincha," p. 67; Rowe, "Kingdom of Chimor," p. 46; Menzel, "Inca Occupation," p. 141.

37. Rowe, "Kingdom of Chimor," p. 45; Castro and Ortega Morejón, "Relación," p. 237.

38. Ibid., p. 239.
39. John V. Murra, "Rite and Crop in the Inca State," in *Culture in History: Essays in Honor of Paul Radin*, ed. Stanley Diamond (New York, 1960), pp. 399-401; Murra, "El 'control vertical' de un maximo de pisos ecológicos en la economía de las sociedades andinas," in Ortiz de Zúñiga, *Visita de Huánuco*, II, 429-468; Lanning, *Peru*, pp. 164-165; Thomas C. Patterson and Edward P. Lanning, "Changing Settlement Patterns on the Central Peruvian Coast," *Ñawpa Pacha*, 2 (1964), 117.
40. Molina, "Relación de muchas cosas," p. 67; Vedia, *Historiadores primitivos*, II, 424; Reginaldo de Lizárraga, *Descripción breve de toda la tierra del Perú, Tucumán, Río de la Plata y Chile*, BAE, 216 (Madrid, 1968), 44; Cobo, *Obras*, II, 301; Menzel and Rowe, "Role of Chincha," pp. 63-64.
41. Noble David Cook, "The Indian Population of Peru, 1570-1620," unpub. diss., University of Texas at Austin, 1973, pp. 98-99.
42. Rowe, "Inca Culture," pp. 212, 252, and 285-286.
43. BNP, A 629.
44. C.T. Smith, "Depopulation of the Central Andes in the Sixteenth Century," *Current Anthropology*, 11 (1970), 455-457 (see also Murra's comments at the end, pp. 461-462).
45. BNP, A 629.
46. Rowe, "Inca Culture," pp. 268-269; see also Woodrow Borah and Sherburne F. Cook, *Essays in Population History: Mexico and the Caribbean* (2 vols., Berkeley and Los Angeles, 1971-1974), I, 18.
47. Kosok argues (*Life, Land and Water*, pp. 34-35, 227) that the valleys south of Huaura now have about the same area under cultivation as they did before the conquest, since these valleys do not have any major abandoned irrigation canals as do those of the north coast.
48. Geertz, *Agricultural Involution*, p. 33; R.H. Tawney, *Land and Labor in China* (London, Allen & Unwin, 1932), pp. 24-25.
49. Garcilaso, *Royal Commentaries*, I, 93; Vedia, *Historiadores primitivos*, II, 423; Jérez, "Verdadera relación," pp. 26-27; Menzel and Rowe, "Role of Chincha," p. 68; Molina, "Relación de muchas cosas," p. 67.
50. Lizárraga, *Descripción breve*, p. 44; Menzel and Rowe, "Role of Chincha," pp. 67-68.
51. Ibid., 66; Rowe, "Kingdom of Chimor," pp. 40-41; see also table 2, above.

*Chapter 2: The Encomienda System*

1. The most recent account of the conquest may be found in John Hemming, *The Conquest of the Incas* (New York, 1970). On the epidemic and its effects, see Henry F. Dobyns, "An Outline of Andean Epidemic History to 1720," *Bulletin of the History of Medicine*, 37 (1963), 494-497. For a different version of the succession crisis, see Burr C. Brundage, *Lords of Cuzco: A History and Description of the Inca People in Their Final Days* (Norman, Okla., 1967), pp. 63, 99-100.
2. Guillermo Lohmann Villena, "Indice del 'Libro becerro de escrituras,'" RANP, 14 (1941), 212, 215, 221.
3. See Elman R. Service, "The Encomienda in Paraguay," HAHR, 31 (1951), 230-252.
4. H.B. Johnson, Jr., "The Donatary Captaincy in Perspective: Portuguese Backgrounds to the Settlement of Brazil," HAHR, 52 (1972), 206-207; "Encomenderos y

encomiendas," RANP, 4 (1926), 7-8; Mario Góngora, *El estado en el derecho indiano: Época de fundación (1492-1570)* (Santiago de Chile, 1951), pp. 104-105; Raúl Porras Barrenechea, ed., *Cartas del Perú (1524-1543)*, vol. III of *Colección de documentos inéditos para la historia del Perú* (Lima, 1959), p. 166; Bertram T. Lee and Juan Bromley, eds., *Libros de Cabildos de Lima* (23 vols., Lima, 1935-1963), I, 352 (hereafter cited as *Cabildos*).

5. James Lockhart, "Encomienda and Hacienda: The Evolution of the Great Estate in the Spanish Indies," HAHR, 49 (1969), 415.

6. See Eduardo Arcila Farías, *El régimen de la encomienda en Venezuela* (Seville, 1957), and Service, "The Encomienda in Paraguay."

7. Diego de Encinas, *Provisiones, cédulas, capítulos de ordenanzas, instrucciones y cartas . . . . tocante al buen gobierno de las Indias. . . .* (4 vols., Madrid, 1596), II, 258.

8. Porras, *Cartas del Perú*, pp. 161-162; Roberto Levillier, ed., *Gobernantes del Perú. Cartas y papeles, siglo XVI; Documentos del Archivo de Indias* (14 vols., Madrid, 1921-1926), III, 65-66.

9. James Lockhart, *Spanish Peru, 1532-1560: A Colonial Society* (Madison, 1968), p. 4; Juan Bromley, *La fundación de la Ciudad de los Reyes* (Lima, 1935), p. 39.

10. José de la Riva-Agüero y Osma, *El primer alcalde de Lima: Nicolás de Ribera el viejo y su posteridad* (Lima, 1935), p. 13; Mamerto Castillo Negrón, *Monografía de la provincia de Pisco* (Lima, 1947), pp. 81-83; Pedro de Cieza de León, *Guerras civiles del Perú*, ed. Marcos Jiménez de la Espada (2 vols., Madrid, 1877-1881), I, 127-128.

11. Lockhart, *Spanish Peru*, p. 158.

12. See tables 2, 3, 4, and 5, in text. Due to the variation between the Chincha and Lima ratios, these calculations may involve errors of up to 30 percent, but these would not be large enough to affect the basic pattern of distribution which is described below.

13. James Lockhart, *The Men of Cajamarca: A Social and Biographical Study of the First Conquerors of Peru* (Austin, Texas, 1972), pp. 209-212, and *Spanish Peru*, p. 45; Riva-Agüero, *El primer alcalde de Lima*; Cristóbal Vaca de Castro, "Ordenanzas de tambos . . . hechas en la ciudad del Cuzco en 31 de Mayo de 1543," *Revista Histórica*, 3 (1908-1909), 450.

14. Lockhart, *Men of Cajamarca*, pp. 146, 307-309, 370-372, 447-455, and *Spanish Peru*, p. 86.

15. Cobo, *Obras*, II, 303-304.

16. *Biblioteca peruana* (Lima, [1968]), ser. 1, I, 433.

17. Ortiz de Zúñiga, *Visita de Huánuco*, I, 35, 45, and Garcí Diez de San Miguel, *Visita hecha a la provincia de Chucuito . . . . en el año 1567*, ed. Waldemar Espinosa Soriano (Lima, 1964), pp. 66, 206. Somewhat lower ratios for the central sierra can be derived from demographic information contained in the *Relaciones geográficas* (see Rowe, "Inca Culture," p. 184), but these figures seem less reliable than those of the visitas. In the case of Yauyos, for instance, the whole province was said to contain 10,000 tributaries, though it had five encomiendas, and at least three of these must have fallen in the "substantial" category judging by the men who held them; see Jiménez de la Espada, *Relaciones geográficas*, I, 155-156, 167, 221.

18. Ibid., p. 160; "Encomenderos y encomiendas," pp. 2-3.

19. Lockhart, *Men of Cajamarca*, pp. 31-37, 209-212, 258-263.

20. The following account is based mainly on Horacio H. Urteaga, "Alonso Martín de Don Benito," RANP, 6 (1928), 1-11.

21. ANP, Notarios, Pedro de Castañeda (1537-38), reg. 2, f. 30.

22. ANP, Títulos, c. 46.

23. Rolando Mellafe, "Frontera agraria: el caso del virreinato peruano en el siglo XVI," in Alvaro Jara, ed., *Tierras nuevas: Expansión territorial y ocupación del suelo en América (siglos XVI-XIX)* (Mexico, 1969), p. 16.

24. Lockhart, *Spanish Peru,* pp. 17-18; Jara, *Tierras neuvas,* p. 7. For a European parallel, see Marc Bloch, *Feudal Society,* trans. L.A. Manyon (Chicago, 1961), pp. 145-160.

25. ANP, Notarios, Pedro de Salinas (1542-43), reg. 2, f. 12. Lockhart (*Spanish Peru,* pp. 31-32) mentions a similar case involving an encomendero in Arequipa.

26. See ibid., p. 80.

27. BNP, A 31; Horacio H. Urteaga, "Don Diego de Agüero y Sandoval, conquistador y poblador del Perú," RANP, 6 (1928), 164; Domingo Angulo, ed., "El testamento del capitán Jerónimo de Aliaga (1547)," RANP, 14 (1941), 169.

28. Urteaga, "Don Diego de Agüero," pp. 163-164; ANP, Real audiencia: procedimientos civiles, leg. 4 (Creditors v. Francisco de Burgos); Cobo, *Obras,* I, 381.

29. Rafael Loredo, *Los repartos* (Lima, 1958), p. 229.

30. Dobyns, "Outline of Andean Epidemic History," pp. 497-501; Alfred W. Crosby, "Conquistador y Pestilencia: The First New World Pandemic and the Fall of the Great Indian Empires," HAHR, 47 (1967), 321-337. For a comparable European case, see A.R. Bridbury, "The Black Death," *Economic History Review,* ser. 2, 26 (1973), 577-592.

31. Diego Gutiérrez de Santa Clara, "Quinquenarios o historia de los guerras civiles del Perú," Juan Pérez de Tudela Bueso, ed., *Crónicas del Perú,* BAE, 164-168 (5 vols., Madrid, 1963-1965), II, 219; see also Guamán Poma de Ayala, *La nueva corónica y buen gobierno,* ed. Luís Bustíos Gálvez (3 vols., Lima, 1956-1966), II, 125-129.

32. Juan de Matienzo, *Gobierno del Perú,* ed. Guillermo Lohmann Villena (Paris and Lima, 1967), p. 99; Hernando de Santillán, "Relación del origen, descendencia, política, y gobierno de los Incas," in Esteve Barba, *Crónicas peruanas,* p. 146.

33. Ricardo Konetzke, ed., *Colección de documentos para la historia de la formación social de Hispanoamérica, 1493-1810* (3 vols. in 5 parts, Madrid, 1953-1962), I, 297, 566, 572; Guillermo Lohmann Villena, "La restitución por conquistadores y encomenderos: Un aspecto de la incidencia lascasiana en el Perú," *Anuario de Estudios Americanos,* 23 (1966), 21-69; Poma de Ayala, *Nueva corónica,* II, 141-150.

34. Porras, *Cartas del Perú,* p. 162; Miguel de Contreras, *Padrón de los indios de Lima en 1613* (Lima, 1968); AA, Testamentos, leg. 1.

35. BNP, A 629 and A 53.

36. For a description of this eruption and its consequences, see Vásquez de Espinosa, *Compendium,* pp. 498-499, 504-505.

37. See J.H. Elliott, *Imperial Spain, 1469-1716* (London, Edward Arnold, 1963), pp. 279-281.

38. "Relación del origen e gobierno que los Ingas tuvieron," CLDP, ser. 2, III, 71-72.

39. See Rostworowski, *Curacas y sucesiones,* pp. 14-17, and Karen Spalding, "Social Climbers: Changing Patterns of Mobility among the Indians of Colonial Peru," HAHR, 50 (1970), 655-659.

40. Matienzo, *Gobierno del Perú,* p. 48.

41. Lizárraga, *Descripción breve,* pp. 100-101; Matienzo, *Gobierno del Perú,* pp. 16-20; Santillán, "Relación," p. 120.

42. Bernard Mishkin, "The Contemporary Quechua," in *Handbook,* II, 441-448.

43. Alberto Rossel Castro, *Historia regional de Ica: Epoca colonial,* I (Lima, 1964), 44; Heraclio Bonilla Mayta, *Las comunidades campesinas tradicionales del valle de Chancay* (Lima, 1965), pp. 45-46.

44. Kosok, *Life, Land and Water,* pp. 135-138.

45. Vásquez de Espinosa, *Compendium,* pp. 484-485, and Cobo, *Obras,* I, 93-94, 255-256.

46. Frederick P. Bowser, *The African Slave in Colonial Peru, 1524-1650* (Stanford, Calif., 1974), pp. 187-189.

47. ANP, Títulos, c. 567; BNP, A 345. See Appendix, below.

48. Lockhart, *Spanish Peru,* p. 12.

49. Ibid., pp. 135-149.

50. Ibid., pp. 143-145; Boleslao Lewin, ed., *Descripción del virreinato del Perú: Crónica inédita de comienzos del siglo XVII* (Rosario, Argentina, 1958), p. 70.

51. Levillier, *Gobernantes,* I, 376, and III, 31-32, 50, 95; Luís Ulloa, ed., "Documentos del virrey Toledo," *Revista Histórica,* 3 (1908), 314-348; Lewin, *Descripción,* p. 42.

52. See Guillermo Lohmann Villena, *El corregidor de indios en el Perú bajo los Austrias* (Madrid, 1957), Book I, and Roberto Levillier, *Don Francisco de Toledo, supremo organizador del Perú: Su vida, su obra (1515-1582)* (3 vols., Madrid, 1935-1942), I, 233-239. The Huaura case is mentioned in a visita of the encomienda which occurred in that year (BNP, A 629). On the tamed encomienda, see Lesley B. Simpson, *The Encomienda in New Spain: The Beginning of Spanish Mexico* (rev. and enl. ed., Berkeley and Los Angeles, 1950), chs. 10 and 11.

53. Lohmann, *El corregidor,* pp. 265-270, 434-437; "Expediente sobre el juicio de residencia tomada a Hernán Vásquez de Puga, corregidor de Cañete," BNP, A 537.

54. Net tribute figures for the early seventeenth century may be found in Vásquez de Espinosa, *Compendium,* pp. 694-720; salary figures in Lohmann, *El corregidor,* pp. 182-184.

*Chapter 3: The Beginnings of Commercial Agriculture*

1. Cobo, *Obras,* I, 380; Porras, *Cartas del Perú,* p. 100; Mellafe, "Frontera agraria," in Jara, *Tierras nuevas,* pp. 23-24; see also Chevalier, *Land and Society,* pp. 84-86.

2. Cobo, *Obras,* I, 383-387; Lohmann, "Indice," RANP, 16 (1943), 63, 73.

3. BNP, A 556; *The Harkness Collection in the Library of Congress: Calendar of Spanish Manuscripts concerning Peru, 1531-1651* (Washington, 1932), p. 141; Urteaga, "Don Diego de Agüero," p. 164; BNP, A 394; BNP, A 32, f. 198.

4. BNP, A 398.

5. BNP, Z 1265; ANP, Real audiencia: procedimientos civiles, leg. 23 (Aliaga v. Alconchel); AHNC, Soc. de Beneficencia, sala 1, est. 5, ana. 7-18 (Navarro v. Valencia).

6. ANP, Real audiencia: procedimientos civiles, leg. 12 (Ocampo v. Ocoña), and leg. 34 (Talavera v. Cárdenas), especially the inventories; *Cabildos,* III, 6; Lewin, *Descripción,* p. 30; Bonilla, *Las comunidades campesinas,* pp. 75-82.

7. Cobo, *Obras,* I, 386; *Cabildos,* IX, 608.

8. ANP, Notarios, Juan Martínez (1549-53), f. 173; Sebastián Vásquez (1551-54), ff. 591, 978; Ambrosio de Moscoso (1554-66), reg. 21; Lockhart, *Spanish Peru,* p. 91.

9. ANP, Notarios, Simón de Alzate (1548-51), f. 869; ANP, Derecho indígena, c. 40; ANP, Real audiencia: procedimientos civiles, leg. 12 (Gallego v. Illescas). The size

of this estancia was not given, but a similar one in the Mala valley contained about 210 acres.

10. Ibid., leg. 12 (Gallego v. Illescas) and leg. 34 (Talavera v. Cárdenas), inventory; ANP, Notarios, Sebastián Vásquez (1553-54), ff. 945, 1141; *Cabildos,* IX, pp. 50-51.

11. Ibid., III, 147; VI, 503; Constantino Bayle, *Los cabildos seculares en la América española* (Madrid, 1952), p. 479.

12. *Cabildos,* IV, 389-390; Guillermo Lohmann Villena, "Apuntaciones sobre el curso de los precios de los artículos de primera necesidad en Lima durante el siglo XVI," *Revista Histórica,* 29 (1966), 95. On the mechanism of supplying cities in Spain, see Carmelo Viñas y Mey, *El problema de la tierra en la España de los siglos XVI-XVII* (Madrid, 1941), pp. 104-105, and Bartolomé Benassar, *Valladolid au siècle d'or: Une ville de Castille et sa campagne au XVIe siècle* (Paris, 1967), pp. 57-69.

13. *Cabildos,* VIII, 438; IX, 113; XII, 103.

14. ANP, Notarios, Ambrosio de Moscoso (1554-66), reg. 19, f. 86; ANP, Notarios de Ica, leg. 9 (Juan de Herrera, 1573), f. 682; Lohmann, "La restitución," pp. 21-69; ANP, Notarios, Juan Cristóbal de Frías (1561-62), ff. 559, 566; Toribio de Mogrovejo, "Diario de la segunda visita pastoral que hizo de su Arquidiocesis . . . ," ed. Domingo Angulo, RANP, 1 (1920), 65-69.

15. CDIA, XVIII, 5-7; Chevalier, *Land and Society,* pp. 95-96, 100; *Cabildos,* III, 61-63; ANP, Notarios, Nicolás de Grados (1564), ff. 135-137; BNP, A 629.

16. Bonilla, *Las comunidades campesinas,* p. 78; Cobo, *Obras,* I, 88. For evidence of transhumant grazing patterns, see BNP, A 84, and Vásquez de Espinosa, *Compendium,* p. 494.

17. Bayle, *Los cabildos seculares,* pp. 87-90; *Cabildos,* IV, 514-515; V, 105, 161; IX, 303-304.

18. Ibid., I, 301; III, 3; Cobo, *Obras,* I, 383.

19. Chevalier, *Land and Society,* pp. 89-90; *Cabildos,* I, 301, 345; Cobo, *Obras,* I, 383. City blocks in Lima were about 420 feet (450 Castilian feet) on a side (Bromley, *Fundación,* p. 74).

20. Bonilla, *Las comunidades campesinas,* pp. 78-80, 82-83.

21. Chevalier, *Land and Society,* pp. 98-100; *Cabildos,* I, 134; III, 130-131, 146; IV, 343, 390, 494; ANP, Notarios, Bartolomé de Quiñones (1555-56), 7/19/55.

22. ANP, Real audiencia; procedimientos civiles, leg. 30 (Guinea v. Mexía de Tovar).

23. ANP, Notarios de Ica, leg. 11 (Tomás de Vallejos, 1568-69), f. 158; ANP, Real audiencia: procedimientos civiles, leg. 30 (Guinea v. Mexía de Tovar).

24. Cobo, *Obras,* II, 302.

25. Lockhart, *Spanish Peru,* p. 12; Huguette and Pierre Chaunu, *Seville et l'Atlantique, 1504-1650* (8 vols. in 10 parts, Paris, 1955-1959), VIII, pt. 1, p. 1099; Alvaro Jara, *Tres ensayos sobre economía minera hispanoamericana* (Santiago de Chile, 1966), p. 103 and fig. 1; Lockhart, *Spanish Peru,* pp. 24-25; Enrique Florescano, "El abasto y la legislación de granos en el siglo XVI," *Historia Mexicana,* 14 (1964-1965), 570.

26. See Murra, "Rite and Crop," p. 400.

27. ANP, Real audiencia: procedimientos civiles, leg. 39 (Vera v. Talavera).

28. Lockhart, *Spanish Peru,* p. 198; Horacio H. Urteaga, "Doña María de Escobar, introductora del trigo en el Perú," RANP, 12 (1939), 183-185.

29. Cobo, *Obras,* I, 408; B.H. Slicher van Bath, *The Agrarian History of Western*

*Europe, A.D. 500-1850*, trans. Olive Ordish (London, 1963), pp. 328-334.

30. Cobo, *Obras*, I, 407. Fixed prices did not of course respond as rapidly to changes in supply or demand as free market prices would have, but they were affected by such changes.

31. Cobo, *Obras*, II, 302-305.

32. *Cabildos*, I, 22, 23, 163; Chevalier, *Land and Society*, p. 60.

33. ANP, Notarios, Pedro de Salinas (1546-48), ff. 134-135.

34. *Cabildos*, III, 157.

35. Lohmann, "Apuntaciones," pp. 89-90.

36. Lockhart, *Spanish Peru*, p. 179.

37. Ibid, p. 103.

38. ANP, Notarios, Diego Gutiérrez (1545-55), ff. 840-841.

39. ANP, Notarios, Sebastián Vásquez. On slave prices, see Lockhart, *Spanish Peru*, p. 179, and Bowser, *African Slave*, Appendix B.

40. ANP, Notarios, Juan de Morales (1572-77), ff. 196-198.

41. ANP, Notarios, Bartolomé de Quiñones (1555-56), ff. 161, 188; Nicolás de Grados (1560), f. 43; Pedro de Salinas (1546-48), ff. 134-135; and Diego Gutiérrez (1545-55), ff. 840-841.

42. ANP, Notarios, Marcos Franco de Esquível (1569-77), f. 383; ANP, Títulos, c. 331; BNP, B 818.

43. ANP, Notarios, Sebastián Vásquez (1551-54), ff. 106, 1069, 1097, 1161; Bartolomé de Quiñones (1555-56), f. 249, f. 26; Lockhart, *Spanish Peru*, pp. 186-187.

44. Ibid., pp. 25, 110; BNP, B 818; ANP, Títulos, c. 567.

45. This was also true in Mexico; see Woodrow W. Borah and Sherburne F. Cook, *Price Trends of Some Basic Commodities in Central Mexico, 1531-1570*, Ibero-Americana, 40 (Berkeley and Los Angeles, 1958), p. 20.

46. ANP, Notarios, Pedro de Salinas (1546-48), f. 934.

47. BNP, A 629, A 537.

48. *Cabildos*, III, 2, 4, 155, 287, 297-298.

49. ANP, Real audiencia: procedimientos civiles, leg. 23 (Aliaga v. Alconchel); ANP, Derecho indígena, c. 40; ANP, Notarios, Simón de Alzate (1548-51), f. 869, and Pedro de Salinas (1546-48), ff. 632-633; Rossel, *Historia regional*, I, 31; Angulo, "Fundación de Cañete," pp. 41, 58.

50. Chevalier, *Land and Society*, p. 55; ANP, Notarios, Bartolomé de Quiñones (1555-56), f. 188; Ambrosio de Moscoso (1550-53), reg. 1, f. 68 and reg. 7, f. 30; *Cabildos*, IV, 277.

51. ANP, Títulos, c. 567; BNP, A 345, A 328; Rossel, *Historia regional*, I, 27-28.

52. ANP, Notarios, Ambrosio de Moscoso (1554-66), reg. 12, and separate sheet dated 6/12/57; Diego Gutiérrez (1545-55), reg. 12, f. 544; Ambrosio de Moscoso (1550-53), reg. 17, f. 86; Sebastián Vásquez (1551-54), ff. 453, 831.

53. ANP, Títulos, c. 82; Lockhart, *Spanish Peru*, p. 198; on Cortés' Mexican sugar enterprises, see Ward Barrett, *The Sugar Hacienda of the Marqueses del Valle* (Minneapolis, 1970), p. 11.

54. ANP, Notarios, Pedro de Salinas (1546-48), f. 658; Vedia, *Historiadores primitivos*, II, 418.

55. Vásquez de Espinosa, *Compendium*, pp. 472-473; Pérez, *Crónicas del Perú*, I, 384; Lockhart, *Spanish Peru*, pp. 184-185; ANP, Notarios, Juan Cristóbal de Frías (1561-62), reg. 2, f. 72.

56. See, for instance, Lockhart, "Encomienda and Hacienda," pp. 411-429, and Robert G. Keith, "Encomienda, Hacienda and Corregimiento in Spanish America: A

Structural Analysis," HAHR, 51 (1971), 431-446. As will be seen below, however, these positions are not irreconcilable.

57. On Chancay, see Robert G. Keith, "Origen del sistema de hacienda: El caso de Chancay," in *La hacienda, la comunidad y el campesino en el Perú*, pp. 49-53, Perú Problema, ed. José Matos Mar, no. 3 (Lima, 1970). On Huaura, see ANP, Títulos, cc. 93 and 646, and Notarios, Alvar García (1551-52), reg. 10 (Toraya, 1599-1602, f. 43; Jorge Juan and Antonio de Ulloa, *A Voyage to South America*, trans. John Adams (2 vols., London, 1758), II, 25.

58. ANP, Real audiencia: procedimientos civiles, leg. 23 (Aliaga v. Alconchel).

59. Angulo, "Fundación de Cañete," pp. 41, 58; the Navarro case can be found in a long lawsuit over the encomienda of Barranca in AHNC, Soc. de Beneficencia, sala 1, est. 5, ana. 7-18.

60. Rossel, *Historia regional*, I, 28-29; Edmundo Guillén Guillén, "Un documento inédito para la historia social y económica de Ica," RANP, 27 (1963), 95-96.

*Chapter 4: The Age of the Gentleman-Farmer*

1. Elliott, *Imperial Spain*, pp. 20-23, 99-102; John Lynch, *Spain under the Hapsburgs* (2 vols., New York, 1964-1969), I, 12-20; Jaime Vicens Vives, *An Economic History of Spain*, trans. Frances M. López-Morillas (Princeton, N.J., 1969), pp. 161-166, 294-296.

2. On servicios and mercedes, see J.H. Elliott, *The Revolt of the Catalans: A Study in the Decline of Spain (1598-1640)* (Cambridge, 1963), p. 67.

3. Levillier, *Gobernantes*, I, 119, 155.

4. Ibid., I, 208, 267.

5. Pérez, *Crónicas del Perú*, II, 72; Garcilaso, *Royal Commentaries*, II, 1427-1428, 1431-1434.

6. CDIHE, XCIV, 151, 155, 162. There are two errors in this version of the list: Zurbano's post is given as "alcalde" instead of *alcaide*, and the name of the fortress is given as "Huaura" instead of Huarco.

7. Levillier, *Gobernantes*, I, 376.

8. Ibid., I, 391; IV, 74, 78.

9. BNP, A 345 and A 328; ANP, Títulos, c. 567. For an example of such a land grant, see Appendix, below.

10. Angulo, "Fundación de Cañete," pp. 34-43; Carlos Romero, "La fundación de Chancay," *Revista Histórica*, 9 (1928-1935), 382-387.

11. AHNC, Soc. de Beneficencia, sala 1, est. 5, ana. 7-18, f. 749 ff. (lawsuit between Antonio Navarro and Ordoño de Valencia over the encomienda of Barranca); Levillier, *Gobernantes*, I, 503.

12. CDIA, VII, 459-460.

13. Levillier, *Gobernantes*, I, 503; III, 366; CDIA, VII, 460.

14. Angulo, "Fundación de Cañete," pp. 43-44; Vedia, *Historiadores primitivos*, II, 424.

15. Levillier, *Gobernantes*, I, 542; Julio E. Sánchez Elías, *Cuatro siglos de historia iqueña* (Lima, 1957), p. 23.

16. Garcilaso, *Royal Commentaries*, II, 998, 1021; ANP, Notarios, Juan de Salamanca (1571-75), reg. 2, f. 414; A.M. Velez Picasso, quoted in José M. Valega, *El virreinato del Perú: Historia crítica de la época colonial, en todos sus aspectos* (Lima, [1939]), pp. 38-39.

17. ANP, Notarios de Ica, leg. 11 (Antonio de Vallejos, 1568-69), f. 130 and leg. 9

(Juan de Herrera, 1573-88), f. 299; ANP, Notarios, Juan de Salamanca (1571-75), reg. 2, f. 414. There is no direct evidence that Flores sold his farm land, but he sold his solares and huertas to Juan Martínez Rengifo, and presumably would have sold his other property in the valley at the same time (see BNP, A 84).

18. Angulo, "Fundación de Cañete," p. 34.

19. Sánchez Elías, *Cuatro siglos,* p. 23; Rossel Castro, *Historia regional,* I, 77; Cristóbal Vaca de Castro, "Ordenanzas de tambos, distancias de unos a otros, modo de cargar los indios y obligaciones de las justicias respectivas hechas en la ciudad del Cuzco en 31 de Mayo de 1543," *Revista Histórica,* 3 (1908-1909), 447-452; AHNC, Soc. de Beneficencia, sala 1, est. 5, ana. 7-18, ff. 969, 977.

20. Rossel Castro, *Historia regional,* I, 70; Angulo, "Fundación de Cañete," p. 38; Levillier, *Gobernantes,* I, 542.

21. Angulo, "Fundación de Cañete," pp. 37-43, 72-81; Sánchez Elías, *Cuatro siglos,* p. 30; ANP, Títulos, c. 6.

22. Angulo, "Fundación de Cañete," p. 37; Romero, "Fundación de Chancay," p. 383; Levillier, *Gobernantes,* I, 542; Navarro-Valencia pleito, f. 750. The Castilian foot was about 2 cm. shorter than the English foot.

23. See above, p. 67n.

24. Angulo, "Fundación de Cañete," p. 56; ANP, Títulos, c. 6.

25. Angulo, "Fundación de Cañete," pp. 43-83.

26. Lizárraga, *Descripción breve,* p. 43. The acequia of Chome is now called San Miguél and that of Hualcara, María Angola.

27. Angulo, "Fundación de Cañete," pp. 45 and 57; AHNC, Soc. de Beneficencia, sala 1, est. 5, ana. 7-18, f. 977.

28. Ibid., ff. 748-749, 971, 977.

29. Angulo, "Fundación de Cañete," pp. 43-44, 58-59, 64-65.

30. Ibid., pp. 40-83.

31. Ibid., pp. 48, 51, 63, 73; ANP, Títulos, c. 115; ANP, Compañía de Jesús: Títulos, leg. 1 (delineation of Rengifo lands) and leg. 2 (Jesuits v. Vargas).

32. Romero, "Fundación de Chancay," pp. 384-386; Mogrovejo, "Diario," RANP, 1 (1920), 79; BNP, A 61. See also Donald L. Wiedner, "Forced Labor in Colonial Perú," *The Americas,* 16 (1959-1960), 357-383.

33. *Cabildos,* VIII, 82, 197; IX, 58, 62, 626.

34. Angulo, "Fundación de Cañete," pp. 47-66, 72-84.

35. Ibid., pp. 84-86.

36. BNP, A 97, A 345, A 84; Keith, "Origen," pp. 34-42.

37. Angulo, "Fundación de Cañete," pp. 84-86; Mogrovejo, "Diario," RANP, 1 (1920), pp. 76-79.

38. Lohmann, "Apuntaciones," pp. 85-88.

39. BNP, A 61.

40. BNP, A 61; Levillier, *Gobernantes,* IV, 105-106.

41. Gibson, *Aztecs,* pp. 235-242; Barrett, *Sugar Hacienda,* pp. 86-87.

42. ANP, Notarios, Juan de Salamanca (1571-72), reg. 9 (Saracho), f. 79.

43. ANP, Títulos, c. 331.

44. Lewin, *Descripción,* p. 40; Vásquez de Espinosa, *Compendium,* pp. 428, 480, 482, 694, 695; Bowser, *African Slave,* pp. 84-94.

45. Ibid., Appendix B.

46. ANP, Notarios, Sebastián Vásquez (1551-54), ff. 739, 1014; ANP, Títulos, cc. 646, 85.

47. BNP, B 1935 and B 1939.

48. Lohmann, "Apuntaciones," pp. 90-94, 104; ANP, Notarios de Ica, leg. 2 (García de Cordova, 1583), ff. 200, 298, 340, and leg. 9 (Juan de Herrera, 1573-88), ff. 204, 452, 649.

49. Fernando Ortiz Fernández, *Cuban Counterpoint: Tobacco and Sugar*, trans. Harriet de Onís (New York, Knopf, 1947), pp. 55-60. For examples of partnerships, see ANP, Notarios, Marcos Franco de Esquível (1569-77), f. 842; ANP, Real audiencia: procedimientos civiles, leg. 10 (Gutiérrez v. Gutiérrez).

50. This account of the Ingenio valley is based on ANP, Títulos, cc. 86, 146, 165, 415, 575.

51. See Charles Jago, "The Influence of Debt on the Relations between Crown and Aristocracy in Seventeenth-Century Castile," *Economic History Review*, ser. 2, 36 (1973), 223-225, on the reluctance of Spanish bureaucrats to approve the sale or mortgaging of entailed property when it was not in the long-term interest of the estate.

52. ANP, Títulos, c. 304.

53. BNP, A 64; ANP, Notarios de Ica, leg. 2 (García de Cordova, 1583), f. 16.

54. ANP, Títulos, c. 205; ANP, Notarios, Juan de Salamanca (1571-75), reg. 9 (Saracho).

55. Cobo, *Obras*, I, 405-406; Tadeo Haenke, *Descripción del Perú* (Lima, 1901), p. 62.

56. See the inventories contained in ANP, Títulos, cc. 92, 93, 646, and W.B. Stevenson, *A Historical and Descriptive Narrative of Twenty Years' Residence in South America* (3 vols., London, 1825), I, 423.

57. On the Jesuit haciendas, see Pablo Macera Dall'Orso, ed., *Instrucciones para el manejo de las haciendas jesuítas del Perú, ss. XVII-XVIII*, in *Nueva Corónica*, vol. 2, fasc. 2 (Lima, 1966).

58. Cobo, *Obras*, II, 316; Haenke, *Descripción*, pp. 183, 185.

59. Lizárraga, *Descripción breve*, p. 14.

60. Cosme Bueno, *Geografía del Perú virreinal (siglo XVIII)* (Lima, 1951), p. 52; Vásquez de Espinosa, *Compendium*, pp. 395-396; Vedia, *Historiadores Primitivos*, II, 419.

*Chapter 5: The Consolidation of the Hacienda System*

1. ANP, Notarios, Juan de Salamanca (1573-75), reg. 7, f. 320, and Juan de Morales (1572-77), reg. 10, f. 335; ANP, Títulos, c. 85.

2. Ibid., c. 133.

3. This hacienda was still called San Martín at the beginning of the eighteenth century and took its later name from its owner at that time, Dr. Francisco Saenz Galeano; see ANP, Títulos, cc. 115, 676.

4. On Rengifo and the Chancay hacienda, see BNP, Z 1279; ANP, Títulos, c. 331; ANP, Compañía de Jesús: Títulos, leg. 1; ANP, Notarios, Marcos Franco de Esquivel (1569-77), f. 842.

5. ANP, Real Audiencia: Procedimientos civiles, leg. 29 (Soto v. Santiago). The extent of Soto's landholdings can also be judged from the fact that in 1593 he was assessed a higher amount for the settlement of his land titles than any of the other Cañete landowners with the exception of the encomendero Diego de Agüero (see Angulo, "Fundación de Cañete," pp. 84-86).

6. BNP, A 84.

7. D.A. Brading, *Miners and Merchants in Bourbon Mexico, 1763-1810* (Cambridge, 1971), pp. 215-219.

8. Cobo, *Obras*, II, 120; Castro and Ortega Morejón, "Relación," pp. 243-244;

ANP, Notarios, Juan de Morales (1572-77), reg. 6.

9. ANP, Derecho indígena, c. 28; Guillén, "Un documento inédito," pp. 95-96.
10. For an example, see the Appendix.
11. ANP, Títulos, c. 1.
12. For some examples, see ibid., c. 240.
13. Ibid., c. 241.
14. ANP, Notarios, Pedro Arias Cortés (1582-99), reg. 10.
15. ANP, Títulos, cc. 133, 156. For other cases, see ibid., cc. 46, 202, 289, and also Derecho indígena, c. 77.
16. ANP, Notarios, Juan de Salamanca (1573-75), reg. 1, f. 32, and Pedro Arias Cortés (1582-99), reg. 3, f. 9; ANP, Títulos, c. 225; ANP, Real audiencia: procedimientos civiles, leg. 29 (Rengifo v. Bayón).
17. ANP, Títulos, c. 82.
18. See above, ch. 4, p. 100n.
19. ANP, Títulos, c. 331. The principal of the censo was 4,410 pesos ensayados or 6,125 pesos corrientes (see Glossary).
20. Guillén, "Un documento inédito," pp. 94-103.
21. ANP, Notarios de Ica, leg. 11 (Tomás de Vallejos, 1568-69), f. 277.
22. ANP, Títulos, cc. 240, 241.
23. Ibid., c. 393.
24. See Chevalier, Land and Society, pp. 52-58.
25. ANP, Títulos, c. 567.
26. Ibid., c. 258. The 1642 title-settlement records for the Ribera hacienda in Chunchanga (Pisco valley) mention 38 fanegadas of "tierras carrizales" which had been set aside by the visitador Maldonado as common pasture for the whole valley (AH, sección colonial, leg. 1, c. 3B).
27. See Chevalier, Land and Society, pp. 265-277.
28. ANP, Títulos, cc. 223, 646; AH, sección colonial, leg. 1, c. 3B.
29. Chevalier, Land and Society, pp. 270-271; Angulo, "Fundación de Cañete," pp. 84-86.
30. The only substantial series of title-settlement records I discovered came from the Pisco valley in 1642-43 and are in AH, sección colonial, leg. 1 and 2.
31. See Eric R. Wolf and Sidney W. Mintz, "Haciendas and Plantations in Middle America and the Antilles," Social and Economic Studies, 6 (1957), 389. On coastal yanaconas, see José Matos Mar, "Las haciendas del valle de Chancay," Revista del Museo Nacional, 33 (1964), 361-364.
32. Ambrosio Cerdán y Pontero, "Disertación sobre las aguas que riegan los valles de Lima," Antiguo Mercurio Peruano (Lima, 1861), VI, 97 (originally published in 1793 in Mercurio Peruano, VII); Vedia, Historiadores primitivos, II, 418.
33. Cerdán, "Disertación," p. 160.
34. Glick, Irrigation and Society, pp. 207-209; Vedia, Historiadores primitivos, II, 418.
35. Cerdán, "Disertación," pp. 123-124, 213-214.
36. Cabildos, I, 93, 223; III, 27; V, 363; VIII, 176.
37. Roberto Levillier, ed., Ordenanzas de Don Francisco de Toledo, Virrey del Perú, 1569-1581 (Madrid, 1929), p. 384.
38. Ibid.
39. BNP, A 306.
40. Levillier, Ordenanzas, pp. 391-399; Cerdán, "Disertación," p. 125, n. 1, and p. 160.
41. Ibid., pp. 120-127, 177-185.

42. Guillén, "Un documento inédito," pp. 95-96; ANP, Derecho indígena, c. 48.
43. Levillier, *Ordenanzas*, pp. 395-396; BNP, A 629.
44. ANP, Aguas, cc. 6, 7.
45. Cerdán, "Disertación," pp. 181-184; José Alejandro Alvarado, *El río de Surco (canal de irrigación) y sus valles: Su transformación a través de 15 años* (Lima, 1934), pp. 77-85.

*Conclusion*

1. On the Oaxaca case, see William B. Taylor, *Landlord and Peasant in Colonial Oaxaca* (Stanford, Calif., 1972), and Brian R. Hamnett, "Dye Production, Food Supply, and the Laboring Population of Oaxaca, 1750-1820," HAHR, 51 (1971), 51-78. On the Peruvian sierra, see Karen Spalding, "Tratos mercantiles del Corregidor de indios y la formación de la hacienda serrana en el Perú," *América Indígena*, 30 (1970), 595-608.
2. Lockhart, *Spanish Peru*, pp. 96-101.
3. Carl O. Sauer, *The Early Spanish Main* (Berkeley and Los Angeles, 1969), pp. 197-204; Murdo J. MacLeod, *Spanish Central America: A Socioeconomic History, 1520-1720* (Berkeley and Los Angeles, 1973), pp. 217-220. As Sauer points out, Spanish difficulties on Española were caused also by the exhaustion of the early gold workings.
4. MacLeod, *Spanish Central America*, pp. 227-228.
5. On plantations and manorial haciendas see Wolf and Mintz, "Haciendas and Plantations," pp. 380-412.
6. Wolf, *Sons of the Shaking Earth*, pp. 204-205.
7. See Chevalier, *Land and Society*, ch. 5.

# Bibliography

Manuscript Sources

The present study is based in large part on local documentary material from the sixteenth and early seventeenth centuries which was found in Peru. With respect to origin, this material fell into three main categories: notarial, judicial, administrative. The notarial documents included wills, bills of sale, rental and labor agreements, contracts for the payment of censos or the repayment of debts; they were generally found in the original registers of the notaries, in later collections of land titles, or in the records of law suits. The judicial documents consisted mainly of cases which came before the audiencia in Lima, but often contained transcripts of earlier proceedings. Among the more important administrative documents were the records of title settlements (usually fragmented and often found in the collections of land titles), and the transcripts of residencias and visitas. The Archivo Nacional proved to have the richest collection of this material, though much of it is uncatalogued and difficult to use efficiently (catalogues for a few sections have been published in the *Revista del Archivo Nacional*). Particularly valuable were the many notarial registers found in the sección notarial, the collections of land titles in Títulos de propriedad, and the judicial cases in Real audiencia: Procedimientos civiles, Derecho indígena, and Aguas. The Biblioteca Nacional has a smaller and somewhat fragmentary collection which is, however, well catalogued and easier to utilize. The Archivo Histórico del Ministerio de Hacienda provided material on the seventeenth-century title settlements, mainly from the Pisco region.

Archivo Arzobispal de Lima
   Causas de visitas: legajos 1, 2, 9, 16, 17, 23
   Censos: legajos 1, 5, 10, 11, 15
   Padrones: legajo 5
   Testamentos: legajo 1
Archivo Histórico del Ministerio de Hacienda y Comercio del Perú
   Sección colonial: legajos 1 and 2
Archivo Histórico Nacional del Cuzco
   Sociedad de Beneficencia: sala 1, est. 5, ana. 7-18
Archivo Nacional del Perú
   Sección histórica

Aguas: legajos 1 and 2 (catalogued by cuadernos)
Compañía de Jesús, Títulos de propriedad: legajos 1 and 2
Derecho indígena: legajos 2-7 (catalogued by cuadernos)
Real Audiencia, Procedimientos Civiles: legajos 3-5, 7-10, 12, 14, 15, 17-26,
    28-34, 36, 39, 41, 42
Residencias: legajos 1-3, 9
Superior gobierno: cuadernos 25, 56a
Títulos de propriedad: legajos 1-19, 21, 23, 28, 29, 33, 34, 35, 40-42, 44 (cata-
    logued by cuadernos)
Sección notarial
    Notarial registers from Lima and Ica
Biblioteca Nacional del Perú
    Documents from the sixteenth and early seventeenth centuries

## Maps and Aerial Photographs

There are few colonial maps of the coastal valleys detailed enough
to be of much help. The Biblioteca Nacional possesses a few nineteenth-century maps and plans of individual valleys, and Bromley and
Barbagelata have published some useful old maps of the lower part of
the Lima valley in *Evolución urbana de Lima*. The most valuable
modern maps of the coastal valleys are those in the *Carta Nacional*
published in Lima by the Instituto Geográfico Militar. The aerial
photographs which made it possible to establish present-day limits of
cultivation and patterns of settlement and to trace the course of irrigation canals were obtained from the Instituto Geográfico Militar and
the Servicio Aerofotográfico Nacional.

## Printed Sources

The published material dealing specifically with the social and
economic history of the Peruvian coast in the sixteenth century is
limited, but a few works deserve special mention. Lockhart's *Spanish
Peru* is the best starting point for the investigation of early colonial
society, and the present book has relied heavily on it. Several general
works of history and geography written during the colonial period contain valuable information on the coast: the *Crónica del Perú* and
*Señorío de los Incas* of Cieza de León, the *Descripción breve* of Lizárraga, and the later works of Vásquez de Espinosa and Cobo. Equally
valuable was Cerdán's eighteenth-century account of the irrigation system of the Lima valley. The *Libros de cabildos de Lima,* edited by Lee
and Bromley, were a mine of useful information on the valleys close to

the city. Finally, the documentary collections published by Levillier provided the clearest picture of the problems of social and economic change as perceived by those responsible for the government of Peru.

Acosta, José de. *Obras.* Edited by Francisco Mateos. Biblioteca de Autores Españoles, 73. Madrid, Ediciones Atlas, 1954.

Alvarado, José Alejandro. *El río de Surco (canal de irrigación) y sus valles: Su transformación a través de 15 años.* Lima, 1934.

Angulo, Domingo de, ed. "El capitán Francisco de Ampuero, conquistador del Perú y vecino de la ciudad de los reyes," *Revista del Archivo Nacional del Perú,* 7 (1928), 55-68.

————, ed. "Don Andrés Hurtado de Mendoza y la fundación de la villa de Cañete," *Revista Histórica,* 7 (Lima, 1921-1925), 21-90.

————, ed. "La fundación y población de la villa de Zaña," *Revista del Archivo Nacional del Perú,* 1 (1920), 280-301.

————, ed. "El testamento del capitán Jerónimo de Aliaga," *Revista del Archivo Nacional del Perú,* 14 (1941), 165-172.

Arcila Farías, Eduardo. *Régimen de la encomienda en Venezuela.* Publicaciones de la Escuela de Estudios Hispano-Americanos de Sevilla, 106. Seville, 1957.

Barrett, Ward. *The Sugar Hacienda of the Marqueses del Valle.* Minneapolis, University of Minnesota Press, 1970.

Bataillon, Marcel. "Les colons du Perou contre Charles Quint: Analyse du mouvement pizarriste (1544-1548)," *Annales: économies, sociétes, civilisations,* 22 (1967), 479-494.

Bayle, Constantino. *Los cabildos seculares en la América espanõla.* Madrid, Sapientia, 1952.

Belaunde Guinassí, Manuel. *La encomienda en el Perú.* Lima, Ediciones Mercurio Peruano, 1945.

Benassar, Bartolomé. *Valladolid au siècle d'or: Une ville de Castille et sa campagne au XVIe siècle.* Paris, Mouton, 1967.

*Biblioteca Peruana: primera serie.* 3 vols. Lima, Editores Técnicos Asociados, [1968].

Bloch, Marc. *Feudal Society.* Translated by L.A. Manyon. Chicago, University of Chicago Press, 1961.

————. *French Rural History: An Essay on its Basic Characteristics.* Translated by Janet Sondheimer. London, Routledge & Kegan Paul, 1966.

Bonilla Mayta, Heraclio. *Las comunidades campesinas tradicionales del valle de Chancay.* Publicaciones del Museo Nacional de la Cultura Peruana, Tesis antropológicas, no. 1. Lima, 1965.

Borah, Woodrow W. *Early Colonial Trade and Navigation between Mexico and Peru.* Ibero-Americana, 38. Berkeley and Los Angeles, University of California Press, 1954.

————. *New Spain's Century of Depression.* Ibero-Americana, 35. Berkeley and Los Angeles, University of California Press, 1951.

Borah, Woodrow W., and Cook, Sherburne F. *The Aboriginal Population of Central Mexico on the Eve of the Spanish Conquest.* Ibero-Americana, 45. Berkeley and Los Angeles, University of California Press, 1963.

————. *Price Trends of Some Basic Commodities in Central Mexico, 1531-1570.*

Ibero-Americana, 40. Berkeley and Los Angeles, University of California Press, 1958.

———. *Essays in Population History: Mexico and the Caribbean.* 2 vols. Berkeley and Los Angeles, University of California Press, 1971-1974.

Borde, Jean, and Góngora, Mario. *Evolución de la propriedad rural en el valle del Puangue.* Universidad de Chile, Instituto de Sociología, Publicación 1-2. Santiago de Chile, Editorial Universitaria, 1956.

Bowser, Frederick P. *The African Slave in Colonial Peru, 1524-1650.* Stanford, Stanford University Press, 1974.

Brading, David A. *Miners and Merchants in Bourbon Mexico, 1763-1810.* Cambridge Latin American Studies, 10. Cambridge, Cambridge University Press, 1971.

Bromley, Juan. *La fundación de la Ciudad le los Reyes.* Lima, 1935.

———, and Barbagelata, José. *Evolución urbana de Lima.* Lima, Editorial Lumen, n.d.

Brundage, Burr Cartwright. *Lords of Cuzco: A History and Description of the Inca People in Their Final Days.* Norman, University of Oklahoma Press, 1967.

Bueno, Cosme. *Geografía del Peru virreinal (siglo XVIII).* Published by Daniel Valcarcel. Lima, 1951.

Busto Duthurburu, José Antonio del. "El capitán Melchor Verdugo, encomendero de Cajamarca," *Revista Histórica,* 24 (Lima, 1959), 318-387.

———. *El Conde de Nieva, Virrey del Perú.* Primera parte. Publicaciones del Instituto Riva-Agüero, no. 43. Lima, 1943.

———. *Francisco Pizarro: El Marqués Gobernador.* Madrid, Ediciones Rialp, 1966.

Cabello Balboa, Miguel. *Miscelánea antártica: Una historia del Perú antiguo.* Lima, Instituto de Etnología, Facultad de Letras, Universidad Nacional Mayor de San Marcos, 1951.

Cabero, Marco A. "El corregimiento de Saña y el problema histórico de la fundación de Trujillo," *Revista Histórica,* 1 (Lima, 1906), 151-191, 337-373, 486-514.

Calancha, Antonio de. *Corónica moralizada del orden de San Agustín en el Peru.* Barcelona, 1638.

Cappa, Ricardo. *Estudios críticos acerca de la dominación española en América.* 20 vols. Madrid, 1889-1897.

Casas, Bartolomé de las. *Obras escogidas.* Edited by Juan Pérez de Tudela Bueso. Biblioteca de Autores Españoles, 95, 96, 105, 106, 110. Madrid, Ediciones Atlas, 1957-1961.

Castillo Negrón, Mamerto. *Monografía de la provincia de Pisco.* Lima, Compañía de Impresiones y Publicidad, 1947.

Castro, Cristobal de, and Ortega Morejón, Diego de. "Relación y declaración del . . . valle de Chincha . . . ." *Quellen zur Kulturgeschichte des präkolumbischen Amerika.* Edited by Hermann Trimborn. Stuttgart, Strecker and Schröder, [1936]. Pp. 236-246.

Castro Pozo, Hildebrando. *El yanaconaje en las haciendas piuranas.* Lima, Compañía de Impresiones y Publicidad, 1947.

Cerdán y Pontero, Ambrosio. "Disertación sobre las aguas que riegan los valles de Lima." *Antiguo Mercurio Peruano,* VI, 90-246. Lima, 1861.

Cespedes del Castillo, Guillermo. "La sociedad colonial americana en los siglos XVI y XVII." *Historia de España y América.* Edited by Jaime Vicens Vives. 2nd ed. Barcelona, Editorial Vicens Vives, 1971.

Cevallos López, Vilma. "La caja de censos de indios y su aporte a la economía colonial (1565-1613): primeras investigaciones para el estudio de esta institución," *Revista del Archivo Nacional del Perú,* 26 (1962), 269-352.

Chamberlain, Robert S. "Castilian Backgrounds of the Repartimiento-encomienda," *Contributions to American Anthropology and History*, 5 (1939), 19-66.

Chaunu, Huguette, and Chaunu, Pierre. *Seville et l'Atlantique, 1504-1650.* 8 vols. Paris, Colin, 1955-1959.

Chevalier, François. "La expansión de la gran propriedad en el Alto Perú del siglo XX, a través de escritor José María Arguedas y de otras fuentes." In *XXXVI Congreso Internacional de Americanistas: Actas y Memorias* IV, 371-378. (4 vols., Seville, 1966).

————. *Land and Society in Colonial Mexico: The Great Hacienda.* Edited by Lesley B. Simpson and translated by Alvin Eustis. Berkeley and Los Angeles, University of California Press, 1963.

————. "Signification sociale de la fondation de Puebla de los Angeles," *Revista de Historia de América,* 23 (1947), 105-130.

Cieza de León, Pedro de. *La crónica del Perú.* In *Historiadores primitivos de Indias,* edited by Enrique Vedia, II (Madrid, 1853), 349-458.

————. *Guerras civiles del Perú.* Edited by Marcos Jiménez de la Espada. 2 vols. Madrid, 1877-1881.

————. *El señorío de los Incas.* Edited by Carlos Araníbar and Pierre Duviols. Lima, Instituto de Estudios Peruanos, 1967.

Cobb, Gwendolin B. "Supply and Transportation for the Potosí Mines, 1545-1640," *Hispanic American Historical Review,* 29 (1949), 25-45.

Cobo, Bernabé. *Obras.* Edited by Francisco Mateos. Biblioteca de Autores Españoles, XCI and XCII. Madrid, Ediciones Atlas, 1964.

*Colección de documentos inéditos para la historia de España.* Edited by Martín Fernández de Navarrete et al. 112 vols. Madrid, 1842-1895.

*Colección de documentos inéditos relativos al descubrimiento, conquista y organización de las antiguas posesiones españoles de América y Oceanía, sacados de los archivos del Reino, y muy especialmente del de Indias.* 42 vols. Madrid, 1864-1884.

*Colección de documentos inéditos relativos al descubrimiento, conquista y organización de las antiguas posesiones españolas de ultramar.* 25 vols. Madrid, 1885-1932.

"Compilación de reales cédulas, provisiones, leyes, ordenanzas, instrucciones y procedimientos sobre repartimientos y composiciones de tierras . . . ," *Revista del Archivo Nacional del Perú,* 19 (1955), 46-61; 20 (1956), 151-170 and 417-446; 21 (1957), 192-235 and 396-474; 22 (1958), 219-229 and 445-471.

Contreras, Miguel de. *Padrón de los indios de Lima en 1613.* Introduction by Noble David Cook. Lima, Universidad Nacional Mayor de San Marcos, Seminario de Historia Rural Andina, 1968.

Cook, Noble David. "The Indian Population of Peru, 1570-1620," unpub. diss., University of Texas at Austin, 1973.

Crosby, Alfred W. "Conquistador y Pestilencia: The First New World Pandemic and the Fall of the Great Indian Empires," *Hispanic American Historical Review,* 47 (1967), 321-337.

Diez de San Miguel, Garci. *Visita hecha a la provincia de Chucuito por Garci Diaz de San Miguel en el año 1567.* Edited by Waldemar Espinoza Soriano. Documentos regionales para la etnología y etnohistoria andinas, I. Lima, Ediciones de la Casa de la Cultura del Perú, 1964.

Dobyns, Henry F. "Estimating Aboriginal American Population 1: An Appraisal of Techniques with a New Hemispheric Estimate," *Current Anthropology,* 7 (1966), 395-416.

————. "An Outline of Andean Epidemic History to 1720," *Bulletin of the History of Medicine,* 37 (1963), 493-515.

————. "The Struggle for Land in Peru: The Hacienda Vicos Case," *Ethnohistory*, 13 (1966), 97-122.

Duby, Georges. *Rural Economy and Country Life in the Medieval West.* Translated by Cynthia Postan. Columbia, S.C., University of South Carolina Press, 1968.

Elliott, J.H. *Imperial Spain, 1469-1716.* London, Edward Arnold, 1963.

————. *The Revolt of the Catalans: A Study in the Decline of Spain (1598-1640).* Cambridge, England, Cambridge University Press, 1963.

Encinas, Diego de. *Provisiones, cédulas, capítulos de ordenanzas, instrucciones y cartas . . . . tocante al buen gobierno de las Indias y administración de la justicia en ellas.* 4 vols. Madrid, 1596. Facsimile edition entitled *Cedulario Indiano.* 4 vols. Madrid, Ediciones Cultura Hispánica, 1945-1946.

"Encomenderos y encomiendas," *Revista del Archivo Nacional del Perú,* 4 (1926), 1-21.

Engel, Frederic. *Geografía humana prehistórica y agricultura precolumbina de la quebrada de Chilca.* Vol. I: Informe preliminar. Lima, Universidad Agraria, 1966.

Esteve Barba, Francisco, ed. *Crónicas peruanas de interés indígena.* Biblioteca de Autores Españoles, CCIX. Madrid, Ediciones Atlas, 1968.

Fals-Borda, Orlando. "Indian Congregations in the New Kingdom of Granada: Land Tenure Aspects, 1595-1850," *The Americas,* 13 (1956-1957), 331-351.

Faron, Louis C. "From Encomienda to Hacienda in Chancay Valley, Peru; 1533-1600," *Ethnohistory,* 13 (1966), 145-181.

Favre, Henri. "Evolución y situación de las haciendas en la región de Huancavélica, Perú," *Revista del Museo Nacional,* 33 (Lima, 1964), 237-257.

Florescano, Enrique. "El abasto y la legislación de granos en el siglo XVI," *Historia Mexicana,* 14 (1964-1965), 567-630.

Foster, George M. *Culture and Conquest: America's Spanish Heritage.* Viking Fund Publications in Anthropology, no. 27. Chicago, Quadrangle Books, 1960.

Friede, Juan. "Proceso de formación de la propriedad territorial en la América intertropical," *Jahrbuch für Geschichte von Staat, Wirtschaft und Gesellschaft Lateinamerikas,* 2 (1965), 75-87.

Fuentes, Manuel A. *Memorias de los Virreys que han gobernado el Perú durante el tiempo del coloniaje español.* 6 vols. Lima, 1859.

Garcilaso de la Vega, el Inca. *Royal Commentaries of the Incas and General History of Peru.* Translated by Harold V. Livermore. 2 vols. Austin, University of Texas Press, 1966.

Geertz, Clifford. *Agricultural Involution: The Processes of Ecological Change in Indonesia.* Berkeley and Los Angeles, University of California Press, 1968.

Gibson, Charles. *The Aztecs under Spanish Rule: A History of the Indians of the Valley of Mexico, 1519-1810.* Stanford, Stanford University Press, 1964.

————. *Tlaxcala in the Sixteenth Century.* New Haven, Yale University Press, 1952.

Gillin, John. *Moche: A Peruvian Coastal Community.* Smithsonian Institution, Institute of Social Anthropology, Publication no. 3. Washington, 1947.

Glick, Thomas F. *Irrigation and Society in Medieval Valencia.* Cambridge, Mass., Harvard University Press, 1970.

Góngora, Mario. *El estado en el derecho indiano: Época de fundación (1492-1570).* Santiago de Chile, Instituto de Investigaciones Histórico-Culturales, Facultad de Filosofía y Educación, Universidad de Chile, 1951.

————. *Los grupos de conquistadores en Tierra Firme (1509-1530): Fisonomía histórico social de un tipo de conquista.* Santiago de Chile, Centro de Historia Colonial, Universidad de Chile, 1962.

_____. *Origen de los inquilinos de Chile central.* Santiago de Chile, Seminario de Historia Colonial, Facultad de Filosofía y Educación, 1960.

Guillén Guillén, Edmundo, ed. "Un documento inédito para la historia social y económica de Ica," *Revista del Archivo Nacional del Perú,* 27 (1963), 88-103.

Haenke, Tadeo. *Descripción del Perú.* Lima, Imprenta de "El Lucero," 1901.

Hagen, Victor W. von. *The Desert Kingdoms of Peru.* Greenwich, Conn., New York Graphic Society Publishers, 1964.

Hammell, Eugene A. *Wealth, Authority and Prestige in the Ica Valley, Peru.* University of New Mexico Publications in Anthropology, no. 10. Albuquerque, 1962.

Hamnett, Brian R. "Dye Production, Food Supply, and the Laboring Population of Oaxaca, 1750-1820," *Hispanic American Historical Review,* 51 (1971), 51-78.

_____. *Politics and Trade in Southern Mexico, 1750-1810.* Cambridge Latin American Studies, 12. Cambridge, Cambridge University Press, 1971.

Hanke, Lewis. *The Spanish Struggle for Justice in the Conquest of America.* Philadelphia, University of Pennsylvania Press, 1949.

Haring, Clarence H. *The Spanish Empire in America.* 1st ed. revised. New York, Oxford University Press, 1952.

*The Harkness Collection in the Library of Congress: Calendar of Spanish Manuscripts concerning Peru, 1531-1651.* Washington, U.S. Government Printing Office, 1932.

Harth-Terré, Emilio. "El esclavo negro en la sociedad indoperuana," *Journal of Inter-American Studies,* 3 (1961), 297-341.

_____. "Incahuasi: Ruinas incaicas del valle de Lunahuaná," *Revista del Museo Nacional,* 2 (Lima, 1933), 106-114.

_____. *Informe sobre el descubrimiento de documentos que revelan la trata y comercio de esclavos negros por los indios del común durante el gobierno virreinal en el Perú.* Lima, Editorial "Tierra y Arte," 1961.

Hemming, John. *The Conquest of the Incas.* New York, Harcourt Brace Jovanovich, 1970.

Heros, Luís de los. *Monografía agrícola del valle de Cañete.* Lima, 1922.

Jago, Charles. "The Influence of Debt on the Relations between Crown and Aristocracy in Seventeenth-Century Castile," *Economic History Review,* 2nd series, 36 (1973), 218-236.

James, Preston E. *Latin America.* 3rd ed. New York, Odyssey Press, 1959.

Jara, Alvaro. *El salario de los indios y los sesmos del oro en la tasa de Santillán.* Santiago de Chile, Centro de Investigaciones de Historia Americana de la Universidad de Chile, 1966.

_____. *Tres ensayos sobre economía minera hispanoamericana.* Economía minera hispanoamericana, 1. Santiago, Centro de Investigaciones de Historia Americana de la Universidad de Chile, 1966.

_____, ed. *Tierras nuevas: Expansión territorial y ocupación del suelo en América (siglos XVI-XIX).* Centro de Estudios Históricos, n.s. 7. Mexico, El Colegio de México, 1969.

Jérez, Francisco de. "Verdadera relación de la conquista del Perú." Urteaga and Romero, *Colección de libros y documentos,* ser. 1, vol. V.

Jiménez de la Espada, Marcos, ed. *Relaciones geográficas de Indias: Perú.* Biblioteca de Autores Españoles, 183-185. 3 vols. Madrid, Ediciones Atlas, 1965.

Johnson, H.B., Jr. "The Donatary Captaincy in Perspective: Portuguese Backgrounds to the Settlement of Brazil," *Hispanic American Historical Review,* 52, no. 2 (1972), 203-214.

Juan, Jorge, and Ulloa, Antonio de. *Noticias secretas de América (siglo XVIII).* Biblio-

teca Ayacucho, XXXI-XXXII. 2 vols. Madrid, Editorial América, 1918.
_____. *A Voyage to South America.* Translated by John Adams. 2 vols. London, 1758.
Keith, Robert G. "Encomienda, Hacienda and Corregimiento in Spanish America: A Structural Analysis," *Hispanic American Historical Review,* 51, no. 3 (1971), 431-446.
_____. "Origen del sistema de hacienda: El caso de Chancay." In *La hacienda, la comunidad y el campesino en el Perú,* Perú Problema, edited by José Matos Mar, no. 3 (Lima, Francisco Moncloa Editores, 1970), 13-60.
Konetzke, Ricardo, ed. *Colección de documentos para la historia de la formación social de Hispanoamérica, 1493-1810.* 3 vols. in 5 parts. Madrid, Consejo Superior de Investigaciones Científicos, 1953-1962.
Kosok, Paul. *Life, Land and Water in Ancient Peru.* New York, Long Island University Press, 1965.
Kutscher, Gerdt. "Iconographic Studies as an Aid in the Reconstruction of Early Chimú Civilization," *Transactions of the New York Academy of Sciences,* series 2, vol. 12, no. 6 (1950), pp. 194-203.
Lanning, Edward P. *Peru before the Incas.* Englewood Cliffs, N.J., Prentice-Hall, 1967.
Larco Herrera, Alberto, ed. *Anales de cabildo, ciudad de Trujillo: Extractos tomados de los años 1566-1571.* Lima, n.d.
Laslett, Peter. *The World We Have Lost: England before the Industrial Age.* London, Methuen, 1965.
Leach, E.R. "Hydraulic Society in Ceylon," *Past and Present,* no. 15 (April 1959), 2-26.
Lee, Bertram T., and Bromley, Juan, eds. *Libros de cabildos de Lima.* 23 vols. Lima, 1935-1963.
Levillier, Roberto. *Don Francisco de Toledo, supremo organizador del Perú: Su vida, su obra (1515-1582).* 3 vols. Madrid, Espasa-Calpe, 1935-1942.
_____, ed. *Audiencia de Lima. Correspondencia de presidentes y oidores; documentos del Archivo de Indias.* Madrid, Imprenta de J. Pueyo, 1922.
_____, ed. *Gobernantes del Perú. Cartas y papeles, siglo XVI; Documentos del Archivo de Indias.* 14 vols. Madrid, Sucesores de Rivadeneyra, 1921-1926.
_____, ed. *Ordenanzas de Don Francisco de Toledo, Virrey del Perú, 1569-1581.* Madrid, Imprenta de J. Pueyo, 1929.
Lewin, Boleslao, ed. *Descripción del virreinato del Perú: Crónica inédita de comienzos del siglo XVII.* Instituto de Investigaciones Históricas, Colección de Textos y Documentos, series B, no. 1. Rosario, Universidad Nacional del Litoral, 1958.
Lizárraga, Reginaldo de. *Descripción breve de toda la tierra del Perú, Tucumán, Río de la Plata y Chile.* Biblioteca de Autores Españoles, 216. Madrid, Ediciones Atlas, 1968.
Lockhart, James. "Encomienda and Hacienda: The Evolution of the Great Estate in the Spanish Indies," *Hispanic American Historical Review,* 49 (1969), 411-429.
_____. *The Men of Cajamarca: A Social and Biographical Study of the First Conquerors of Peru.* Latin America Monographs, no. 27. Austin, University of Texas Press, 1972.
_____. *Spanish Peru, 1532-1560: A Colonial Society.* Madison, University of Wisconsin Press, 1968.
Lohmann Villena, Guillermo. "Apuntaciones sobre el curso de los precios de los artículos de primera necesidad en Lima durante el siglo XVI," *Revista Histórica,* 29

(1966), 79-104.

_____. *El corregidor de indios en el Perú bajo los Austrias*. Madrid, Ediciones Cultura Hispánica, 1957.

_____. "Indice del 'Libro becerro de escrituras,' " *Revista del Archivo Nacional del Perú*, 14 (1941), 209-240; 15 (1942), 87-96, 215-220; 16 (1943), 59-100, 175-219; 17 (1944), 51-69.

_____. "La restitución por conquistadores y encomenderos: Un aspecto de la incidencia lascasiana en el Perú," *Anuario de Estudios Americanos*, 23 (1966), 21-69.

Loredo, Rafael. *Los repartos*. Lima, 1958.

Lynch, John. *Spain under the Hapsburgs*. 2 vols. New York, Oxford University Press, 1964-1969.

McBride, George M. *Chile: Land and Society*. American Geographical Society, Research Series, no. 19. New York, 1936.

MacLeod, Murdo J. *Spanish Central America: A Socioeconomic History, 1520-1720*. Berkeley and Los Angeles, University of California Press, 1973.

Macera Dall'Orso, Pablo, ed. *Instrucciones para el manejo de las haciendas jesuítas del Peru (ss. XVII-XVIII)*. *Nueva Corónica*, vol. 2, fasc. 2. Lima, Universidad Nacional Mayor de San Marcos, 1966.

Mason, John A. *The Ancient Civilizations of Peru*. Baltimore, Penguin Books, 1957.

Matienzo, Juan de. *Gobierno del Perú*. Edited by Guillermo Lohmann Villena. Travaux de l'Institut Français d'Etudes Andines, XI. Paris and Lima, 1967.

Matos Mar, José. "Las haciendas del valle de Chancay," *Revista del Museo Nacional*, 33 (1964), 283-395.

_____ et al. *El valle de Lurín y el pueblo de Pachacamac: Cambios sociales y culturales*. Serie Monografías Etnológicas, III. Lima, Universidad Nacional Mayor de San Marcos, 1964.

Melendez, Juan de. *Tesoros verdaderos de las Yndias en la Historia de la gran provincia de San Juan Bautista del Perú de el orden de Predicadores*. 3 vols. Rome, 1681-1682.

Mendiburu, Manuel de. *Diccionario histórico-biográfico del Perú*. 2nd ed. 11 vols. Lima, 1931-1934.

Menzel, Dorothy. "The Inca Occupation of the South Coast of Peru," *Southwestern Journal of Anthropology*, 15 (1959), 125-142.

_____. "Style and Time in the Middle Horizon," *Ñawpa Pacha*, 2 (1964), 1-105.

_____, and Rowe, John H. "The Role of Chincha in Late Pre-Spanish Peru," *Ñawpa Pacha*, 4 (1966), 63-77.

Miranda, Cristóbal de. "Relación de los oficios que se proveen en el Perú . . . ." In *Juicio de límites entre el Perú y Bolivia: Prueba peruana*, edited by Victor M. Maúrtua, I (Barcelona, 1906), 153-280.

Miranda, José. *La función económica del encomendero en los orígenes del régimen colonial (Nueva España, 1525-1531)*. Cuadernos: Serie Histórica, no. 12. 2nd ed. Mexico, Instituto de Investigaciones Históricas, Universidad Nacional Autónoma de México, 1965.

Mogrovejo, Toribio de. "Diario de la segunda visita pastoral que hizo de su Arquidiocesis . . .," edited by Domingo Angulo, *Revista del Archivo Nacional del Perú*, 1 (1920), 49-81, 227-279, 401-419; 2 (1921), 37-79.

Molina, Cristóbal de, el Almagrista [attributed]. "Relación de muchas cosas acaecidas en el Perú." In *Crónicas peruanas de interés indígena*, edited by Francisco Esteve Barba (Madrid, 1968), pp. 57-95.

Montenegro y Ubaldi, Juan Antonio. "Noticia de la ciudad de Santa Catalina de Guadalcázar de Moquegua," *Revista Histórica,* 1 (1906), 70-109, 255-268, 321-336.

Moore, John Preston. *The Cabildo in Peru under the Hapsburgs: A Study in the Origins and Powers of the Town Council in the Viceroyalty of Peru, 1530-1700.* Durham, N.C., Duke University Press, 1954.

Moore, Sally Falk. *Power and Property in Inca Peru.* Morningside Heights, N.Y., Columbia University Press, 1958.

Moseley, M. Edward. "Assessing the Archaeological Significance of Mahamaes," *American Antiquity,* 34 (1969), 485-487.

Murra, John V. "An Aymara Kingdom in 1567," *Ethnohistory,* 15 (1968), 115-151.

———. "Cloth and its Functions in the Inca State," *American Anthropologist,* 64 (1962), 710-728.

———. "Guamán Poma de Ayala," *Natural History,* 70 (1961), no. 7, pp. 34-37, and no. 8, pp. 52-63.

———. "Herds and Herders in the Inca State." *Man, Culture and Animals: The Role of Animals in Human Ecological Adjustments.* Edited by Anthony Leeds and Andrew P. Varda. American Association for the Advancement of Science, Publication 78. Washington, D.C., 1965.

———. "New Data on Retainer and Servile Populations in Tawantinsuyu." In *XXXVI Congreso Internacional de Americanistas: Actas y Memorias* (4 vols., Seville, 1966), II, 35-45.

———. "On Inca Political Structure." In *Systems of Political Control and Bureaucracy in Human Societies,* edited by Vernon F. Ray, Proceedings of the 1958 Annual Spring Meeting of the American Ethnological Society (Seattle, 1958), pp. 30-41.

———. "Rite and Crop in the Inca State." *Culture in History: Essays in Honor of Paul Radin,* edited by Stanley Diamond (New York, Columbia University Press, 1960), pp. 393-407.

———. "Social Structural and Economic Themes in Andean Ethnohistory," *Anthropological Quarterly,* 34 (1961), 47-59.

Ortiz de Zúñiga, Iñigo. *Visita de la provincia de León de Huánuco en 1562.* Edited by John V. Murra. 2 vols. Huánuco, Peru, Facultad de Letras y Educación, Universidad Nacional Hermilio Valdizán, 1967-1972.

Ots Capdequí, José María. *España en América: El régimen de tierras en la época colonial.* Mexico and Buenos Aires, Fondo de Cultura Económica, 1959.

———. *El estado español en las Indias.* 4th ed. Mexico and Buenos Aires, Fondo de Cultura Económica, 1965.

Parry, John H. *The Age of Reconnaissance.* New York, World, 1963.

———. *The Audiencia of New Galicia in the Sixteenth Century: A Study in Spanish Colonial Government.* Cambridge, England, Cambridge University Press, 1948.

———. *The Spanish Seaborne Empire.* New York, Alfred A. Knopf, 1966.

———. *The Spanish Theory of Empire in the Sixteenth Century.* Cambridge, England, Cambridge University Press, 1940.

Parsons, Jeffrey R. "The Archaeological Significance of *Mahamaes* Cultivation on the Coast of Peru," *American Antiquity,* 33 (1968), 80-85.

Patterson, Thomas C., and Lanning, Edward P. "Changing Settlement Patterns on the Central Peruvian Coast," *Ñawpa Pacha,* 2 (1964), 113-123.

Pérez de Tudela Bueso, Juan, ed. *Crónicas del Perú.* Biblioteca de Autores Españoles, CLXIV-CLXVIII. 5 vols. Madrid, Ediciones Atlas, 1963-1965.

Piel, Jean. "Sur l'evolution des structures de domination interne et externe dans la société péruvienne," *L'Homme et la Société,* 12 (1969), 119-137.

Pizarro, Pedro. "Relación del descubrimiento y conquista de los reinos del Peru." *Crónicas del Peru,* edited by Juan Perez de Tudela Bueso, V, 159-242.

Polo de Ondegardo, Juan. *Informaciones acerca de la Religión y Gobierno de los Incas. Colección de libros y documentos referentes a la historia del Perú.* Edited by Horacio H. Urteaga and Carlos A. Romero. 1st series. Vols. 3 and 4. Lima, Librería y Imprenta Gil, 1916-1917.

Poma de Ayala, Guamán. *La nueva corónica y buen gobierno.* Edited by Luís Bustíos Gálvez. 3 vols. Lima, Talleres de Imprenta "Gráfica Industrial," 1956-1966.

Porras Barrenechea, Raúl, ed. *Cartas del Perú (1524-1543). Colección de documentos inéditos para la historia del Perú,* vol. III. Lima, Edición de la Sociedad de Bibliófilos Peruanos, 1959.

————. *Las relaciones primitivas de la conquista del Perú.* Lima, Instituto Raúl Porras Barrenechea, 1967.

Prescott, William H. *History of the Conquest of Peru.* 2 vols. New York, 1847.

Price, Barbara J. "Prehispanic Irrigation Agriculture in Nuclear America," *Latin American Research Review,* 6, no. 3 (1971), 3-60.

*Recopilación de leyes de los reynos de las Indias.* 4 vols. Madrid, 1681.

Riva-Agüero y Osma, José de la. *El primer alcalde de Lima: Nicolás de Ribera el viejo y su posteridad.* Lima, Librería y Imprenta Gil, 1935.

Romero, Carlos A. "La fundación de Chancay," *Revista Histórica,* 9 (1928-1935), 381-388.

Romero, Emilio. *Geografía económica del Perú.* 5th ed. Lima, 1966.

————. *Historia económica del Perú.* 2nd ed. 2 vols. Lima, Editorial Universo, [1968].

Romero, Fernando. "The Slave Trade and the Negro in South America," *Hispanic American Historical Review,* 24 (1944), 368-386.

Rossel Castro, Alberto. *Caciques y templos de Ica.* Lima, Talleres de la Penitenciaria de Lima, [1954].

————. *Historia regional de Ica: Epoca colonial.* Vol. I. Lima, Imprenta de la Universidad Nacional Mayor de San Marcos, 1964.

Rostworowski de Diez Canseco, María. *Curacas y sucesiones: Costa norte.* Lima, Imprenta "Minerva," 1961.

————. *Pachacutec Inca Yupanqui.* Lima, Imprenta Torres Aguirre, [1953].

Rowe, John H. "Inca Culture at the Time of the Spanish Conquest." In *Handbook of South American Indians,* edited by Julian H. Steward, II (Washington, 1946), 183-330.

————. "The Incas under Spanish Colonial Institutions," *Hispanic American Historical Review,* 37 (1957), 155-199.

————. "The Kingdom of Chimor," *Acta Americana,* 6 (1949), 26-59.

————. "Urban Settlements in Ancient Peru," *Ñawpa Pacha,* 1 (1963), 1-27.

Sánchez Elías, Julio E. *Cuatro siglos de historia iqueña.* Lima, Editorial Victory, 1957.

Sanders, William T. and Price, Barbara J. *Mesoamerica: The Evolution of a Civilization.* Random House Studies in Anthropology. New York, 1968.

Santillán, Hernando de. "Relación del origen, descendencia, política y gobierno de los Incas." In *Crónicas peruanas de interés indigena,* edited by Francisco Esteve Barba (Madrid, 1968), pp. 97-149.

Sarmiento de Gamboa, Pedro. "Historia Índica." In Roberto Levillier, *Don Francisco de Toledo,* III (Madrid, 1942), 1-159.

Sauer, Carl O. *The Early Spanish Main.* Berkeley and Los Angeles, University of California Press, 1969.

Service, Elman R. "The Encomienda in Paraguay," *Hispanic American Historical Review,* 31 (1951), 230-252.

_____. *Spanish-Guaraní Relations in Early Colonial Paraguay.* University of Michigan Museum of Anthropology, Anthropological Papers, no. 9. Ann Arbor, 1954.

Simpson, Lesley B. *The Encomienda in New Spain: The Beginning of Spanish Mexico.* Revised and enlarged ed. Berkeley and Los Angeles, University of California Press, 1950.

_____. *The Exploitation of Land in Central Mexico in the Sixteenth Century.* Ibero-Americana, 36. Berkeley and Los Angeles, 1952.

Slicher van Bath, B. H. *The Agrarian History of Western Europe, A.D. 500-1850.* Translated by Olive Ordish. London, Edward Arnold, 1963.

Smith, C.T. "Depopulation of the Central Andes in the Sixteenth Century," *Current Anthropology,* 11 (1970), 453-464.

Solórzano Pereira, Juan de. *Política indiana.* 5 vols. Madrid, 1647.

Spalding, Karen. "Social Climbers: Changing Patterns of Mobility among the Indians of Colonial Peru," *Hispanic American Historical Review,* 50 (1970), 645-664.

_____. "Tratos mercantiles del Corregidor de indios y la formación de la hacienda serrana en el Perú," *América Indígena,* 30 (1970), 595-608.

Stevenson, W.B. *A Historical and Descriptive Narrative of Twenty Years' Residence in South America.* 3 vols. London, 1825.

Steward, Julian H., ed. *Handbook of South American Indians.* Bureau of American Ethnology, Bulletins. 7 vols. Washington, U.S. Government Printing Office, 1946-1959.

Stumer, Louis M. "Population Centers of the Rimac Valley of Peru," *American Antiquity,* 20 (1954-1955), 130-148.

Taylor, William B. "Cacicazgos coloniales en el valle de Oaxaca," *Historia Mexicana,* 20 no. 1 (1970), 1-41.

_____. *Landlord and Peasant in Colonial Oaxaca.* Stanford, Calif., Stanford University Press, 1972.

Torres Saldamando, Enrique. *Apuntes históricos sobre las encomiendas en el Perú.* Comentarios del Perú, 7. Lima, Universidad Nacional Mayor de San Marcos, [1967]. Originally published in *Revista Peruana,* vols. III and IV (1879 and 1880).

Trewartha, Glen T. *The Earth's Problem Climates.* Madison, University of Wisconsin Press, 1961.

Ulloa, Luís. "Documentos del virrey Toledo," *Revista Histórica,* 3 (1908), 314-348.

Urteaga, Horacio H. "Alonso Martín de Don Benito," *Revista del Archivo Nacional del Perú,* 6 (1928), 1-11.

_____. "Doña María de Escobar, introductora del trigo en el Perú," *Revista el Archivo Nacional del Perú,* 12 (1939), 183-191.

_____. "Don Diego de Agüero y Sandoval, conquistador y poblador del Perú," *Revista del Archivo Nacional del Perú,* 6 (1928), 149-170.

_____, and Romero, Carlos A., eds. *Colección de libros y documentos referentes a la historia del Perú.* 24 vols. in 3 series. Lima, Imprenta y Librería Sanmartí (1st series) and Librería y Imprenta Gil (2nd and 3rd series), 1916-1935.

Vaca de Castro, Cristóbal. "Ordenanzas de tambos, distancias de unos a otros, modo de cargar los indios y obligaciones de las justicias respectivas hechas en la ciudad del Cuzco en 31 de Mayo de 1543," *Revista Histórica,* 3 (1908-1909), 427-491.

Valega, José M. *El virreinato del Perú: Historia crítica de la época colonial, en todos sus aspectos.* Lima, Editorial Cultura Ecléctica, [1939].

Vargas Ugarte, Rubén, S.J. *Historia general del Perú.* 6 vols. Lima, Milla Batres, 1966.

——. *Títulos nobilarios en el Perú.* 4th ed. Lima, Librería y Imprenta Gil, 1966.

Vásquez de Espinosa, Antonio. *Compendium and Description of the West Indies.* Edited and translated by Charles Upson Clark. Smithsonian Miscellaneous Collections, 102. Washington, U.S. Government Printing Office, 1942.

Vedia, Enrique de, ed. *Historidores primitivos de Indias.* Biblioteca de Autores Españoles, 22 and 26. Madrid, 1852-1853; reprint, Madrid, Ediciones Atlas, 1946-1947.

Vicens Vives, Jaime. *An Economic History of Spain.* With the collaboration of Jorge Nadal Oller. Translated by Frances M. López-Morillas. Princeton, N.J., Princeton University Press, 1969.

Villarán, Manuel Vicente. *Apuntes sobre la realidad social de los indígenas del Perú ante las leyes de Indias.* Lima, Talleres Gráficos P.L. Villanueva, 1964.

Villar Córdova, Pedro Eduardo. *Las culturas pre-hispanicas del departamento de Lima.* Lima, Talleres Gráficas de la Guardia Civil y Policía, 1935.

Viñas y Mey, Carmelo. *El problema de la tierra en la España de los siglos XVI-XVII.* Madrid, Consejo Superior de Investigaciones Científicos, 1941.

Weber, Max. *The Theory of Social and Economic Organization.* Translated by Talcott Parsons. New York, Oxford University Press, 1947.

Willey, Gordon R. *Prehistoric Settlement Patterns in the Virú Valley, Peru.* Bureau of American Ethnology, Bulletin 155. Washington, U.S. Government Printing Office, 1953.

Wittfogel, Karl A. *Oriental Despotism: A Comparative Study of Total Power.* New Haven, Yale University Press, 1957.

Wolf, Eric R. *Sons of the Shaking Earth.* Chicago, University of Chicago Press, 1959.

——, and Mintz, Sidney W. "Haciendas and Plantations in Middle America and the Antilles," *Social and Economic Studies,* 6 (1957), 380-412.

Wrigley, E.A. *Population and History.* World University Library. New York, McGraw-Hill, 1969.

Zárate, Agustín de. *Historia del descubrimiento y conquista del Perú.* Edited by Jan M. Kermenic. Lima, D. Miranda, [1944].

Zavala, Silvio A. *De encomiendas y propriedad territorial en algunas regiones de la América española.* Mexico, Antigua Librería Robredo de J. Porrua y Hijos, 1940.

# Glossary

ACEQUIA: irrigation canal

ALCALDE: magistrate and cabildo member

AUDIENCIA: court of appeals which also had administrative functions

BALDÍAS: vacant lands

CABILDO: municipal council

CACIQUE: Indian chief or local ruler; curaca

CARNECERÍA: slaughterhouse

CASADO: married man or head of a household

CENSO: rent-charge or mortgage imposed on real estate (see p. 100n.)

CHACRA: parcel of Indian agricultural land; small or medium-sized Spanish farm

COMPOSICIÓN: settlement of a (sometimes dubious) title to land by means of a monetary payment to the crown

CORREGIDOR DE INDIOS: administrative official in Indian districts

CORREGIMIENTO: the area governed by a corregidor

CURACA: Indian chief or local ruler; cacique

DEHESA: communal pasture land

ENCOMENDERO: holder of an encomienda

ENCOMIENDA: grant of Indians, primarily as tribute payers

ESTANCIA: livestock ranch; land granted to early Spanish settlers around Lima

FANEGA: unit of solid measurement equal to about 1½ bushels; unit of area equal to one-third of a fanegada

FANEGADA: unit of area equal to 7.2 acres or 2.9 hectares at Lima and in most of the coastal valleys (see p. 67n.)

GARÚA: dense fog and drizzle which affects the Peruvian coast during the winter months

GUANO: manure of sea birds, used as fertilizer

HACIENDA: farm or estate

HOYA: excavated pit in which crops were grown with underground water which seeped up through the soil

INGENIO: water mill, especially for grinding sugarcane

LOMA: desert land which received sufficient moisture from the garúa to support vegetation during part of the year

MERCED: grant, usually of land

MITA: Inca system of draft labor which was taken over by the Spaniards

MITMAQ: Indian colonist sent to live in a satellite settlement established outside the territory of his ethnic group

PESO CORRIENTE: monetary unit worth 9 reales in the sixteenth century and 8 reales for most of the seventeenth

PESO DE ORO: monetary unit used down to the 1570's; theoretically equal to 450 Spanish maravedís

PESO ENSAYADO: monetary unit of account; equal to 12½ reales or 425 Spanish maravedís

REAL: a silver coin worth 34 Spanish maravedís

REDUCCIÓN: the concentration of a scattered Indian population into a larger town; a town where Indians were resettled

REPARTIMIENTO: early name for the encomienda

RESIDENCIA: trial of an official which was automatically held at the end of his term of office

RIEGO: unit for measurement of irrigation water

SOLAR: building or house lot

SOLDADO: soldier; Spaniard who lacked the means to support himself

TAMBO: inn for travellers

TOMÍN: coin roughly equal to 1 real

VECINO: citizen of a town

VISITA: tour of inspection made by a representative of the government or the church hierarchy

VISITA DE TIERRAS: tour for the inspection and settlement of land titles and the sale of crown lands

VISITADOR: official who conducted a visita

YANACONA: hired Indian agricultural laborer

# Index

# Harvard Historical Studies

83. *John W. Padberg, S.J.* Colleges in Controversy: The Jesuit Schools in France from Revival to Suppression, 1813-1880. 1969.

84. *Marvin Arthur Breslow.* A Mirror of England: English Puritan Views of Foreign Nations, 1618-1640. 1970.

85. *Patrice L. R. Higonnet.* Pont-de-Montvert: Social Structure and Politics in a French Village, 1700-1914. 1971.

86. *Paul G. Halpern.* The Mediterranean Naval Situation, 1908-1914. 1971.

87. *Robert E. Ruigh.* The Parliament of 1624: Politics and Foreign Policy. 1971.

88. *Angeliki E. Laiou.* Constantinople and the Latins: The Foreign Policy of Andronicus, 1282-1328. 1972.

89. *Donald Nugent.* Ecumenism in the Age of the Reformation: The Colloquy of Poissy. 1974.

90. *Robert A. McCaughey.* Josiah Quincy, 1772-1864: The Last Federalist. 1974.

91. *Sherman Kent.* The Election of 1827 in France. 1975.

92. *A. N. Galpern.* The Religions of the People in Sixteenth-Century Champagne. 1976.

93. *Robert G. Keith.* Conquest and Agrarian Change: The Emergence of the Hacienda System on the Peruvian Coast. 1976.